The Handmaid's Tale
and Philosophy

Popular Culture and Philosophy® Series Editor: George A. Reisch

For full details of all Popular Culture and Philosophy® books, visit www.opencourtbooks.com.

Popular Culture and Philosophy®

The Handmaid's Tale and Philosophy

A Womb of One's Own

EDITED BY

RACHEL ROBISON-GREENE

OPEN COURT
Chicago

Volume 123 in the series, Popular Culture and Philosophy®, edited by George A. Reisch

To find out more about Open Court books, visit our website at www.opencourtbooks.com.

Open Court Publishing Company is a division of Carus Publishing Company, dba Cricket Media.

The Handmaid's Tale and Philosophy: A Womb of One's Own

This book has not been prepared, authorized, or endorsed by the creators or producers of *The Handmaid's Tale*.

ISBN: 978-0-8126-9992-0

This book is also available as an e-book (ISBN 978-0-8126-9996-8).

Library of Congress Control Number: 2018959069

*For all the kind, brilliant, inspirational
women in my life.*

Contents

Contents

Contents

Thanks

I'd like to express my thanks to all of those who helped with the production of this book. In particular, a debt of gratitude is owed to David Ramsay Steele and George Reisch at Open Court and to the contributors to this volume. Special thanks, as always, to my wonderful, supportive husband, Richard Greene, and to my son, Henry Greene.

Resisting Dystopia

The Handmaid's Tale is one of my favorite books. It is one of those rare reading experiences that you feel compelled to carry on, even if it makes you deeply uncomfortable—perhaps *because* it makes you deeply uncomfortable.

It's no surprise that people report responding to the television series in the same way. I've been told by friends that while viewing the show, they needed to take breaks to cry or to otherwise decompress; the subject matter is *so heavy*, but *so important*.

The story has this effect on us because it reminds us that our grasp on our most fundamental civil liberties is often tenuous at best. As a result, it's crucial that we pay careful and active attention to the way that political events unfold. We must be ever on the alert for warning signs. We must avoid letting others tell us how we should understand our purpose or personal worth.

The Handmaid's Tale reminds us that our value or purpose as human beings, and as women in particular, is not reducible to the state of our physical bodies. It is not reducible to our weight, height, race, ethnicity, or age. Our value is not determined by our physical potentiality. We are not *things*— not *incubators*. Our value is not determined by the extent to which we are physically attractive or sexually available. We are not commodities to be controlled and regulated.

The Handmaid's Tale encourages us to remember that providing care for others is an act of love. The fact that women may often be motivated by an instinct to do caring work in various ways does not imply that they should be subordinated by those who are motivated by other considerations. The act of providing care is a powerful act, not a weak one.

The Handmaid's Tale imparts the invaluable lesson that we should never let individuals and institutions convince us that facts are malleable or non-existent things. There are truths. There are good critical thinking practices that provide us with reliable access to truths about the present and the past. A full appreciation of where we are requires an understanding of where we've been. The facts, not the politicians, should control the narrative.

If we fail to pay attention, or fail to put forth our best effort, or if we are the unfortunate recipients of terrible luck, we may find ourselves under the control of institutions set on moving backward rather than forward. In these moments, we must find the courage to find our political voices and make them heard.

Nolite te bastardes carborundorum.

Part I

But They Were Godless

1
A Great Darkness Filled with Echoes

ANNA DE VAUL

From the moment the first episode of *The Handmaid's Tale* began, we were hooked. There was the sound of sirens, the careening car, Luke urging June and Hannah to run ahead through the woods, and then the gunshot.

Within minutes Hannah was being ripped from her mother's arms, both of them screaming. It's not how the novel begins, but it's the beginning of the story all the same, the single event that, more than any other, shapes who June is and dictates her future. This is her, and our, entry into Gilead.

Gilead is, by all accounts, a strange place (though, as Aunt Lydia says, ordinary is what you are used to). Despite the strangeness, though, we recognize elements of our own world in it. That's how cautionary tales work. They convince us that the events they show us are just a few steps away from becoming real. *The Handmaid's Tale*, like most dystopian stories, is meant to be a graphic warning of what might happen if we don't change our ways.

The novel won multiple awards when it was published, and it helped establish Atwood as an important voice in literature, but that was in 1985, more than thirty years ago. So why and how is the story of June and her life in Gilead considered so relevant today, even more so than other popular dystopian stories?

Cycles of the Non-biological Kind

History, and the political movements that shape it, tend to be cyclical, just like trends in fashion. We see renewed efforts to outlaw abortion or limit LGBTQ rights in the present day just like we see the return of the plaid flannel Luke wears in hipster fashion.

This isn't a new idea. Ancient philosophers and historians like Plato and Aristotle in Greece, and Sima Qian in China wrote about the cyclical nature of history. Philosophers, historians, and sociologists have come up with many different versions of social cycle theories, but all of these theories are based on the idea that what happened before is likely to happen again.

Social cycle theory is an important part of *The Handmaid's Tale*. The idea that history repeats itself helps shape the story. It's part of what makes both the novel and the TV show a cautionary tale. Gilead, in all its oppressive glory, is the result of political and historical cycles repeating themselves, and bringing things we thought were long past into the present day.

All This Has Happened Before, All This Will Happen Again

Dystopian stories warning us about oppressive governments are nothing new. Still, while I enjoyed *The Hunger Games*, I can't imagine hundreds of women dressing up like Katniss to protest political events or changes. Panem, Katniss's country, just doesn't feel realistic—*real*—in the way that Gilead does.

That's partly because every aspect of Gilead and of June's experiences there, down to the clothing she wears, is based on things that had already happened or that already existed in the real world. There are no fantastic technologies, no genetically-engineered jabberjays or tracker jackers, no dresses made of fire. There are only things that we recognize as real.

It's not only the little details that are borrowed from the real world. Everything that happens, everything the Sons of

Jacob do, has its roots in history. The Eyes don't need jabber-jays or tracker jackers to help them spy on people. All they need to do is borrow from Stalinist Russia or the McCarthy era or any number of other examples when organizing their constant surveillance and purges of anyone who doesn't toe the party line.

That heart-breaking scene in which June and Hannah are separated? In an interview with Patt Morrison, Atwood herself pointed out that, "Totalitarianism always has views on who shall be allowed to have babies and what shall be done with the babies." Consider the Nazi practice of taking blond children and giving them to German officials, the sad history of residential schools, the many programs set up to spare families the "shame" of unwed young mothers, in the USA and abroad.

In an interview with *The Guardian*, Atwood said, "when I wrote it I was making sure I wasn't putting anything into it that humans had not already done somewhere at some time." This insistence on including only what is real or what already exists is what makes the story speculative fiction, rather than science fiction. And this is what allowed Atwood, and allows the creators of the TV show, to present Gilead as a believable step in our real-world social cycles, rather than as a comfortably distant sci-fi story like *The Hunger Games*.

But wait a second. *The Handmaid's Tale* is still fiction. It's not as if the events in the story are really going to happen. We'd never let it get that far. Or at least that's what we tell ourselves.

This is part of Atwood's point in focusing on social cycles in the story. We tend to view history as something distant, rather than cyclical, and we think we wouldn't fall into the same traps we've read about. We'd stop the Nazis before they started shipping people off to concentration camps. We'd take a stand against slavery and we'd fight back against Stalinist purges. But in the Season One episode "Late," June tells us, "I was asleep before. That's how we let it happen." This is really Atwood and the writers of the show talking, and what they're saying is that bad things happen when we don't pay attention to history and its cycles. We let history repeat itself.

Those Pesky Puritans

In a recent interview at the *Restorying Canada* conference at the University of Ottawa, Atwood said she had three major influences when writing *The Handmaid's Tale*. The first was seventeenth-century Puritan New England. Atwood called this America's foundational center, and said, "It comes back periodically, in one form or another, ever since. And we're seeing one of those moments right now."

The Puritan influence in Gilead is pretty obvious. We can see it in small details like the sheet with its carefully embroidered hole laid out for Eden and Nick's wedding night. We can see it in the larger social structures, too. The Particicutions, the portrayal of women as immoral temptresses, the violent suppression of other religions, the keeping of the Bible (the supposed basis for all laws) under lock and key—all these have their roots in Puritan New England.

Atwood's second influence was the 1980s resurgence of the religious right in America, which she connected to the periodic return of Puritan influences. She said she was particularly concerned with "writing by them saying what they would do if they got the chance." This came shortly after Iran's 1979 revolution and the rise of the Islamic Republic, which also influenced her as she wrote the novel.

So when June walks by the wall and sees hanging bodies bearing signs that identify them as abortion providers or as gay or as Muslim or Catholic, it's an echo of past violence. Think witch trials, think scarlet letters, think lynchings. There are parallels with Stalin's purges and with the Holocaust here, too, and with the Inquisition and any number of less well-known crackdowns on people considered to be different in some way. This is Atwood, and now the TV show's writers, showing us what they think might happen if the cycle of history brings puritanical politicians back into power in America.

Under Whose Eye?

Gilead isn't just a puritanical state. It's also a totalitarian state, meaning that the governing Sons of Jacob have almost unlimited power to control every part of the people's public and private lives. And it's a fascist state—the Sons of Jacob have created a strictly regimented economy and society, they use extreme force to crush any opposition to their rule, and they believe the success of the state is more important than the happiness of the people. As Commander Waterford says, "You can't make an omelette without breaking eggs"—and Gilead breaks a whole lot of eggs.

We associate the rise of totalitarianism and fascism with the beginning of World War II. After the war, there was a surge in dystopian fiction as writers tried to make sense of what had happened. Many famous dystopian stories deal with one or both kinds of governments. In fact, one of the most famous dystopian novels, George Orwell's *Nineteen Eighty-Four*, was written shortly after World War II as a response to the role of these systems of belief and government.

Atwood said her third major influence was her interest in dystopias as a literary form, particularly *Nineteen Eighty-Four*. In many ways, *The Handmaid's Tale* is Atwood's reply to *Nineteen Eighty-Four*—she's written and spoken about the connections many times. While *Nineteen Eighty-Four* was a man's story in a male-dominated totalitarian and fascist society, Atwood gave us a woman's story. At the *Restorying Canada* conference, she said she asked herself, "If the United States were to have a totalitarian dictatorship, what kind of totalitarian dictatorship would it be?" Her answer, based on her understanding of social cycles in America and abroad, was Gilead.

Nineteen Eighty-Four reappeared on best-seller lists in 2017, the same year the TV adaptation of *The Handmaid's Tale* hooked us all. In a fine example of social cycles, the same concerns and conditions that inspired Orwell and Atwood to write felt relevant once again.

You and Me Up Against the Wall, Baby

Atwood shows us the effects of the historical and political cycle coming around again in not only the structure of Gilead as a whole but also in the individual characters' lives.

Consider June's relationship with her mother (called Holly on the TV show) and with Moira. Holly is a staunch second-wave feminist. Where first-wave feminists focused primarily on voting and property rights, second-wave feminists sought equality in domestic life, in reproductive rights, in the workplace, and in many other areas. Holly pokes fun at June's marriage and seems frustrated with her lack of interest in politics. On the TV show, she's the only person, for example, who seems unimpressed when June announces she's taken a job as an editor. TV-show Holly is an abortion practitioner, and the daughter she fought to have and raised attending feminist rallies is beloved but, politically speaking, a bit of a disappointment. "As for you, she'd say to me, you're just a backlash. Flash in the pan. History will absolve me" (p. 121).

If June is the disinterested younger generation who takes for granted what her mother fought for, Moira is the next generation of feminist. She's politically active and aware. She warns June about what's happening, but June doesn't listen to her any more than she listens to her mother. Even as the Moira of the novel memorizes and destroys mailing lists for fear of the persecution that is coming, June seems curiously unconcerned, until it's too late.

"Look out, said Moira to me, over the phone. Here it comes.

Here what comes? I said.

You wait, she said. They've been building up to this. It's you and me up against the wall, baby" (p. 174).

June is happy with the sort of domestic life her mother once saw women trapped within, and Moira rejected. Of course, June chooses her life with Luke and their daughter. But the freedom to choose was short-lived, a small moment on a larger cycle, as both Holly and Moira predicted.

Cycles within Cycles

Most social cycle theory deals with long spans of time. Puritanism isn't something that returns seasonally like pumpkin spice lattes, after all. Atwood and the TV show writers take it a step further, though, and show us history repeating itself on the small scale in daily life as well.

When June first discovers "Nolite te bastardes carborundorum" scratched into her closet wall, she sees it as a message from the former Offred, the handmaid who came before her. Later she realizes, of course, that the former Offred learned it from Commander Waterford. Like June, she was invited into his study, played Scrabble with him, had non-Ceremony sex with him, and was found out by Serena Joy. It's very possible that Serena may have arranged for the former handmaid to sleep with Nick, as well. In many ways, June is repeating her story, but the key difference is that, unlike her and unlike the Ofglen of the novel, June doesn't hang herself when the black van comes for her. Instead she steps inside, in part to protect the baby she's carrying.

When June escapes on the TV show, she is taken in by Omar and Heather. She later sees Omar hanging on the wall, a placard with a crescent moon for Muslim hanging around his neck, and learns that Heather is now a Handmaid. Their son Adam, like June's daughter Hannah, has been assigned to a new family. Because they sheltered her, Omar, Heather, and Adam have met the same fate as June's own family. The knowledge that she has caused history to repeat itself in this way makes June break down, and submit to Aunt Lydia and the regime. After all, if she runs again, she risks inflicting the same cycle on yet another family.

And then there's Hannah. All we see of the unnamed daughter in the novel is her mother's memories of her and a photograph of her in a white dress, "her face a closed oval" (p. 174). But in Season One, June sees Hannah from a distance. Hannah is dressed all in pink, in an outfit reminiscent of a Handmaid's, and it is an Aunt who leads her out of a building marked with the same symbol we saw on the floor and walls of the Red Center. The implication here is troubling. Will that pink someday change to red? Or will it change to blue, with an accompanying Handmaid somewhere behind her in the shadows? Either way, Hannah's fertility will dictate her life, just as it has dictated June's life.

When June sees Hannah in Season Two, their reunion is brief. She's not ready to let Hannah go when the time comes, and so her daughter is torn from her arms, both of them screaming once again. It's a deliberate echo of the past, and there are many more. Luke's lover at Jezebel's guesses he doesn't want to sleep with her because of "the Handmaid" and a season later his wife Eden guesses the same thing. Serena Joy tells June not to get upset because it isn't good for the baby, and June later says the same thing to her. These little details remind us that what has happened before will happen again, and they also remind us that this is partly because all of these people are living in the same society, with similar (though definitely not the same!) sets of circumstances.

Echoes in the Dark

The TV adaptation also plays with the idea of history repeating itself when it shows us unconscious parallels, such as when we watch the beginning of June's relationship with Luke play out in flashbacks as her relationship with Nick begins in the Season One episode, "Faithful." This is an exercise in compare and contrast. The differences and similarities are both poignant. We can't help but feel for June, and for Luke and for Nick.

In some ways June is repeating past patterns here, and in others she is not—and the same is true of Gilead as a whole. Social cycle theory doesn't claim that the past will repeat itself exactly. We learn and change as individuals and as a society, and our circumstances change, too. June finds love within the limits of her circumstances.

On a much larger scale, the circumstances of our world change. Just think about nuclear bombs. The power and spectacle of the bombings of Hiroshima and Nagasaki helped usher in the end of World War II. But can you imagine how the war would have played out differently if the states involved had nuclear bombs at the start of the conflict? Technology is just one factor that affects our decision-making and so affects our cycles.

Social progress is another factor. Most social cycle theory doesn't claim that we can't advance or learn or grow. Most of these theories don't claim we'll be stuck in the same patterns forever, with no possibility of breaking out of them. We can change, and we can evolve.

There's hope, is what I'm saying. That's why so many cautionary tales and dystopian stories like *The Handmaid's Tale* exist—to warn us and inspire us to change. There may be unhappy endings for some individuals, but as a society we can break out of our cycles.

The Unhappy Ending

Most readers will tell you that the novel ends at the same point as Season One. June is taken by the Eyes to the dreaded black van. She tells us, "And so I step up, into the darkness within; or else the light" (p. 296). At that point, we're left to decide for ourselves what happens next.

That's not quite the whole story, though. The novel contains an epilogue. It's a transcript of a talk at a fictional academic conference held nearly two hundred years after June steps into the van, and after the fall of Gilead. The conference takes place in Denay, Nunavit. There's a pun here—Deny None of It. It's another not-so-subtle reminder from Atwood to pay attention to our past.

We learn that the Handmaid's tale was recorded onto cassette tapes, which were transcribed by two male academics, Professors Pieixoto and Wade. In the process of transcribing them, these men decided what order to present the story in, and edited as they saw fit. It turns out June's story is not hers at all—it's a reconstruction presented by the same men who called it a "tale" as an admittedly vulgar pun on "tail."

Pieixoto casually dismisses women and peppers the talk

with crude sexual jokes. He says we shouldn't judge the people of Gilead, like the Sons of Jacob, too harshly because they were under pressure and their choices were shaped by their culture—they didn't know any better. In an echo of the doubt often faced by women who report trauma and abuse, he questions the authenticity and honesty of the handmaid's story, though he offers no reasons she might have lied.

What *is* questionable about this tale is what the academics left out. We know Anne Frank's father edited her diary before it was published, removing, for example, sections about menstruation. There's a lot of blood in one form or another in the Handmaid's reconstructed tale, but that doesn't mean there aren't gaps, things cut because the professors didn't think they were important or didn't believe them or because they wanted a better or more complete story.

Maybe June didn't sleep with Nick. Maybe she did sleep with Serena. Maybe she lost the baby. Maybe she cleansed herself with vinegar, or did any of one hundred other prosaic things the male professors might have found irrelevant. The point is that we will never know, because she has been removed as the author of her own story. It is the final form of violence inflicted on her.

This epilogue, entitled "Historical Notes" in another pointed pun, is Atwood's closing message to her reader. This isn't an example of social evolution. Rather than learning from the past, becoming more enlightened, Pieixoto's society is repeating the same behaviors we see now. History is cycling back around.

In the Historical Notes, Atwood is making sure we understand that this is a story about social cycles, in case we somehow missed it before. Pieixoto tells us, "The past is a great darkness, and filled with echoes" (p. 311). In many ways this sums up the novel. This is Atwood reminding us to pay attention to the past and to those echoes. If we don't, she's saying, the future may not be Gilead, but it probably won't be rosy.

2
Dystopia from a Woman's Point of View

RACHEL ROBISON-GREENE

In 2013, Margaret Atwood wrote a piece for *The Guardian* called "My Hero: George Orwell" in which she described the ways Orwell's work inspired her, particularly when she began work on *The Handmaid's Tale*. She said:

> The majority of dystopias—Orwell's included—have been written by men and the point of view has been male. When women have appeared in them, they have been either sexless automatons or rebels who've defied the sex rules of the regime. I wanted to try a dystopia from the female point of view—the world according to Julia, as it were. ("My Hero: George Orwell")

It's easy to see why a work like *Nineteen Eighty-Four* would captivate Atwood's imagination—I was similarly captivated. Recently, I read both books one after the other and immediately a cluster of questions came to mind. What common features make the works dystopic? What common practices make for a successful dystopia? What features of a dystopia would be particularly interesting from a woman's point of view? What do dystopic stories tell us about what it is to be a flourishing human being?

In *Nineteen Eighty-Four*, the main character is a man named Winston. He lives in a place called Oceania under the totalitarian party Ingsoc. Life in Oceania shares features in common with life in Gilead, but there are quite noteworthy differences as well.

Ignorance Is Strength in Gilead

The most dangerous threat to a totalitarian government is a critical thinker. If enough people are thoughtful enough to challenge the "received wisdom" of the party, perhaps the public will no longer receive it. Both Oceania and Gilead have instituted programs designed to keep citizens uneducated.

I noticed three main strategies that Gilead has employed to dumb down its citizenry. First, it prohibits women from reading. Second, it revises existing texts to ensure that those texts are consistent with the objectives of the Sons of Jacob. Third, Gilead has seriously restricted the conditions under which women can speak to other members of the community. These policies serve as significant roadblocks on all of the traditional paths to knowledge acquisition and growth.

We learn very early on in *The Handmaid's Tale* that, in Gilead, Handmaids are not permitted to read. Even the wooden signs that hang outside of shops have pictures on them to indicate the kinds of things they sell. No words. There is a beautiful irony to this. As readers and viewers we are, after all being entertained (and horrified) by a Handmaid's *tale*—a story. When we read this story, our minds race. We consider the implications. We make comparisons. We think about the lessons we should take with us in our own lives and for our own communities. If this is what a person tends to do when they read a story, no wonder totalitarian governments desire to eliminate stories altogether or, at the very least, control the narrative.

Gilead does not ban all books. It needs to locate the source of its authority *somewhere*, and they've decided on the Bible. It turns out to be fairly easy to manipulate people using the Bible for a number of reasons. First, the majority of people in the country are already aware of the Bible and many of them already view the book as a source of authoritative guidance. Second, the Bible is long and is written in language that is not contemporary and is therefore foreign to many people. This results in several convenient states of affairs for the Sons of Jacob.

Because the Bible is long, frankly, many of Gilead's citizens haven't read it, or at least haven't read it all the way through. Those who have read it all the way through couldn't possibly remember every passage, and even in the unlikely event that they could remember every passage, much of the language requires interpretation. These features make the Bible malleable for the Sons of Jacob—it's putty in their hands. They use the Bible to control the narrative—to *change* the narrative. It is useless to re-write the Bible in this way unless *someone* is allowed to read it. The community members who are the most ideologically committed—the Commanders and the Aunts—are the gatekeepers of the new Gileadean Bible. The narrative shift is most striking in one of Offred's reflections in particular:

> Not every Commander has a Handmaid: some of their wives have children. *From each*, says the slogan, *according to her ability; to each according to his needs.* We recited that three times, after dessert. It was from the Bible, or so they said. St. Paul again. In Acts. (*The Handmaid's Tale*, p. 117)

Now wait a second. You're reading a book about philosophy. I'm sure your first response when you read that passage was the same as mine. The bones of that quote aren't found in the Bible. It's Marx! But Marx wasn't talking about distribution of resources in the form of *the bodies of fertile women*! The Handmaids are out of luck. If they are suspicious about the true origin of this passage, there's no way for them to confirm their suspicions. If they *know this didn't come from the Bible and was, instead, a bastardization of Marx* there is no way for them to *prove* that fact. Because of the fear tactics that have been employed, there is no receptive audience to prove it to anyway.

15

Ignorance Is Strength in Oceania

Winston works for the Ministry of Truth—the branch of government responsible for shaping the putty of recorded history into the shape the party wants it to take. In particular, he works for the Records Department. In this capacity, he regularly alters news stories and changes the recorded history of the past. O'Brien, a party leader of Ingsoc, reveals the motivation for such a practice: "Who controls the past controls the future; who controls the present controls the past" (*Nineteen Eighty-Four*, p. 248).

In *The Use and Abuse of History*, Friedrich Nietzsche describes ways in which history can be used dangerously. One way of using (and abusing) history is to be what Nietzsche calls a *monumentalist*. Monumentalists use history in mythic and self-aggrandizing ways, often to reinforce their political agenda. Nietzsche says:

> monumental history is the theatrical costume in which they pretend that their hate for the powerful and the great of their time is a fulfilling admiration for the strong and the great of past times. In this, through disguise they invert the real sense of that method of historical observation into its opposite . . . Their motto: let the dead bury the living.

The totalitarian regimes of *The Handmaid's Tale* and *Nineteen Eighty-Four* engage in monumentalism to terrifying affect. They take the elements of history that cast their regime in a favorable and undisputedly authoritative light, and add the elements they need to tell the story it is useful for them to tell. Whether the details are right or not makes little difference. Once an authoritarian regime of this type owns the present, it can change the past, at least in the popular mind.

Another, less destructive approach to the use of history is the critical approach. There is something liberating in the idea of living *unhistorically*—of living lives that are unconstrained by what has come before. That's not an option for human beings. As reflective creatures, we are bound to the past. Nietzsche thinks that we shouldn't go too far in the other direction, we shouldn't become *superhistorical*—we shouldn't be stuck in the past, bound too tightly to what has come before. In standard Nietzschean fashion, he maintains that we should live for *this life*. History should be in the service of the living. That service shouldn't be to purely monumentalize the past. The critical approach to history allows us to look back on the virtues and vices of the past and use them to guide the future.

The monumentalism of Gilead and of Oceania deprives their respective citizens of the ability to use history critically. The citizens are reflective; they aren't chickens or hamsters. They can't live *unhistorically*, they know that *there has been a past*. They just have no way of determining what that past *actually looked like*. Of course, none of us can have perfect knowledge of such a thing. The citizens of these countries are, at worst, totally deluded about history, and, at best, kept in a perpetual skepticism about it.

Nineteen Eighty-Four introduces the concept of "thought-crime." What a notion! This is the idea that a person can violate an obligation they have to their government *simply by having internal mental states!* This feature of dystopic novels, and some of the other closely related features I've mentioned in this chapter, is very telling about human nature.

Aristotle identifies rationality as the essential human function; it is what sets us apart from other living beings. I'd wager that most people wouldn't have to read their Aristotle to come to this conclusion—it's a fairly intuitive idea. Consider stories like *The Jungle Book* or *Tarzan*. In both of these pop culture classics, for better or for worse, rationality is a dominant feature of humans and a main driving plot point in stories about humans living with non-human animals. Unsurprisingly, we value that rationality in ourselves. When authors imagine a dystopia—the worst system of government they can conceive of—they time and again conceive of a world in which our capacity to engage in critical thought is severely restricted or eliminated altogether. This really says something about our values and what we think it means to be a human being.

Ignorance and Strength from a Woman's Point of View

Nineteen Eighty-Four and *The Handmaid's Tale* both effectively demonstrate the value of critical thinking and the manipulative power governments can have over their citizens when critical thinking is viewed as inappropriate or even unlawful. As we've seen, Atwood has explicitly indicated that this tale is a tale of a dystopia from a *woman's* point of view. Which of these insights about the value of critical thinking are particularly useful or insightful from a uniquely female perspective?

First, when critical thinking is undermined in a culture, it is easier to reduce groups to stereotypes. Stereotypes often have their origins in the contingent biological features of individuals and groups. A subset of women are capable of giving birth. This is, of course, a crucial element of human life and the continuation of the species. In a culture that discourages critical thinking, however, it may be easy to push the narrative that because women are *capable* of giving birth, their *value is reducible* to the ability to give birth. The same is true for other forms of work that have, traditionally, been performed by women—thus, the creation of categories like Marthas, Aunts, and Jezebels.

If these kinds of characterizations of women strike you as confined exclusively to the pages of a dystopian novel, believe me, the history of philosophy is swimming with depictions of women that influenced public opinion and generated, in the popular mind at the time, constraints on the intellectual, physical, and social possibilities for women.

As Simone de Beauvoir pointed out in *The Second Sex*, women often play a significant role in their own oppression (look no further than the Aunts in *The Handmaid's Tale* for an example of this). When critical thinking skills are not emphasized, otherizing and stereotyping in ways that harm women are often perpetrated by men and women alike.

The Value of Language

We learn a similar lesson about humanity by looking at the use of language in both *The Handmaid's Tale* and *Nineteen Eighty-Four*. Fans of *The Handmaid's Tale* are familiar with the epilogue to that work in which, in a distant future, an academic conference is held on the subject of The Republic of Gilead. *Nineteen Eighty-Four* contains a similarly fascinating appendix that reads in very similar way. It is titled *The Principles of Newspeak*. Newspeak is the language of Oceania, introduced and routinely revised by Ingsoc. I'll let one of the architects of the language, Syme, describe Newspeak:

> By 2050—earlier, probably—all real knowledge of Oldspeak will have disappeared. The whole literature of the past will have been destroyed. Chaucer, Shakespeare, Milton, Byron—they'll exist only in Newspeak versions, not merely changed into something different, but actually changed into something contradictory to what they used to be. Even the literature of the Party will change. How could you have a slogan like "freedom is slavery" when the concept of freedom has been abolished? The whole climate of thought will be different. In fact there will *be* no thought, as we understand it now. Orthodoxy means not thinking—not needing to think. Orthodoxy is unconsciousness.

The totalitarian program of Ingsoc is bottom up. They don't simply want to tell citizens what to think. They want utter domination. Complete control. They want the power to *keep citizens from thinking at all*. Descartes proclaims "I think, therefore I am!" In Oceania existence is bleak and might take place in the utter absence of thought.

In these two dystopic novels, language is used to "otherize." In *Nineteen Eighty-Four*, Orwell introduces the notion of an *unperson*. In *The Handmaid's Tale*, this type of language is used to further discourage oppression of distinct groups such as *unwomen* and *unbabies*.

Orwell also introduces the concept of "doublethink"—which is, essentially, to believe two contradictory propositions at once. Both writers suggest that doublethink is,

19

somehow, crucial for totalitarian control and for individual survival in a totalitarian government:

> Winston sank his arms to his sides and slowly refilled his lungs with air. His mind slid away into the labyrinthine world of doublethink. To know and not to know, to be conscious of complete truthfulness while telling carefully constructed lies, to hold simultaneously two opinions which cancelled out, knowing them to be contradictory . . . Even to understand the word "doublethink" involved the use of doublethink. (*Nineteen Eighty-Four*, p. 53)

Doublethink is useful for totalitarian control because (this is a fact about logic) anything at all follows from a contradiction. If, as Ingsoc does to Winston near the end of *Nineteen Eighty-Four*, you can get a person to believe that two plus two equals five, you can get that person to believe anything.

Doublethink is crucial to survival in totalitarian regime for the same reason. If an oppressed citizen can believe a contradiction—can *hope for both contradictory parts* of the contradiction *at the same time*—they can *hope* for anything. Even a seemingly impossible future free from oppression.

The concept of doublethink shares features and, perhaps, philosophical lessons in common with Søren Kierkegaard's ideas about absurdity. Many existentialist thinkers had theories of the absurd, but Kierkegaard's religious conception of the phenomenon was that believing in the absurd involved belief in that which is contrary to reason. He uses the Biblical example of Abraham and Isaac. Abraham is promised by God that he and his wife Sarah will have a child. Abraham has faith in the satisfaction of God's promise, even though reason would lead him to the conclusion that Sarah was too old to bear children. After Abraham's son, Isaac, is born, God commands Abraham to sacrifice Isaac. Abraham is prepared to do what God commands even though he believes that an all good God would not command such a thing. To believe the contradiction—to act against the dictates of reason, is to take what Kierkegaard calls a "leap of faith."

Atwood makes use of doublethink and her characters take Kierkegaard's leap of faith. Offred imagines what must of happened to Luke. She pictures three distinct paths his life might have taken. First, she imagines that he is lying face down in a thicket—a mere skeleton, wasting away to nothing. Second, she imagines him in a prison somewhere, scarred and tortured. Third, she pictures him free, a member of the resistance, taking all the steps necessary to save her from her servitude. Of these possibilities, she says:

> The things I believe can't all be true, though one of them must be. But I believe in all of them, all three versions of Luke, at one and the same time. This contradictory way of believing seems to me, right now, the only way I can believe anything. Whatever the truth is, I will be ready for it. (*The Handmaid's Tale*, p. 106)

What are the lessons we can learn from the ways in which ownership by the government is taken over language in these two dystopic novels? First, these texts motivate reflection on the relationship between language and thought. Language gives us the tools we need to engage in good reasoning practices. Without language, humans could never have given voice to their discovery of logic. Language allows us to insist that *we can make sense out of the world*. Language allows us to proclaim, "There are objective truths!" Language allows us to talk back to our oppressors—to make use of reasons to establish conclusions. When even the very language of a culture is controlled, the citizens are left naked, without their most essential protective tools.

Women and Language

Does the perspective from the feminine lens present in *The Handmaid's Tale* give us more to think about when it comes to language? I think it does. As we have already seen, language contributes substantially to the process of otherizing people or groups. These categories are then used as markers to determine whose autonomy should be recognized and whose well being should be taken seriously.

Language in *The Handmaid's Tale* isn't just a useful tool that the Sons of Jacob use to control the citizens of Gilead. Language is also central to the construction of identity *for the individual*. When an individual is given a name or a label, that individual comes to see herself in a certain way. She comes to see the roles and names given to others in contradistinction to her own names and roles. Society doesn't merely construct, through language, the way individuals are seen by others, they construct large portions of the very identity of the *individuals themselves*. Offred clings to her former identity, the language associated with that identity gives it life:

> My name isn't Offred, I have another name, which nobody uses now because it's forbidden. I tell myself it doesn't matter, your name is like your telephone number; useful only to others; but what I tell myself is wrong, it does matter. I keep the knowledge of this name like something hidden, some treasure I'll come back to dig up, one day. (p. 84)

Language use in Gilead is hyperbolic—it shows us the worst of the worst (hopefully, it shows us something that is worse than things will ever get). This feature of the tale has real-world implications. It should cause us to think about the ways in which language plays a central role in developing the expectations people have for themselves and for others. Language is a crucial part of who we are, in more ways than one.

War Is Peace

> Oceania was at war with Eastasia: Oceania had always been at war with Eastasia.
>
> —*Nineteen Eighty-Four*

Another way these governments keep their citizens in line is to convince them that they are perpetually at war, perpetually in danger. Many citizens are ready and willing to give up all sorts of rights and liberties if they feel it is required for keeping themselves and their loved ones safe (been to the airport recently?).

Perpetual threat is a significant theme in *Nineteen Eighty-Four* and *The Handmaid's Tale*. In *Nineteen Eighty-Four*, there are three major world powers, Oceania, Eastasia, and Eurasia. The totalitarian government convinces its citizens that they are always at was with one of these powers. Reports on the conflict are regular features of daily life.

The same is true in *The Handmaid's Tale*. Gilead soldiers are referred to as "Angels," because, of course, they're out fighting for the righteous cause of Gilead. Offred watches a piece of war propaganda in which an enemy soldier is taken prisoner.

> I look into this man's eyes, trying to decide what he's thinking. He knows the camera is on him: is the grin a show of defiance, or is it submission? Is he embarrassed at having been caught?
>
> They show us only victories, never defeats.
>
> Possibly he's an actor. (p. 83)

As a group, human beings aren't very good at avoiding conflict. If we can't avoid ceaseless conflict, we at least want to feel that we're fighting *for something*. We want a good and evil story—every victory in battle should carry with it the moral certainty we feel when we think of Nazis defeated during World War II. The idea that the struggle is meaningless and that it carries with it such senseless suffering, causes more existential anguish than we can bear.

The feminine lens also adds something useful to this aspect of the discussion. In *The Handmaid's Tale*, women may easily feel that if people (Angels, no less) are fighting and dying for the safety and security of Gilead, the least she can do is play her role dutifully. Her life isn't on the line, after all. Conflict and war have ramifications for individuals and groups far beyond those who are actually fighting (if anyone is actually fighting at all).

Love and Sex

> The old civilizations claimed that they were founded on love and
> justice. Ours is founded upon hatred.
>
> —*Nineteen Eighty-Four*, p. 267

Perhaps the most striking similarity between the two novels
is the way in which the governments of Oceania and Gilead,
respectively, view sex and love as their natural enemies—restrictions of their power.

In Oceania under the rule of Ingsoc, sex is reserved exclusively for the purpose of reproduction. Young women in
particular are taught from a very early age that sex for reproduction should properly be viewed as joyless and unfortunate but is, nevertheless a duty to the Party. "There were
even organizations such as the Junior Anti-Sex league which
advocated complete celibacy for both sexes." Ideally, all children would be created by artificial insemination and then
raised by the state. This didn't happen in all cases, but it was
a theoretical ideal. Ingsoc carefully controls which members
of the Party are allowed to marry each other; they only sanc-
tion unions in which sexual desire is clearly not present.

> It was not merely that the sex instinct created a world of its own
> that was outside the Party's control and which therefore had to be
> destroyed if possible. What was more important was that sexual
> privation induced hysteria, which was desirable because it could
> be transformed into war fever and leader worship.

This element—the revolutionary implications of love and
sex—is of *fundamental* importance in both works. The relationship between Winston and Julia and the relationship between Offred and Nick are courageous acts of pure freedom
in a totalitarian state. All four characters are, at least for a
little while; bold enough to act on their *own desires* and to
utterly commit themselves, mind and body, to something
other than the ideals of the Party.

In *Nineteen Eighty-Four*, Winston and Julia engage in an
illicit love affair. They are ultimately caught and punished

for their treachery against the Party and subjected to intense, unimaginable tortures. Under this pressure, they confess everything. They even confess to completely fabricated offenses, just to get the pain to stop. The mental and physical torture goes on for days, months, *years* perhaps—it's unclear. Winston utterly changes, mind and body. Through it all, however, some small but defining part of him still revolts. The following is an exchange between Winston and O'Brien, his torturer:

> We have beaten you, Winston. We have broken you up. You have seen what your body is like. Your mind is in the same state. I do not think there can be much pride left in you. You have been kicked and flogged and insulted. You have screamed with pain, you have rolled on the floor in your own blood and vomit. You have whimpered for mercy, you have betrayed everyone and everything. Can you think of a single degradation that has not happened to you?
>
> Winston had stopped weeping, though the tears were still oozing out of his eyes. He looked up at O'Brien.
>
> "I have not betrayed Julia," he said.
>
> O'Brien looked down at him thoughtfully. "No," he said, "No; that is perfectly true. You have not betrayed Julia." (p. 273)

Technically, of course, Winston *had* betrayed Julia. He had confessed every crime against the Party that she had committed and a little extra for good measure. But Winston remained faithful to Julia in a more radical and subversive way. He had never stopped loving her—that's something the Party had not been able to control.

"How sweet," you might be thinking. Probably not. If you've read this far into this chapter, it's likely that you know that this doesn't end well for our star-crossed lovers. Winston *does* betray Julia in the end. This is the point at which the Party *really* owns him.

O'Brien orders that Winston be brought to room 101 of, presumably, The Ministry of Love. In this room, party leaders devise truly demented methods of torture, tailor-made for the particular people to which they'll be meted out. Winston is particularly horrified by rats. They devise a mask to put on his face that is connected to a cage full of a ravenous pack of them. When O'Brien pulls a lever, the rats will be released into the mask, the mask will swing shut and Winston's head will be trapped, with the bloodthirsty creatures burrowing into his face. As the mask gets closer and closer to his face, Winston cries:

> Do it to Julia! Do it to Julia! Not me! Julia! I don't care what you do to her. Tear her face off, strip her to the bones. Not me! Julia! Not me! (p. 286)

Winston may have prevented the rats from boring into his inner depths, but the party has done just that. By depriving Winston of that last dignity—his love for and commitment to another human being—the party has deprived him of the last remaining thing that made him *a person at all*. Sure, Winston is still a living, breathing, conscious human being. But he is no longer a person. He is a husk—empty and dry. He is now a thing, a resource for the party to use in its Sisyphean pursuit of power for its own sake.

A Woman's Perspective on Love and Sex

Here, too a female voice has something to add to the narrative. The Sons of Jacob are engaging in *monumentalist* history—they are appealing to the perceived greatness of some time in the past. In particular, they're appealing to a "better" time before women were sexually emancipated. It's difficult to use some glorified version of history to justify the oppression of men, since there was no time in the past in which men were subordinated purely on the basis of their gender.

In the face of war and other threats, the relative comfort of history seems like a reasonably safe place to turn for guidance toward safety and security. The Sons of Jacob control the narrative of the past, and that narrative determines the "appropriate" parameters of the sex and love lives of female citizens. The Sons of Jacob magnify and distort the facts, but the oppression of women *did exist* in the past, and that fact is likely part of the collective consciousness of those who are old enough to remember a time before the new regime. This kernel of truth may serve to lend legitimacy, in the eyes of many, to what Gilead is doing.

Like Winston's affair with Julia, Offred's relationship with Nick is an act of rebellion. The intimacy of this relationship is precisely the kind of thing the Party wants to prevent. Offred even tells Nick her name; this relationship helps to revive the identity that Offred created and now continues to create *for herself.*

The Handmaid's Tale also explores the rebellious nature of love of a different sort—love for a child. We see again and again throughout the book and television series that love for a child is important enough that parents will risk the wrath of the government for the sake of the child. This kind of bond doesn't need to be biological, and seems to be a more powerful motivating factor than sexual or romantic love. In fact, the power of this kind of love appears to be stronger than the Sons of Jacob bargained for. Our love for our children transcends worries for our own being.

A Woman's View of Dystopia

Stories involving dystopias can help us to recognize the most fundamental human values: rationality, the ability to communicate our ideas through the use of language, sexual desire, romantic love, and the love of children.

Nineteen Eighty-Four motivates deep reflection on these issues, but *The Handmaid's Tale* allows us to see dystopia from a woman's point of view.

3
Gestational Totalitarianism

LEIGH KELLMANN KOLB

A woman's place. A woman's work. These phrases are immediately identifiable in twenty-first-century America, but their origins and evolutions can be traced back to Aristotle's division of human life into separate spheres—*polis* as the public, political sphere; *oikos* as the private, domestic sphere.

While ancient Greek life and thought helped inform these ideals, what is most familiar to us is the distinction between the two spheres that emerged in the Victorian era and Industrial Revolution in the nineteenth century. The gendered nature of the spheres became even more pronounced as the cult of domesticity took hold and work outside of the home was valued financially and ideologically. In capitalism, value is tied to financial reward.

As feminism fought against the relegation of women to the private sphere, the aim for equality had its eye on the *polis*, since that is where decisions, and money, are made. As women made gains outside the home, there were *oikos* revolutions happening as well: a great deal of housework became automated, and technological advance allowed for safe and reliable birth control. Aristotle imagined an open flow between public and private; however, Christian (especially Puritan) capitalism did not.

In Hannah Arendt's *The Human Condition*, she spends a great deal of time examining how modernity has blurred the lines between the private and public—specifically, what used to be the private domain had been thrust into the public realm, and a third definition, the *social*, had emerged, which made the "society" take the place of the family.

While many have regarded Arendt's discussion of this as anti-feminist, her argument is not necessarily that women should get back into the kitchen and go into hiding. Her argument is much broader, focusing on how modernity has obliterated a balance between private lives and public politics, and how what she calls *Viva Activa* (the "human condition" of labor, work, and action) is increasingly out of balance. Arendt is saying: what we are doing isn't working.

Margaret Atwood's *The Handmaid's Tale* is rightfully considered a feminist classic—a dystopia that shows a too-familiar near-future where in the Republic of Gilead totalitarian Christian patriarchal rule has overthrown the American government. Women are put in their place. Atwood consistently says that she didn't put anything in the book that hasn't happened (or isn't currently happening). The text also makes a point to not only emphasize the horrors of conservative theological patriarchy, but also the difficult contradictions of what women have gained, and what feminism's end goal might look like. Atwood is also saying: what we are doing isn't working.

Arendt's focus on the human activity of labor, and Atwood's premise that the catalyst that resulted in Gilead used the rationale or pretext of falling fertility and birth rates (due to environmental factors and women's choices), both consider the role of reproduction in society. The private realm became political when women fought for—and patriarchal forces fought against—equality and access to reproductive control.

However, when reproduction is the means of production, women's labor is targeted and controlled. Aunt Lydia says, "There is more than one kind of freedom. Freedom to and freedom from. In the days of anarchy, it was freedom to. Now you are being given freedom from. Don't underrate it" (*The Handmaid's Tale*, p. 24). Society overcorrects, and totalitarianism—where an authoritarian government dictates public and private life—takes hold.

Labor Day

In *The Human Condition*, Arendt delineates the "three fundamental human activities" and names them *Viva Activa*: Labor ("the human condition of labor is life itself"); Work ("the human condition of work is worldliness"); and Action, which is the plurality of humans ("men, not Man, live on the earth and inhabit the world") (pp. 7–8). She goes on to say:

> All three activities and their corresponding conditions are intimately connected with the most general condition of human existence: birth and death, natality and mortality. Labor assures not only individual survival, but the life of the species. Work and its product, the human artifact, bestow a measure of permanence and durability upon the futility of mortal life and the fleeting character of human time. Action, in so far as it engages in founding and preserving political bodies, creates the condition for remembrance, that is, for history. (pp. 8–9)

While she points out that modernity has emancipated women and slaves (allowing them to participate in all human activities), she also notes that Karl Marx advocated for the abolishment of labor, not the emancipation of laborers, in his arguments. We have, through advances in technology (industrial, household, and reproductive), come closer to abolishing labor. However, automation plus modern capitalism results in a modern life that is seemingly futile and meaningless. We consume; we don't produce.

In the realm of biological creation of life and the labor of reproduction, the blurring of lines of human activities, the automation of control, and abolishment of labor takes on new meaning, since controlling women and their reproduction is such a cornerstone of Western patriarchal societies. In Gilead, the focus is not on eradicating capitalism, fixing the environment, or empowering women to want to have more children.

Instead, the answer is to situate women firmly in the private sphere, divide their labor based on their fertility or infertility, and remove any capacity for free thought, speech, or action.

This is a society—like our own—that has contempt for labor, but needs it, and forces it, on women and a re-established slave class. Wives, Handmaids, Marthas, Econowives, Unwomen, Jezebel workers—division of labor at its finest. Arendt and Atwood both encourage us to not say "It cannot happen here," because it has and it can again.

Birth Day

In *The Human Condition*, Arendt focuses on birth as the great hope for humanity. A new life, a new individual: "the new beginning inherent in birth can make itself felt in the world only because the newcomer possesses the capacity of beginning something anew" (p. 9). In Gilead, the rhetoric is similar, though their "newness" is a "return to traditional values." Babies are the product; babies are the goods.

In most societies, a plummeting birth rate and low fertility is cause for great concern. However, in Gilead/Puritan/totalitarianism/Christian patriarchal ideology, falling birth rates are an urgent excuse to encourage or force birth not by giving women options via reproductive technology, health care, or childcare—the Commander says "Damn Cubans. All that filth about universal daycare" (*The Handmaid's Tale*, p. 209). Instead, the solution is to remove reproductive rights and control women's bodies and their births. This is common in totalitarian regimes (the Nazi Lebensborn program, for example), and is the basis of Gilead.

In this social tension—the need for natality for a functioning society, and the rights of women to have bodily autonomy—Aunt Lydia's promise of "freedom from" is turned upside down. If babies are the product, as Offred acknowledges when she sardonically refers to herself as a "national resource" (p. 65), she is both a laborer and a worker.

Arendt defines two kinds of laborer: the *Animal laborans*, who labors in solitude, and the *Homo faber*, who is a creator.

Meaning is found in creation, and not in solitary automation. While we may associate childbirth with creation, society has more commonly relegated slave labor and women's labor into *Animal laborans*, denigrating the creation of life itself, since it's a bodily function carried out by an oppressed group.

The modern world has offered access to contraception, abortion, and reproductive technologies, so that creating life can be more of a *Homo faber* experience, as we can create and control life with tools. This was June's pre-Gilead world. In Gilead, fertility is a resource, yet the patriarchal Christian framers are against any sort of reproductive technology. Women must not have control. When birth is forced, and the woman is regarded as a carrier, then she loses the creative freedom of *Homo faber* and is relegated to *Animal laborans* status. Arendt's reverence for natality, and women's roles as life laborers, is feminist if we consider her regard for the *Homo faber*.

Arendt says:

> That individual maintenance should be the task of the man and species survival the task of the woman was obvious, and both of these natural functions, the labor of man to provide nourishment and the labor of the woman in giving birth, were subject to the same urgency of life. Natural community in the household therefore was born of necessity, and necessity ruled over all activities performed in it. (*The Human Condition*, p. 30)

The strict division of labor is a hallmark of modern industrialization, and of Gilead. Arendt sees the division of labor as a loss of workmanship; the specialization of work has been lost to mass production (p. 125). Of course, she also consistently speaks of women and slaves being seen as operating in the same oppressed class. She acknowledges that the emancipation of slaves and women in the nineteenth and twentieth centuries was part of this merging of private and public, and the elevation of the social.

Arendt's nuanced thoughts about this make it clear that she is not advocating a return to a spherical structure that keeps those with unequal status out of the public sphere of influence; she points out that the household is an incredibly unequal space (with the male as the head of the household). It is not at all anti-feminist to assert that modernity is out of balance.

Scholars have considered how Arendt might have viewed reproductive technology in the modern world (see the works by Seyla Benhabib, Kimberley Curtis, and Maren Klawiter). Can natality that is controlled by human "tools" be *Homo faber*? That is ideal, but hard to imagine in a patriarchal society.

Liberal thought and feminism often agree in matters of the importance of women's bodily autonomy and the freedom and possibilities that come with being able to plan reproduction. When thinking about modern society's failings, we can also often agree that automation and mechanization have created a lack of meaning in individuals' lives—we are more concerned with consuming and controlling. These ideologies are often complementary, until we more deeply consider the nature of reproduction and what it means to be a laborer vs. creator.

The Handmaid's Tale television show is a remarkable adaptation of the novel, and gives us more insight into the pre-Gilead society. Moira is shown in a flashback being a surrogate. This choice, which came with a large profit, was agonizing. We squirm when we are faced with these tensions, largely because what we consider the alternative to be (patriarchal control of women's choices) seems all too real a threat.

Season Two depicts the transformative power of skin-to-skin contact and breastfeeding, and the powerful, animalistic solitary birth scene is juxtaposed with flashbacks to June's hospital birth. Serena Joy could very possibly gestate her own child if she had access to reproductive technology. Gilead (and Christian patriarchy) have a contempt for medicine and nature when it comes to women. Where reproduction and parenting are concerned, our modern world certainly doesn't have it all figured out. However, removing choice and disempowering women is not the answer.

Arendt's criticism of the social (the seeping-out of the private into the public) is not inherently anti-feminist, especially considering her deep familiarity with totalitarianism, as she outlines in *The Origins of Totalitarianism* (1951). She does not suggest a return to the way things were. Instead, she suggests we must rethink where we are and where we are going. Much like the dichotomy of Serena Joy and Offred's mother in *The Handmaid's Tale*, we cannot simplify ideologies.

Atwood draws Offred and her mother's relationship as a difficult one—her mother's second-wave feminism was more radical than she was comfortable with, and the activism competed for her daughter's attention. Serena's activism led to oppression she didn't imagine. Patriarchy forced them both into extremes; liberal feminists fight against the current, conservative anti-feminists paddle with the current, but neither is in charge of the water's flow. We can all recognize, as Arendt is asking us to, that modernity is broken in numerous ways. *The Handmaid's Tale* shows us clearly that totalitarianism is a horrifying threat.

We cannot help gendering the spheres because of our shared history, our Puritan roots. However, a radical rethinking of modern society and modern capitalism—with natality, the regenerative necessity of both—is needed.

Transition

When Janine/Ofwarren gives birth, she screams in her last stage of labor. Ofglenn thinks, at first, that she should remember the pain from her first birth, but then says, "But who can remember pain, once it's over? All that remains of it is a shadow, not in the mind even, in the flesh. Pain marks you, but too deep to see. Out of sight, out of mind" (p. 125).

The transition phase of labor—the third and final stage—is often marked by the greatest pain, a dramatic and intense shift right before the birth. It's often also forgotten, women report, when it's all over. Forgetting lets you do it again.

Aunt Lydia refers to Offred's generation as transitional as well: "You are a transitional generation. It is the hardest for you. . . . For the ones who come after you, it will be easier. They will accept their duties with willing hearts" (p. 117). The kind of forgetting that is necessary for post-totalitarian revolution is essential to tyrannical rule. "I must beware of inertia," Offred says. She lulls herself into a kind of comfort with Nick. She says, "Being here with him is safety; it's a cave, where we huddle together while the storm goes on outside. This is a delusion, of course." Plato's "Allegory of the Cave" is an easy connection to make here; the discomfort of being faced with the truth can be avoided by staying chained up and watching the shadows. Gilead's totalitarian regime must fight the transitional generation to get to the more subdued future, when "girls will soon only remember being silent" (p. 219).

Offred remembers being a child and watching a documentary with her mother about the Holocaust. One of the interviews was with a mistress of a concentration camp supervisor: "The woman said she didn't notice much that she found unusual. She denied knowing about the ovens. . . . What could she have been thinking about? Not much, I guess; not back then, not at the time. She was thinking about how not to think" (p. 145).

This is a deeply unsettling and powerful anecdote, because our shared understanding about the Holocaust is that it somehow couldn't happen here. We are taught about the genocide, but not how Germany shifted into a place where it could happen. And that's how Gilead came to be. The transition may be painful, but not if you don't think about it too much. If you forget, it will become ordinary: "Ordinary, said Aunt Lydia, is what you are used to. This may not seem ordinary to you now, but after a time it will. It will become ordinary" (p. 33).

It's Nature's Plan

How does it happen? How does Gilead seem so horrifically plausible in the twenty-first century? In *The Origins of Totalitarianism*, Arendt says that unlike in the past, in modern tyrannies "terror is no longer used as a means to exterminate and frighten opponents, but as an instrument to rule masses of people who are perfectly obedient" (p. 6). Modernity is fertile grounds for isolation (in the political realm) and loneliness (in private life). Arendt shows that this combination dangerously keeps the door ajar for totalitarian rule to take over. She says that tyrannical governments push to isolate, and then terror can "rule absolutely" (p. 474). But again, this isn't terrorism against enemies; it is terrorism against their own.

A kind of terror used to instill totalitarianism is a threat of terror. Offred tells us how it happened pre-Gilead when "they shot the president and machine-gunned the Congress and the army declared a state of emergency. They blamed it on the Islamic fanatics, at the time. . . . That was when they suspended the Constitution" (p. 174).

This form of terrorism grew into more literal terrorism: Guardians everywhere, the Wall displaying dead bodies, Salvagings. Offred remembers her mother telling her that humanity is adaptable; it's "amazing" what we can get used to. The early changes—women couldn't use their bank cards, were released from their jobs—were able to be brushed off by even progressive men (she remembers Luke telling her he would take care of her, and "It's only a job"). She was glad to see the pornography stands go. But by then, it's too late.

If we consider Arendt's great study into the "origins" of totalitarianism, and think also of natality as being a kind of origin story, it's easy to understand on a macro and micro level how the control of birth would be incredibly important to both tyrannical leaders *and* to the laborers—birth mothers—in society. *The Handmaid's Tale* shows what happens when the gain of women is overthrown by the ideology and capitalism of the Gilead patriarchy. It's this beginning, this origin, that is both so powerful and the control of which is so threatening, that is central to Gilead.

In Christianity, the origin story involves a woman, the fall of sin involves a woman, and the birth of Jesus of Nazareth involves a woman (a virgin *and* mother—the ideal woman). In Gilead, during the Prayvaganza, the Commander leads the service and wills women to dress modestly and to "learn in silence with *all* subjection. . . . For Adam was first formed, then Eve. And Adam was not deceived, but the woman being deceived was in the transgression. Notwithstanding she shall be saved by childbearing," he continues (p. 221).

In a footnote in *The Human Condition*, Arendt points out that there are two versions of the creation story: the teachings of Jesus of Nazareth vs. Paul. Jesus says, "he which made them at the beginning made them male and female"; Paul says the woman was created "of the man" and "for the man" (p. 8n). She says here and again in the text that Jesus of Nazareth valued action, but Christianity has elevated contemplation over action" (p. 318). Clearly, the Puritanical Christianity that shaped American patriarchy, and is shown in its extreme in Gilead, prefers Paul's version of the creation story.

Throughout *The Handmaid's Tale*, biblical scripture is used—most notably, the story of Rachel and Jacob using their maid Bilhah as a forced surrogate—to shape policy and enforce behaviors. The text is cherry-picked and revised, and used for patriarchal and totalitarian ends. Even Marx is twisted into the mix: "*From each*, said the slogan, *according to her ability; to each according to his needs*. We recited that, three times, after dessert. It was from the Bible, or so they said. St. Paul again, in Acts" (p. 117). Maybe Atwood read Arendt's footnote. Chastity and childbearing: salvational labor, national and natural resources.

The Bomb of Gilead

"The aggressiveness of totalitarianism," writes Arendt, "springs not from lust for power, and if it feverishly seeks to expand, it does so neither for expansion's sake nor for profit, but only for ideological reasons . . . it is necessary for totalitarianism to destroy every trace of what we commonly call human dignity" (*Origins of Totalitarianism*, p. 458). The conflation of power and ideology, especially in its reliance upon terror against "obedient" people and ensuring isolation and loneliness, makes for an overwhelming enemy.

In *The Human Condition,* Arendt examines how strength refers to the individual, and power refers to a collaborative group (p. 200). She says, "The vehement yearning for violence . . . is a natural reaction of those whom society has tried to cheat of their strength" (pp. 203–04). As the past and future are explored in the TV adaptation, we see attempts at revolution. Ofglen detonates a suicide bomb at the dedication of the new Rachel and Leah Center ("First Blood").

We know that the violent protestors who attacked Serena did not win; nor do we expect Ofglen's actions to make a difference. The desperation is palpable. In the following episode, though ("After"), Serena asks Offred to help her write and edit new laws. When Offred clicks the pen open, the image is parallel to Oflgen's clicking the bomb detonator. In "Smart Power," smuggled letters to Canada from Gilead were made public and the Canadian government refused to meet further with the Commander. The argument is clear: violence is tempting, but thoughtfulness and literacy are the only hopes to fight totalitarianism. Action and speech, Arendt says, cannot be done in isolation (*The Human Condition*, p. 188). This, then, is the power of totalitarianism and the challenge of revolution. Women in Gilead—like women throughout history—are kept from action and speech, from the political sphere and the written word.

Breathe, Breathe, Breathe. Push, Push, Push

Arendt writes, "The subterranean stream of Western history has finally come to the surface and usurped the dignity of our tradition. This is the reality in which we live. And this is why all efforts to escape from the grimness of the present into nostalgia for a still intact past, or into the anticipated oblivion of a better future, are vain" (*The Origins of Totalitarianism*, p. ix).

And in her prologue to *The Human Condition*, she contemplates this new era that seems to be marked by a desire to escape earth, specifically in the reactions to the earliest successful space exploration by Sputnik. She says, "it is the same desire to escape from imprisonment to the earth that is manifest in the attempt to create life in the test tube" (p. 2). She is not against scientific advances, but wants us to consider our present and our future without denying our past. She goes on to say, "What I propose in the following is a reconsideration of the human condition from the vantage point of our newest experiences and our most recent fears . . . to think what we are doing" (p. 5).

Atwood asks us to do the same in *The Handmaid's Tale*. She shows what is possible in our future by weaving together our past and present realities, and showing how Puritan Christian extremes, patriarchy, capitalism, and feminism that conforms to modernity instead of creating a new modernity can quickly lead to totalitarianism. The TV show, with its in-depth flashbacks and continued storytelling digs deeper into explaining how our current maladaptation to modern life leaves us ripe for totalitarianism.

The Handmaid's Tale confronts us with the realities of religious extremism and patriarchy. It also confronts us with the realities of feminism and modern society—which demanded that we be most concerned with the *polis* instead of the *oikos*, and entering the public sphere instead of balancing and de-gendering the spheres. Arendt and Atwood confront the fact that what we are doing is not working. And if we don't radically rethink our modern society, Gilead doesn't seem so far away.

4
The United States of Gilead?

RICHARD GREENE

Margaret Atwood published her best-selling dystopian novel *The Handmaid's Tale* in 1985, but its popularity is currently at an all-time high. This can be accounted for in at least in part by the success of the television adaptation of *The Handmaid's Tale*, but part of the story lies in the fact that many people believe that the United States may well be in the early stages of a dystopian era that is not entirely dissimilar to the fictional state of Gilead, as depicted by Atwood. In fact, that perception likely better explains the success of the television version of *The Handmaid's Tale* than does the success of the television series account for the recent rise in popularity of the novel. Not that the situation here in the United States perfectly mirrors life in Gilead (at least is doesn't yet)—that would be an alternative fact—but, as we shall see, there are some disturbing parallels.

Women, Fire, and Dangerous Things

Much of the content in the early chapters of *The Handmaid's Tale* is devoted to Offred, our trusted narrator, describing daily life in the Republic of Gilead. The most salient features are that it is a totalitarian state in which, due to a series of environmental disasters just before and during the overthrow of the government of the United States of America, many of the women of Gilead are infertile.

Certain unmarried women of childbearing years who are thought to be fertile (based on their previously having had a child), become Handmaids. (Offred is married, but due to her marrying Luke, who was married previously, her marriage is not recognized by the state.) Handmaids are essentially taken prisoner, trained (read: conditioned) to be subservient, assigned to a family to be impregnated, and raped each month during ovulation, until they get pregnant. Upon delivery of a child they are reassigned to another family. As bleak as that sounds, it actually gets much worse.

Since a totalitarian regime is in control in Gilead, they tolerate no dissension, and any and all possible threats to their authority must be thwarted. This plays out in a number of ways. To begin with, the citizens of Gilead (I'm using the term "citizens" very loosely here) are made to live in fear at all times. If anyone speaks out, questions authority, actively attempts to work against the goals of the regime, violates laws, complains, or merely discusses their situation in anything but the select glowing terms that have been provided to them as part of their indoctrination, they are punished severely.

During the indoctrination process, punishment might include being shocked with a cattle prod or having your hands and feet beaten. After the indoctrination process this might include such things as being shot on sight by government spies (known as Guardians), hanged in the public square to serve as an example for other would-be dissenters, or being sent off to be forced into prostitution. The Handmaids are not allowed to possess property, talk to one another or others (with a handful of exceptions related to mundane tasks such as shopping or fulfilling their duties as Handmaids), talk to others who are not Handmaids (again with the same exceptions), obtain or share information, or do anything that might be considered pleasurable. Access to information is strictly forbidden (more on this later).

Thus far, the comparisons between The Republic of Gilead and the United States of America are not all that direct. Dissenters are not killed or sold into prostitution in the United States. We have free speech. Anyone can pretty much speak with whomever they like whenever they like. We have prohibitions against cruel and unusual punishment (this means that hands and feet don't get beaten), people are not sold into slavery (at least not by the government), and no one is supposed to get shot on sight (although it happens with striking frequency to black citizens at the hands of white police officers). And while punishment frequently occurs in such a way as to make those punished into public examples, it generally doesn't involved displaying their rotting corpses in public places as a warning to all.

That said, there are some striking similarities. We have a culture that increasingly tries to control women, and in particular what they can do with their own bodies. There has been much legislation of late designed to chip away at abortion rights. Some of that legislation involves draconian laws requiring women to view pictures or motion picture media of aborted fetuses prior to having an abortion (related legislation requires physicians to show the pictures and the media to women who are considering having an abortion).

There is legislation designed to make birth control more difficult, if not impossible to obtain. (I'm reminded here of Republican political candidate financial backer Foster Friess exclaiming that in his day women didn't need contraceptives, because they could just put a Bayer aspirin between their legs to keep their legs closed.) There is further legislation (and subsequent court rulings) that allows pharmacists to deny women contraceptives on the basis of a religious objection. More recent legislation has granted insurance companies the same rights to deny funding for birth control. Without a doubt, many women feel that to a great extent, their rights to choose what to do with their own bodies, are being limited and controlled by the government.

Another similarity between Gilead and the United States has to do with the perpetuation of rape culture. Most people know lots of things about our current president, Donald Trump, but even if one knows next to nothing about him, one likely knows that he famously said, while campaigning for president, that because he was a celebrity, women would let him "grab them by the pussy." This comment was nearly universally condemned, but his defenders employed a defense that was not universally condemned. They suggested things such as "boys will be boys," and this kind of speak was just "locker room talk." (One argument that appeared to gain traction at the time came from Trump campaign surrogate Scottie Nell Hughes stating that she prefers to have a red-blooded president, implying that he's a real man, and that anyone who considers themselves a real man would exhibit similar behaviors.)

Defenders of Trump's remark also pointed to examples of women saying similar bawdy things about men, when they were in the company of other women. Effectively, what they did was to attempt to normalize behaviors such as these. And to some extent they were successful. In a society where women have to fear for their safety when out alone, or in remote places such as on hiking trails, or at the beach, or pretty much anywhere at night when there aren't a lot of other people around, the effects of normalizing this sort of speech can have, and has had, devastating consequences.

It doesn't, however, stop there. As a television personality, as a candidate for President, and as President, Trump has has characterized women in the most reprehensible ways, from his body shaming of Rosie O'Donnell to his depicting Megyn Kelly's line of questioning as a journalist as having "blood coming out of her whatever" (a thinly veiled reference to a popular stereotype of menstruating women as being irrational and not worthy of serious consideration) to his describing political opponents, such as both Hillary Clinton and Carly Fiorina as essentially not being attractive enough to be president (not that their physical attributes had any bearing on their ability to do the job; rather, Trump was suggesting that "we" just don't want an unattractive woman leading our country). Many hoped that this sort of behavior would end once he became president, but it only seems to have gotten worse. More recently he has called former White House staff member, Omarosa Manigault-Newman a "dog." So, while superficial similarities between Gilead and the United

States with respect to the treatment and characterization of women are scant, at deeper levels the two nations share much in common.

Fear Factor

Another area where life in Gilead parallels, but not directly, the United States, has to do with fear tactics. Trump, who prides himself on being a "counter-puncher"—which is a strange euphemism for someone who will retaliate without measure or discretion against anyone who criticizes or calls him out on anything (even when the criticism is warranted)—lashes out at anyone who does not go along with his agenda. Moreover, he will incite his base to either act against his critics, or, at minimum, will destroy their professional reputations in the eyes of his supporters. For example, Republican politicians who speak out against any of his proposals (even the most innocuous ones) find themselves struggling to win primaries against Trump-backed opponents.

White House staffers who do not march in lock-step are fired and attacked publicly. Of course, those who deign to investigate him, such as Robert Mueller, have their professional reputations smeared (I'm hard pressed to think of anyone who has had a more honorable and distinguished public career than Robert Mueller). Very recently, high ranking former officials who have criticized him have been threatened with revocation of their security clearances. And in the case of former Central Intelligence Director, John O. Brennan the threat came to fruition.

This didn't just begin when Trump became president. During the 2016 Republican primaries, it became clear that any of his opponents who spoke out against him, would suffer more public attention at the hands of Trump than most candidates (who aren't named "Trump") can handle. Suddenly everyone had heard of "Low-Energy" Jeb Bush, "Lil'" Marco Rubio (a jab at the size of his, shall we say, manhood), and "Lying" Ted Cruz, just to name a few—believe me, the lists goes on and on.

Of course, fear is precisely how order and control are maintained in Gilead, from the aforementioned threats of execution, and threats of being sold into the sex slave industry, to fear of not ever seeing one's loved ones again, and, as is always the case with religious societies, fear of eternal damnation and the shame of being unworthy in the eyes of God.

How Did We Get Here?

Before we consider the more direct similarities between the full-on totalitarian regime in Gilead and the burgeoning totalitarian state we find in the United States, it might be useful to see how each came to be.

Gilead came about when a group of religious fanatics, with the help of the United States Armed Forces, levied an attack on Congress and the Office of the President that left nearly all politicians dead (they were assassinated virtually at once). The coup was partially motivated by the declining state of the environment (the very causes of the infertility!).

It seems that left-leaning activists actually played a role in bringing the right-wing Gilead government to power. This was not, however, the main circumstance that fostered the revolution. Rather, it had to do with growing moral outrage over the relaxing of sexual mores, and an increase in the amount of prostitution, pornography, and more casual attitudes toward sex, especially in women.

Our current predicament in the United States is much more complicated (this is almost always the case when comparing fiction to reality). But, of note, our current situation has more to do with a lack of concern for environmental issues. Politicians and conservative political commentators on the right have been very effective in convincing independents and right-leaning voters that climate change is part of a vast liberal conspiracy, designed to take their jobs in hopes of promoting a socialist agenda (in reality their jobs were shipped overseas, by the very Republican leaders and their financial backers, whom independents and right-leaning middle-class voters have been convinced to vote for). Furthermore, more than anything, the election of our current president has to do with a racist reaction to the ascendency to power of Barack Obama—the United States' first black President. Trump, of course, was leading the charge from the beginning of Obama's presidency, by being perhaps the most vocal of the anti-Obama birtherists.

For our purposes, the salient point is that what the two states have in common need not lie in the particulars of their respective situations. All that is required for ugly revolutions of the types we find in both Gilead and the United States is a real dissatisfaction among citizens, and a promise to make things better (even if the details of such promises are never explicated). The popular "drain the swamp" slogan of the Trump campaign would have been right at home in Atwood's pre-Gilead world of sexual permissiveness, pornographers, and prostitution. This is where the more striking similarities between Gilead and the United States really begin.

It's Almost Like Looking in a Mirror

There are five features that the Republic of Gilead and the United States have in common that are so remarkably close, that one actually wonders whether Atwood had a time machine: othering, the separating of parents from their children, gaslighting, the discrediting of those who would speak out against them, and lying.

The first feature that Gilead and the United States have in common is that the leaders of each is particularly good at what is called "othering." Othering is the practice of suggesting that members of different groups from one's own are so different, that they reside in a place that is beyond one's ability to empathize. This typically involves creating a two-dimensional stereotype of another group, to which they can be reduced. This makes them completely unrelatable. In Gilead, the Aunts (these are the cattle prod wielding women who are responsible for indoctrinating and overseeing the handmaids) do a fantastic job of "othering" a number of different groups: those slutty women from the pre-Gilead United

States, the women who are not sufficiently subservient, people with different religious views, and so on.

Similarly, Trump's rise to power during the 2016 Presidential campaign involved great amounts of othering. His followers came to see Mexicans as rapists and criminals, Muslims as terrorists, who needed to be kept out of our country, liberals as elitist idiots who wanted to take the guns and jobs from his base. Trump rallies often turned violent against anyone who showed even the slightest sign of dissent (especially if the dissenting voice was that of a person of color).

The second feature that Gilead and the United States share is the taking of children from their parents, against the will of their parents, for redistribution. The sole reason that handmaids exist in Gilead is to produce children, who are then taken from them and given to the family to which they've been assigned. Moreover, if a Handmaid has a child already, that child is taken from her. This is precisely what happened to Offred. For most of the book she doesn't know what became of her daughter or whether she is even alive. When you "other" a group of people, it makes it much easier to take their children.

We see something similar going on in Trump's immigration camps for illegal immigrants coming across our southern border. While the primary motive of the United States government is not to take children from their parents, they do so, just the same. It serves as a scare tactic. As recently as May 2018 there were over ten thousand children in these detention centers, many of whom were separated from their parents, plenty of whom were put into the foster care system, where they could be adopted by US citizens, and a great number of whom, due to faulty record keeping, cannot be reconciled with their parents (who, in most instances, have been deported).

The description of the Red Center (i.e., the place where the handmaids are kept during their initial training and indoctrination)—a large gymnasium full of Army cots, where Aunts walk around shocking people with their prods—seems almost identical to Trump's detention centers. The babies in

Gilead that are mutant or deformed end up in cages. The children in Trump's detention centers end up in make-shift jail cells that resemble cages.

The third similarity—the gaslighting of the Handmaids—is one of the dominant recurring themes of *The Handmaid's Tale*. The Handmaids are constantly being told how bad the women were in the 1970s (again the othering comes into play), they are told they are safer now (which seems like a really tough sell—the argument ultimately boils down to women back then were so promiscuous that they were constantly at risk of being raped or murdered, but you are safer now that you routinely get raped, and if you step even the slightest bit our of line, you will be murdered). They were told that if men did anything bad to them, it was their own fault (one particularly horrific instance of this is when the Aunts get Janine to accept responsibility for the time she got gang raped). The Aunts convince the Handmaids that it is better for them to think of their loved ones as dead. At one point in the book, Offred spews a bunch of contradictory things, claims to believe all of them, and then claims to not know what to believe. This is classic gaslighting at its finest.

Similarly, we see the Trump Administration routinely attempts to gaslight people—to get them to believe that they cannot trust their own senses, and he is somewhat effective at it. A famous example of this occurred just during his inauguration. The news media reported that his inauguration ceremony was sparsely attended as compared with his predecessor. Trump reported that it was the largest crowd in history for a presidential inauguration. When presented with overwhelming evidence (including pictures, video footage, reports from the transportation agencies, and dozens of eyewitnesses), Trump insisted that he was correct and the visual evidence was false. He has also engaged in a fair amount of gaslighting pertaining to Robert Mueller's investigation into the firing of James Comey and Russian meddling in the 2016 presidential election. Repeatedly we hear that Mueller's investigation has produced nothing even though there have been a number of indictments, guilty pleas, and convictions. The press keeps reporting these things, and Trump keeps telling his base the opposite.

Fourth (and very much related to the third similarity) we find that in both Gilead and currently in the United States there is a concerted effort to discredit dissenting voices. In Gilead this is done mostly through restricting of access to other opinions. Handmaids are not allowed to read, speak to one another about anything that doesn't pertain to their duties, have access to the news, share information of any sort, listen to music, or come into contact with anything that might motivate them to believe anything other than what the Aunts tell them.

One of Trump's most common refrains is that the news is fake. This is right out of the totalitarian playbook. The news (both print and broadcast) watch Trump like a hawk and point out every transgression. In every case, he just asserts that the news is fake. He has so discredited the news with his base, that they've become dubious of any attempt to provide evidence. It's remarkable that so many people could come to believe that as honored an institution as the press, could become discredited by the word of one man, and a known con-artist at that, as the lawsuit against Trump University has demonstrated.

The final direct similarity between the Republic of Gilead and the United States has to do with the role of lying. In fact, Gilead was founded on a lie. After the coup and subsequent overthrowing of the United States government, citizens were informed that the corrupt government that led to the devastating environmental problems and ultimately led to so many people becoming infertile would be replaced by a new democratic institution (one that isn't corrupt), but that they needed a temporary government to keep things running until elections could be set up. Of course, those elections never came. Something like martial law was imposed instead. Many other lies were told to the Handmaids, for example, that other countries were at war and that conditions were worse there, and so forth.

Seemingly, the thing that is most noteworthy about Trump is the frequency with which he lies. On average, according to the *Washington Post* (although it's probably fake news) through nearly two years as president, he has lied or misled on average 7.4 times per day. That's nearly 4,300 false or misleading claims. When called out on his lies, in addition to screaming that the news is fake, he lays claim to something called alternative facts. This is the similarity that I find most disturbing.

Truthiness

Notice that each of the five great commonalities discussed in the previous section in some significant way pertain to truth. Philosophers don't entirely agree on what constitutes truth, but most, or at least most in the English-speaking world, accept some variation on what is known as the Correspondence Theory of Truth.

The Correspondence Theory holds that something (either a belief or a statement) is true if and only if it corresponds with the way that the world is. So, my belief that my dog is on the rug next to my chair is true, if, in fact, my dog is on the rug next to my chair.

To be blunt, truth is extremely important. We count on people to be truthful with us, and especially demand this from our leaders. Societies that don't put a premium on truth are likely doomed to failure, but even if they don't fail, they will have difficulty functioning properly. We count on the press to be unbiased. We count on our leaders to be honest with us. We count on our children to be forthcoming, etc. All these things are in some sense necessary if we are to be productive, lead meaningful lives, raise good children, and so forth.

For a very long time, there has been dissatisfaction in the United States with the general level of truthfulness of our leaders. That dissatisfaction has stemmed from our politicians being occasionally willing to lie, and frequently willing to mislead or spin information. That level of dishonesty is not good (and it plays a large role in the current level of gridlock that our government experiences), but common sense along with a trusted and diligent press have kept us in a position of making generally informed decisions.

Things, however, have recently changed for the worse. Trump's propensity to lie, gaslight, and otherize with such great frequency, combined with his thorough discrediting of the press, has left many citizens in a very precarious position. When Trump and his surrogates discuss alternative facts they are literally accepting and propositions and forming beliefs that do not correspond with reality. The very notion of an alternative fact is an oxymoron. The only thing that is alternative to a fact is something that is not a fact.

This, I maintain, is the reason that many people feel that we're on the verge of becoming a dystopian society and that the comparisons to Atwood's Gilead and Orwell's *Nineteen Eighty-Four* are so apt. If people don't know what to believe, and their leaders are willing to have them believe things other than what is true, it's a small step from what we currently have to something truly horrific.

Part II

Faith Is Only a Word, Embroidered

5
Inside Gilead's Misogynist Parlors

> Now Sarai, Abram's wife, had borne him no *children*. And she had an Egyptian maidservant whose name was Hagar. So Sarai said to Abram, "See now, the LORD has restrained me from bearing *children*. Please, go in to my maid; perhaps I shall obtain children by her." . . . And Abram heeded the voice of Sarai. So he went in to Hagar, and she conceived. And when she saw that she had conceived, her mistress became despised in her eyes.
>
> —Genesis, New King James Version, 16

Accounts in other versions of Scripture describe Hagar as an Egyptian slave—a gift from Pharaoh. And other versions invoke euphemisms: We learn that Abraham "slept" with Hagar. "Sarai" becomes "Sarah" late in life after she finally conceives, and "Abram" eventually changes his name to "Abraham."

Let's unravel the Genesis narrative to reveal the rationalizations for Gilead's misogynist parlors. What's overlooked is amusing. What's ignored in the rest of Scripture—namely the Sermon on the Mount—reveals Gilead's depravity. The depravity, of course, is painfully obvious. In the name of Christianity, the patriarchy mocks the faith's highest ideals. Jesus would be anathema in Gilead. I'd like to see a dream sequence when Jesus appears before Aunt Lydia and demands to know why she has forsaken Him. Where is her

55

compassion and kindness, and passion for social justice? No wonder Nietzsche quipped: "There was only one Christian and He died on the cross."

Exegesis Freaks

What in God's name is exegesis? Indeed, what—*in God's name*—are the commanders doing to these hapless women? At the risk of revealing trade secrets, exegesis is simply interpretation of texts, especially interpretation of Scripture. Interpretation can be the life project of a scholar committed to understanding a text, or it can be the nefarious efforts of propagandists broadcasting official reality for personal aggrandizement and social control. Gilead's patriarchs can't be accused of being dedicated scholars.

The Genesis story raises questions and invites interpretation; the *Handmaid's* retelling of the story encourages speculation about how it might end. In the original handmaid's tale—a saga supposedly improvised in Gilead—we find Abraham, God's chosen patriarch, wedded to Sarah, his (Gasp!) half-sister. (Gilead patriarchs, as of this writing, haven't resorted to incest to seek sexual gratification and to reproduce the race.) It seems that despite their sibling ribaldry, many long decades came and went before Sarah produced a child. In the interim Abraham—lacking Christian forbearance—wanted offspring sooner not later, preferably a son. The marriage was on the rocks. Then, a comely possibility presented itself—Hagar, Sarah's handmaiden. And so it came to pass that "He went in to Hagar." What could go wrong?

But who was Hagar? Did she consent to intimacy with Abraham—perhaps a good career move for a slave? Or was she coerced? Now *that's* a matter of interpretation. Some interpreters say Hagar was a maid. That doesn't work for me: Maids are employees *voluntarily* contracted regarding hours, wages, and working conditions. They may—if they have a strong union—enjoy medical benefits, grievance procedures, and a retirement package.

Abraham's tent wasn't unionized—no collective bargaining. Hagar was an Egyptian slave, a gift from Pharaoh. The Handmaids, Marthas, and colonial slaves could use a strong union. Of course, interpreters often reveal more about themselves than the subject at hand. Could it be that, like certain interpreters of Scripture, Gilead's sanctimonious patriarchs call women like Offred (a.k.a. June) Handmaids to candy-coat their actual status—sex slaves?

Sisterhood was neither powerful in Abraham's tent nor in Gilead misogynist parlors. Just as Sarah became jealous of Hagar when she conceived, Serena Joy became jealous when Offred became pregnant. To preserve a modicum of marital bliss, Abraham told his wife: "Behold, your maid is in your power; do to her as you please." She did. Hagar, with child, wound up in the desert. God took pity as she suffered a wilderness experience that wasn't exactly Club Med; luckily God led them to an oasis. Even so, He commanded Hagar to return to Abraham's household and submit to Sarah. Likewise—as we twitch nervously during Season Two—Offred flees into the industrial wilderness only to return and submit to Serena Joy's rule.

There Is a Bomb in Gilead

The *Genesis* and *Handmaid* narratives intertwine—till we watch "First Blood." There's no slave rebellion in *Genesis*—after all Abraham's rule was anointed by the grace of God. Commander Waterford probably convinced himself that God was on his side, but events proved otherwise. Ofglen—whose tongue was torn out for various infractions—found an unmistakable voice in the Mayday Rebellion, a rebellion that among other things, would destroy the Commander's dream.

The Commander, currying favor with his superior, boasted about the completion of the Rachel and Leah Center—a state of the art facility for inducting new sex slaves. Ofglen immolates herself in a massive explosion that destroys the center. Commander Waterford is severely injured but survives to rape another day. Other officials are injured or killed. However, there's a troubling realization that should spin your moral compass: Innocent Handmaids and other blameless individuals also perished in the blast.

A Womb of One's Own

Offred, of course, survives—what would the series be without her? But will she also produce an heir for the Commander? There's good news and bad news. It seems promising indeed: Offred looks fifteen months pregnant in Season Two's "Smart Power." The possible bad news: What if the Commander learns that Offred was impregnated by Luke? Indeed, will there be more startling departures from the Abrahamic script?

Speaking of such departures, we find Serena enjoying a near-normal interlude with an attractive gentleman at a bar during her visit to Canada. Mark Tuello, an agent of the US Government in Exile, broaches an unthinkable thought that hits below the belt: Perhaps many of the men—such as Commander Waterford—are sterile. In any case, he assures her that due to better living through chemistry it is possible for her to have a womb of her own. So Mark makes an offer he thinks Serena can't refuse: a new life in Hawaii and liasons with new men. Oscar Wilde usually got it right: The best way to deal with temptation is to give in. Not this time. Serenea turns Mark down—no treason and coconuts for her. Nevertheless she departs with a tiki torch matchbook—just in case.

He Who Laughs Last

Meanwhile, back in Abraham's tent: in the fullness of time, God revealed to Sarah that, at long last, the inconceivable— or rather the conceivable—would occur: She would bear a child at age ninety. (Now laughter is notably absent in the Bible, but I can't resist the temptation to paraphrase Nietzsche one again: I can't believe in a God that can't laugh.) Sarah and Abraham found the revelation laughable, but came to realize that God didn't have a sense of humor: It wasn't a laughing matter for God (even though some say God must have a peculiar sense of humor for creating our species).

When God reproached the couple, Sarah denied laughing, but there's no plausible deniability standing before an omniscient God. She bore a long-awaited son and named him Isaac (funny thing; "Isaac" means "he who laughs.") A marriage on the rocks became the Rock of Ages. And blessed day! After a century, Abraham became Father Abraham. Will an aging Serena Joy also bear a son in Season Twenty? Stay tuned.

Returning to the ancient narrative, all was not well in Abraham's newfound family: Ishmael thought he'd have the last laugh; He mocked his half-brother amid a feast, a hallowed celebration honoring Isaac. The poet Berthold Brecht quipped: "He who laughs last hasn't heard the terrible news." Bad news indeed for Hagar and son: Sarah—never fond of the two—demanded their banishment. At first Abraham refused such a cruel demand. But God sided with Sarah: a rare event indeed, for God usually favors patriarchy.

Hagar, once again in the wilderness, was rescued by angels (the Muslim tradition of the Haj commemorates Hagar's eventual destination—Mecca) and Ishmael got down to the business of founding nations. Faithful to the ancient narrative, Offred doesn't have a womb of her own; it's the private property of the Waterfords. In Season Two—compounding insult and injury—we learn that like Hagar, Offred will be banished upon giving birth. Unable to hide her resentment, Serena Joy asks her slave a rhetorical question: "Wouldn't you agree? Haven't we had enough of each other?"

Following Isaac's miraculous birth, God tips off Abraham about His sacred Covenant with the Patriarch and all his male associates and descendants—they must be circumcised. At this juncture the Commander and his comrades quickly part company from the Biblical narrative: they don't line up for circumcisions. Of course God—sounding more like the dictator of North Korea—doesn't merely settle for genital mutilation; He demands unquestioned obedience—the highest virtue among the faithful of Gilead.

God commands Abraham to sacrifice Isaac, his beloved son: It's no joke for Isaac—despite his namesake. The Patriarch is less than candid with Isaac, who grows suspicious. Journeying up the sacrificial mountain the boy asks: "Behold the fire and the wood: but where *is* the lamb for a burnt offering?" Abraham replies no worries: "My son, God will provide himself a lamb for a burnt offering." Just as Isaac realized *he* was the lamb, an angel of the Lord stopped the slaughter in the nick of time. Would it surprise you if the series concluded with Commander Waterford sacrificing his son? Would the Commander explain that just as God sacrificed His Son to redeem humanity, the Commander would do the same to redeem Gilead?

Spinning Your Moral Compass

It's customary for professors to conclude lectures by making students uncomfortable by afflicting them with discussion questions. It gives students incentive to attend the next class to seek comfort and, perhaps, to preview answers for the midterm. I depart from custom. Watching *The Handmaid's Tale* is uncomfortable, if not obscene—but it has redeeming social value: It raises perennial philosophical questions that afflict the comfortable.

The show raises questions that should spin your moral compass. The questions, to understate the case, elude easy answers; indeed, maybe they're unanswerable. No wonder philosophy gets bad press when pundits dismiss the discipline as "unintelligible answers to insoluble problems." Even so, we're haunted by questions that probe our deepest values—unavoidable dilemmas. Conversations about these dilemmas promote a humbling recognition of our limits and fallibility—a proper antidote to fanaticism.

Who Gets a Pass?

Right now your moral compass points to repugnant as you read Genesis, watch *The Handmaid's Tale*, and page through history: not a pretty story as you discover slavery, incest, human sacrifice, and murder—to name but a few varieties of human folly and perfidy. But spin your moral compass: Aren't people—even the most villainous—blameless, simply products of their time? Everyone deserves a break, right? How dare we impose our contemporary standards on those ancient days in Abraham's tent, or anything else for that matter? Aren't we reflecting our parochial bias in indicting Gilead? Indeed, who's to say what's right and wrong? To invoke Nietzsche again, is ethics anything more than self-confession? In passing judgment on Gilead, don't we merely reflect the sensibilities of our culture or emotional reactions?

Philosopher Richard Rorty urged us to acknowledge our all-too-human predicament by becoming aware of our socialization: beset by radical doubt, "The ironist worries about the possibility that she may have been initiated into the wrong tribe or taught to play the wrong language game" ("Ironists and Metaphysicians," pp. 101–02). Had we been initiated into Abraham's tribe we very likely would have deemed slavery, incest, and blind obedience natural and desirable, if not virtuous—if we even thought about it.

Likewise, are you certain that, were you born and raised in Gilead, you wouldn't accept its mores—especially if you're a privileged male? Given our appreciation of multi-culturalism and tolerance, we are judgmental and indignant about those who are judgmental. After all, we don't take our cue from the missionaries who insisted that natives couldn't be naked, even in the tropics.

All that said, it seems we can't avoid thoughts of Hitler: Despite our "radical doubt," don't we ache to condemn certain practices even though we realize that individuals didn't choose their tribe? Does everyone get a pass because he or she is a product of his or her time—even Hitler?

Are the tyrants of Gilead fanatical true believers who don't know any better or shameless opportunists who are far from clueless? What of the silenced majority? Like any wise student in doubt, I answer: *both of the above*. True, some cases seem clear: Aunt Lydia—a cross between Nurse

Ratched and Ann Coulter—is a true believer. If Jesus appears to her in that dream, perhaps He would pray: "Father forgive her; she knows not what she does."

But what of Commander Waterford? Maybe Fred shouldn't get a pass because he knows better, or does he? He has occasional brushes with morality as he shows kindness to Offred. Being true to professed ideals is a cornerstone of morality, yet he thrives on parties that any fraternity boy would envy: is he an opportunist who gives hypocrisy a bad name? Fred, of course, is only human, but are certain actions unforgivable? Might Jesus appear to the Commander and pray: "Father forgive him—although he knows what he does?"

And what of the quiescent, non-rebellious Handmaids, and other denizens of Gilead experiencing quiet despair? Indeed, what of June? Spoiler alert! In a recent preview of coming attractions we find June resigned to her feckless fate as she morphs back into Offred. Are we humans infinitely malleable? Camus's Stranger comes to mind when he laments, "You can get used to anything."

There Is a Bomb in Gilead

In Season Two the resistance strikes back raising a question that is anything but hypothetical amid our wars without end: Is violence—especially violence against the innocent—ever justified? Check your moral compass: is it permissible to kill the innocent (euphemistically called collateral damage) in pursuit of a higher end? You're in holy company if you can't answer with confidence: even the saints of the Catholic Church could not agree: St. Francis advocated unconditional pacifism; St. Thomas fashioned a just war doctrine that prevails to this day; and St. Bernard enthused about holy war.

This is not the place for a full account of the doctrine, but several criteria are salient in evaluating the fictitious world of Gilead and, to be sure, our troubled, all-too-real world, a world beset by seemingly intractable moral dilemmas and conflicts.

Pacifism, to be sure, is not always effective in achieving a just cause—nonviolent resistance may permit more violence and mayhem. The same can be said, of course, for violent resistance! Any advice you care to hazard for the Mayday Rebellion?

What are the chances for success of nonviolence and violence? Can this question be answered with confidence; do we have the luxury of prescience? Ofglen didn't know; she didn't live to find out. And what of the track record of those who put young men and women in harm's way? Their record doesn't inspire confidence. The Iraq War began with "Shock and Awe" and ended with "Aw, shucks." When I team-taught a class with an Army major we disagreed about whether civilian deaths justified deposing Saddam Hussein. I told noted just war theorist Michael Walzer about the disagreement. His only advice: "Keep talking."

The violence must be proportional, but who's to judge? Apparently, members of the Gilead Resistance thought the death of the innocent at the Center was lamentable but necessary. The Canadian refugees didn't share their view.

Human Nature

The Handmaid's Tale invites us to ponder a fundamental—perhaps *the most* fundamental—question: Is there a human nature; if so, what's its essence? Once again, I wouldn't presume to answer this question in this context or any other for that matter. However, whether it be due to nature or nurture, the historical record marks the tragic failure of utopian schemes.

Theologian Reinhold Niebuhr indicted this phenomenon as the unwarranted faith of the "Children of Light." History may not be on a trajectory bending toward harmony and social justice. Indeed, Marx—one of these children—got it wrong: The workers of the world didn't unite; they warred against one another. This came as no surprise to Freud, a Child of Darkness, who lamented:

> Men are not gentle creatures who want be loved. . . . Their neighbor tempts them to satisfy their aggressiveness on him, to exploit his capacity for work without compensation, to use him sexually with his

consent, to seize his possessions, to humiliate him, to cause him pain, to torture and kill him. ("Thoughts on War and Death," p. 214)

Did Freud get it right? Is *The Handmaid's Tale* an immorality play about the dystopian fate of utopian schemes, be they Soviet-style communism, Nazism, or (what I call) utopian capitalism? Does the drama take existing trends to their illogical conclusions? Even now high officials offer Biblical justifications for separating young children from their parents, and Congressmen advocate hanging women who have abortions. Perhaps *The Handmaid's Tale* is more than impure fiction.

Linking fact and fiction, could it be that utopian capitalism's wars without end and faith in the neo-liberal marketplace led to the devastation and pollution that fomented the tyranny and gynecological disaster starkly depicted in *The Handmaid's Tale*? Or perhaps the disaster isn't entirely women's fault. Seems Mark Turillo had seminal thought: There's evidence that sperm counts have markedly decreased due, perhaps, to environmental factors.

Unlike other utopian schemes Gilead was not founded upon a benign, let alone optimistic, view of human nature; the children of darkness conceived it. The founders, the Sons of Jacob, presupposed the intractable depravity of human nature—citizens had to be watched, regulated, and totally administered. Accordingly, they created a police and surveillance state that would be the envy of the Taliban. But as thinkers from Plato to Niebuhr would remind them, given the depravity of human nature, history cannot be managed; the corruption and decay of Gilead is virtually inevitable.

6
Serena Joy, Miserable, Despicable

CHARLENE ELSBY

June remembers seeing Serena Joy on the Growing Souls Gospel Hour, and she recalls that Serena Joy "could smile and cry at the same time, one tear or two sliding gracefully down her cheek, as if on cue, as her voice lifted through its highest notes, tremulous, effortless."

What a revolting character is expressed in this one sentence—a woman having the practiced capacity to restrain emotion for the sake of performance, and then to emulate the same emotion *for the appearance* of having it. To calmly, serenely execute a practiced tear of joy, in the effort *to appear* (but not *to be*) so impassioned by the content of her song that it results in not one but *two contradictory* emotional responses, and *all of it part of the spectacle*.

We'd like to conceive of Serena Joy as a classic villain—someone who has her own, self-determined (but evil) motivations. But that's a patriarchal vision of the villain. Serena Joy is something else entirely. Having negated any concept of her own capacity to self-determine, she becomes the empty vessel, a machine through which to enact the visions of others (Gilead).

Classical theories of ethics wonder if it's possible to act against your own best intentions, and we might try to apply those kinds of frameworks to Serena Joy. Serena Joy purposefully and determinedly enacts measures against herself and her whole kind (women), and she does so by actively and

65

consistently annihilating any thought of her own interest. What she's doing is negating her own humanity (in the existential sense of negating her own freedom, which is the human condition, according to Simone de Beauvoir). She has, by virtue of being a living human, the capacity to self-determine, but she actively, willfully, takes on the roles of others, making her own freedom just an extension of the will of Gilead.

Is her oppression of other women the result of *her own* systematic oppression? In a way, sure. Does that mean we should interpret her actions as "mixed" (in the Aristotelian sense)—the result of some element of both free decision and of coercion? What's relevant is that the traditional ethical theories seem only to apply if we assume people are making *free* decisions to act freely. They generally consider it a *special case* when by chance those decisions become *in any way* coerced. What if decisions didn't work that way for the *majority* of the population? Then how would we determine the blameworthiness of actions?

On the one hand, we want to grant some leniency to Serena Joy, because she's a member of an oppressed class whose purpose in life is supposed to be living for some Commander, whose self-aggrandizing title tells us enough about him (and all the other "Commanders") to give us a hint of what it must be like to *live through* the days of her life. But just because she is oppressed doesn't mean she *isn't* a terrible human being. How might we comprehend the moral decisions of people whose actions are never freely determined?

Freedom and Responsibility

There's a well-known relation between freedom and responsibility. In order for us to claim to have responsibility, there must be a corresponding freedom that allows us to be responsible. It's apparent in Aristotle's vision of the ethical realm.

We can deliberate only over problems that are ours to solve. I can't think to myself the best way of going about colliding the sun and the earth. (Without a powerful gravity ray, this remains to me an impossibility.) There are certain decisions that aren't open to someone who is not free to make them. If your actions aren't going to have an effect on whatever situation it is you're considering, you're not really deliberating. You can fantasize about what it would be like to not be a handmaid in Gilead, but it's a whole different thing to book the van and get someone to drive it.

The connection between freedom and responsibility matters, because if someone is not free to perform actions that will affect a situation, we absolve them of responsibility. The question is whether this tendency is something we can or should do in the case of Serena Joy. Serena Joy is subjugated by her husband, and she in turn holds June down while he rapes her. Is that all right with us? We don't tend to think so. We have some sympathy for the character, but we also wonder why Serena Joy isn't poisoning the Commander's corn flakes at the first available opportunity.

Serena Joy is also a special case, because it seems to us she played an integral role in ensuring her own subjugation. In the show, Serena Joy wrote the books professing the values she now embodies, for instance, that women shouldn't be allowed to write books. How she can suffer through the cognitive dissonance of that one is through bad faith. But before I go into that, we should first try to figure out what responsibility Serena Joy has for her current lack of freedom—the lack of freedom that seems to absolve her of responsibility.

The vast majority of ethical systems—at least, those most commonly represented as constituting the history of moral philosophy—depend on the idea that we act in relative freedom. We say that someone does something voluntarily if we think they had the option to do otherwise than they did. We say they acted involuntarily if they were somehow forced into doing what they did.

The question then becomes: What's the definition of "forced"? Does oppression by a patriarchal society count as force? Then things get complicated. We consider the differences between force, coercion and exploitation. We put at the far end of the spectrum actions in which we had no involvement at all—for instance, if I were carried away by the wind, and my body ended up having some effect on the universe that I didn't intend. Perhaps it blew through someone's window. Would I be responsible for that window breaking? We want to say no, even though all of my female readers know that I would feel bad about it anyway and offer to pay for the damage.

Then there's the "bad upbringing" argument. This isn't a new argument, but one Aristotle touched on 2,500 years ago. Is the situation in which we live to be considered, when we attempt to figure out whether they are morally responsible for some action, which seems to be the result of their situation? Is the starving man responsible for the fact that he stole bread? Is it at least a different consideration than if we were to consider an affluent man who stole bread for kicks?

Aristotle goes so far as to determine that there are some people who are never capable of being morally responsible. If some people are not raised in a situation where they have the option of making moral decisions, where they're constantly focused on survival instead of a lofty consideration of their fellow humans, then Aristotle thinks they aren't moral beings. Neither do they have the freedom to make moral decisions, nor are they responsible for the moral implications of their actions.

While it seems kind of us to account for mitigating circumstances, this is actually one of the first "people are animals" arguments that we encounter in the history of philosophy, and we might consider it to be morally reprehensible in itself. On the one hand, it seems merciful of us to say that someone did something worthy of moral reproach, but only because of their circumstance. On the other hand, this consideration conceives of that person as no better than a cat who eats the family bird.

Humanity's Freedom

Existentialist ethics do better than Aristotelian ethics in figuring out the relation between human responsibility and human freedom. In *Being and Nothingness*, Jean-Paul Sartre goes on about how humanity is responsible for everything over which it has the freedom to act. And he is willing to cover the spread with this claim.

If we have to choose between subjugation and death, and we choose subjugation, Sartre would say that we freely chose our subjugation, and are therefore responsible to some extent. To what extent? Is the person who chooses subjugation over death responsible for their subjugation? Obviously not—the whole idea of subjugation is that it is perpetrated by someone (usually someones) else. The person who chooses subjugation over death is responsible for choosing subjugation over death (and that's it).

According to Sartre, it is the human condition to be free; in that condition, we're responsible for what we do. If I set something on fire, I'm responsible for it burning. But am I *morally* responsible? Sartre, at least, believes that you can specify to what extent I am responsible for the fire, as a cause, without specifying whether I'm also blameworthy. It's like saying that water is responsible for water damage, without making the inference that we should blame the water and punish it accordingly.

Sartre leaves it as an open question whether or not we would be more responsible if we were completely free, or if we take into account the fact that we always act within a particular situation. He writes, a few lines before ending *Being and Nothingness*, "In particular, will freedom by taking itself for an end escape all situation? Or on the contrary, will it remain situated? Or will it situate itself so much the more precisely and the more individually as it projects itself further in anguish as a conditioned freedom and accepts more fully its responsibility as an existent by whom the world comes into being."

If I take freedom as the ultimate value of human existence, will I enact that freedom better when I am not constrained by an environment (like Serena Joy's particular position in Gilead), or will I better enact my freedom *because* of my environment? In the *Handmaid's Tale*, Serena Joy is conflicted just because on the one hand, her abstract values led to this society she lives in, but now that she's in it, it seems that she's very much responsible for *this* rape of June, perpetrated by *her* husband. Are we more responsible when we form abstract principles, like "Women should have children," or when we lock June up in her room for a month, waiting for her to ovulate again so that the Commander can rape her?

Simone de Beauvoir takes up the challenge of providing us with an existentialist ethics, and she's willing to specify that as free beings, we're responsible for valuing that freedom, maintaining that freedom, and ensuring the freedom of others as well. Her *Ethics of Ambiguity* goes into detail about the specifics of an ethics that values freedom as its end. At the same time, she recognizes that marginalized groups feel less responsible for the state of the world, and therefore less free to make the world conform to their ideals. Beauvoir gives what I take to be a psychological explanation of Serena Joy at the end of *The Second Sex*, explaining how women in general don't feel as if they *can* change the world:

> The men that we call great are those who—in one way or another—have taken the weight of the world upon their shoulders; they have done better or worse, they have succeeded in recreating it or they have gone down; but first they have assumed that enormous burden. This is what no woman has ever done, what none has ever been *able* to do. To regard the universe as your own, to consider yourself to blame for its faults and glory in its progress, you must belong to the caste of the privileged; it is for those alone who are in command to justify the universe by changing it, by thinking about it, by revealing it; they alone can recognize themselves in it and endeavor to make their mark upon it.

To consider changing the world, we must consider that what we want to change about it is within our control. If Serena Joy can't change the world, we don't want to hold her responsible for not doing it. But at the same time, she was definitely complicit in the process of how her world came to be as it is. We want to think that, because of her situation, she's less blameworthy for the harm that comes to herself and others. At the same time, she's responsible for putting herself and others in that situation.

Serena Joy and Bad Faith

"Embrace your biological destiny!" Serena Joy screams at an angry crowd in Season Two's "First Blood." Is it Serena Joy's biological destiny to profess this opinion in very public venues and ensure the subjugation of women? Surely not. The idea that she can express a well-reasoned opinion to the effect that she should be focused on making babies instead of expressing well-reasoned opinions is contradictory.

What's more interesting than the answer to "Is Serena Joy morally responsible, to what extent, and how should we punish her?" is the question, "How did she even happen?" How can Serena Joy act against her own interests, and with such zeal, and not have it ever occur to her that, hey, maybe you shouldn't give public lectures that recommend the enslavement of your own kind? Instead of asking how many blame units we should impose on her, we would do better to ask, what is wrong with this woman?

Serena Joy is doing what anyone might do in her situation, but which the existentialists recommend explicitly against. She's acting in bad faith. She is able to justify her own actions to herself using various conceptual twists and turns, and she deludes herself into thinking she's doing the right thing. Whereas we try to conceive of her as the embodiment of evil, doing so would be lazy philosophy. All of our human experience tells us that there's no such thing as an evil human, who just wants to harm for the sake of doing harm. We're all aiming at the good, in one way or another, and so is Serena Joy. She just has her very own twisted conception of what's good, which includes things that are objectively bad.

Bad faith is the opposite of good faith. When we say someone's acting in good faith, we mean that they made an honest attempt, they really tried, they're authentic or sincere. There are a few ways to deviate from this model into the territory of bad faith. A simple way of describing Serena Joy's situation is that she's lying to herself. But as Sartre points out, you can't lie without knowing the truth and intending to deceive someone. Bad faith is something else—it's how we try to make it so that we *don't* know the truth, so that some of our more abhorrent actions will be easier to swallow.

The idea that "Some people aren't people" is meant to justify despicable acts towards our fellow humans. After all, if these people are not people, we would not have to afford them all of the rights that we afford people. If Aristotle is right, and some people are not capable of moral action, some other people will try to justify not treating them as people by claiming that they are, indeed, animals. The Republic of Gilead is a theocratic regime that seems to buy into this way of thinking. There's a long history of religious philosophy that aims to justify such absurd conclusions (which I argue can be held only in bad faith). For example, Boethius in Book IV of the *Consolation of Philosophy* suggests that if a person does evil things, they are literally turned into animals. The kind of animal depends on what kind of evil the person does:

> One man, a savage thief, pants after and is ravenous for the goods of other people—you can say that he is like a wolf. Another man, vicious, never resting, has his tongue always in motion in lawsuits—you can compare him to a dog. One man, the hidden plotter, lying in wait, is glad to steal by his deceptions—he can be said to be the same as the foxes. Another roars, giving free rein to his anger—he may be believed to have within him the spirit of the lion. One man, a coward, is quick to turn tail, afraid of things that he need not fear—he is thought to be like the deer. Another, indolent and slack-jawed, is simply inert—he lives the life of an ass. One man, fickle and flighty, changes his interests constantly—he is not at all different from birds. Another wallows in foul and unclean lusts—he is held under by the physical delights of a filthy sow. And so it is that anyone who has ceased to be a human being by deserting righteousness, since he has not the power to cross over into the divine condition, is turned into a beast.

The Republic of Gilead is doing the same thing when they split up women into the classes of women and "unwomen"—

women who aren't women. This kind of thinking can only happen with a strong application of bad faith. "Some people aren't people" is an obvious contradiction, and for someone actually to believe it, they have to do some rigorous mental gymnastics. It's a statement of the form "A is not A," which is a blatant contradiction. In order to make it work, you have to replace one of those terms and say something else instead, like, "These birds aren't people." At the same time, the people who say, "These people aren't people" don't believe that "these people" are *actual birds* and if they did, they wouldn't be holding them morally responsible for their actions.

No, in order to say that, "Some people aren't people," you would first have to admit that they *are people* who are morally responsible, and then convince yourself that, because they are morally responsible for their actions, they should be treated like animals. "These women aren't women" is the same thing. It's a bad faith reasoning process all around.

Serena Joy goes through her own bad-faith reasoning process. She has the idea that she's acting toward a greater good. The survival of the species depends on her locking June in a room and designing a ceremony to make all the raping more palatable. At first, it might appear as if one big right is overpowering a little wrong. That would be a utilitarian conception—some have to sacrifice for the good of the many. What's going on with Serena Joy is more insidious. She no longer conceives of raping June as a wrong that nevertheless must be committed; raping June comes to be conceived of the *means by which* a right is accomplished.

It comes to appear as a good in itself. This is made possible by bad faith—in this case, an intentional obscuring of an obvious truth, "Raping people is bad." The concepts get twisted, until she can find some way to make herself believe that, "Raping people is good." She believes that it's June's biological destiny to produce children. If only June would do it willingly, it wouldn't be rape, she comes to think. But June is so rebellious.

Serena Joy comes to think of June as a traitor, whose suffering is due to her own unwillingness to accept her destiny.

With that twist of thinking, she is able to deny herself any responsibility for what's happening. She has shifted the blame. On some level, she's thinking to herself that they all must make sacrifices for the sake of the common good, and that while she herself is playing her role in the new social order, June is forsaking her duties. It's not Serena Joy who's acting unjustly, on her own account. It's June who doesn't seem to care about the future of the species, who would rather not put up with a pregnancy for the sake of a child, and who is so lucky as to enjoy a household such as hers rather than being sent to the colonies, like some other unfortunate women. Accepting the role of subjugation, Serena Joy thinks that June should do the same, and because she doesn't, she suffers.

This kind of thinking leads to unspeakable cruelty. Simone de Beauvoir mentions this offhand in the conclusion to *The Second Sex*, speaking about the capacity for women to be cruel to men, just because men are part of the privileged class and women are not. She says, "Here we find the explanation of the cruelty that woman often shows she is capable of practicing; she has a good conscience because she is on the unprivileged side."

The same *kind* of thinking goes on when Serena Joy attempts to justify her cruelty to June and the other handmaids. She classifies herself among the unprivileged, and so any act of rebellion by June becomes an act against the unprivileged. Not only can she conceive of June as willfully denying her responsibility for the continued existence of the human race, June is also acting against Serena Joy, the unprivileged, and is therefore another kind of oppressor, who must be dealt with accordingly.

Taking all of this into account, we can comprehend why and how Serena Joy behaves as she does. But the fact that her actions are comprehensible doesn't mean they're not also morally reprehensible. In the contemporary age, we're learning more and more that what we might have tried earlier to dismiss as incomprehensible evil is, in fact, very comprehensible.

We can understand how she comes to believe what she believes, and why she acts how she acts—but she's still abhorrent, and so is what she's doing to June. We understand why she is how she is, but she doesn't have to be that way, and she shouldn't.

7
Remix in Gilead

SETH M. WALKER

Our Father who art in Heaven . . . Seriously? What the actual fuck?

—Matthew 6:9

Okay, so that's not exactly what you'd find at Matthew 6:9 in a typical Christian Bible. But what Offred is doing here is actually something we see a lot of throughout Margaret Atwood's *The Handmaid's Tale* and the television show: remix.

"Wait, what does this have to do with music?" you might be wondering—a creative practice all but outlawed in its entirety throughout Gilead. I'm not exactly—well, not *specifically*—talking about music (those Holy Rollers are certainly *music* to someone's ears, right?). The metaphorical extension of "remix" as a concept in areas outside audio-visual applications has been gaining momentum in the field of remix studies: *all* of culture's productions—like Old Dutch Cleanser and an admiration for Geoffrey Chaucer's witty titles—can be *sampled* and *remixed* into something *new*. And we see this happening all over the place through Gilead's selective sampling of Old Testament scripture and Christian theology in its authoritarian mashup state.

In the "Historical Notes" section at the end of the book, Professor James Darcy Pieixoto of the future Gileadean Research Association tells us "there was little that was truly original with or indigenous to Gilead: its genius was synthesis" (*The Handmaid's Tale*, p. 307). This reuse of cultural artifacts (sampling source material) in the production of something new (a remixed work) is marked by its transformative qualities—elements that many remix scholars point out as key features of remixed works. In other words, the Christian theology and scripture being reworked involves a transformation of that *original* content to effect new meaning and value in a much different context.

From the compelled mantra-like expressions (Blessed Be the Fruit, May the Lord Open, Under His Eye, Praise Be), simultaneous polygamy (though not exactly voluntary or referred to in that way), extreme patriarchy, the labeling for shops and storefronts (like Milk and Honey, Loaves and Fishes, and Daily Bread), and even the name Gilead itself—a biblical area near the Jordan River—to the grounding of the "Ceremony" in the biblical story of Jacob and his wives' handmaids, the association of Queen Jezebel with the underground lifestyle among Gilead's elite, and various personnel and groups (like Guardians of the Faith, Commanders of the Faithful, Eyes of God, Angels of the Apocalypse, and Children of Ham), it's clear that the Sons of Jacob (another good example!) have pointedly sampled certain elements to craft their own theocratic society revolving around biblical tenets: the Gileadean Redux, we might playfully call it.

You Must Feel Pretty Ripped Off

But should we understand this Gileadean Redux as an *authentic* manifestation of Christianity? Atwood herself doesn't think this biblical theopolitical cherry-picking is the real deal, since it lacks certain features compared to what *is* emphasized: "core" behaviors, she shared in an interview with *Sojourners* in 2017, like loving your neighbor *and* your enemy. And the story aims to make sure we understand that as well: Offred regularly talks to "God" throughout both the book and series, she constantly prays to herself, and the television series has her going as far as creating an altar for those killed at the *Boston Globe* building ("Unwomen")—all of which lead us to believe she views Gileadean ideology as something *other*.

While Atwood didn't really elaborate much more on this "core" that makes or breaks the Christian label, it's helpful to point out that this tends to be the way we think about a lot of different things: what needs to be present for something to be considered one thing and not another? How do we know what *counts* as Christianity, and how can we be certain Gilead isn't it? "You must feel pretty ripped off," Offred ponders in her version of the so-called Lord's Prayer (Matthew 6:9–13). "I guess it's not the first time," she adds. Given the role of Christian traditions in countless atrocities and violent regimes throughout history, it's easy to side with her and assume Gilead isn't much different in the greater scheme of things. But thinking about all of this in terms of remix might help us better understand how theocracies like the Republic of Gilead are formed and sustained.

Coupled with Atwood's public remarks, the tale's particular representation of Christian elements leads readers and viewers to recognize what is happening in Gilead as not *really* being Christianity. But why might we— Atwood included—be so quick to draw that sort of comparative conclusion or assume that there exists an *authentic* or *original* Christianity against which something like Gilead can be judged or evaluated?

Should "God" actually feel ripped off?

I Knew They Made That Up . . . They Left Things Out, Too

The process of emphasizing and excluding certain Christian elements we see in Gileadean culture—and behind Atwood's judgment of authenticity—is a great demonstration of how the transformation of *original* content to effect new meaning and value actually works. Offred tells us that the so-called Beatitudes (Matthew 5) were read to them every day during their training at the Rachel and Leah Center. As we all know, "Blessed are the meek" (Matthew 5:5) is a favorite recurring line throughout the book and series. But (and prompting a cattle prod to the jaw in "Late" for reminding Aunt Lydia) Offred notes that the Aunts in charge of their indoctrination always left some stuff out, such as the "for they shall inherit the Earth" line immediately following it. The Aunts also made some stuff up entirely: "Blessed are the silent" they tell their subjects. The problem, of course, Offred states, is that the Handmaids don't really have a way to cross-check any of this. And what good would it do anyway?

Remember Your Scripture

This is far from the only instance, too. In passing, Offred quotes, "From each, according to her ability; to each according to his needs" (p. 117) when discussing the distribution of Handmaids in Gilead (not everyone was as lucky as Commander Waterford). It's from the Bible—St. Paul, in the Acts of the Apostles—she tells us, "or so they said." But here's the thing: it's not. It's actually a popular slogan from *Critique of the Gotha Program* (1875) by Karl Marx (1818–1883)—a letter addressing strategies for class shifts during the transition from capitalism to communism. And actually, it's been remixed a little as well ("her" instead of "his").

You've got to love the irony here too, given how Marx felt about theistic, otherworldly forms of religion: they're effectively opiates that keep the working class unquestioningly in line, warding off the potential for revolution since the subordinated merely look to some other realm for their salvation rather than under their noses and raising arms. The Aunts do cover their ground a little, I suppose: Acts 4:32–35 does address "distribution" according to need, but the emphasis on common possession is certainly skewed.

The selective sampling taking place in Gilead is part of a focused exercise in making sure this all still appears to be *Christian*. And it's reminiscent of a popular form of musical remix: a restrictive remix—one that follows rules, templates, and algorithms in its construction rather than "anything goes." One of the most famous examples of this (sometimes referred to as an A-B mashup) is Danger Mouse's *Grey Album* (2004): a mashup of The Beatles' *White Album* (1968) and Jay-Z's *Black Album* (2003). In an A-B mashup, the remixer is *restricted* to sampling the instrumental track (The Beatles) from one recording and playing the vocal track (Jay-Z) from another on top of it.

We're seeing the same sort of thing with Gilead in the creation of a theopolitical system under certain, restricted parameters. The producers of the series missed a great soundtrack opportunity in "Jezebels" as well. But in Gilead, it's a question of what both *needs* to be there for it to remain "Christian" for its followers and converts and what's *available* in the cultural "archive" of Christian theological elements. Seventeenth-century Puritan society is an acknowledged source. We might recognize some elements of dominionism and Christian reconstructionism as well: the foundation of society resting on biblical law and scripture, specifically. The Sons of Jacob apparently had some choices to make.

The Wives Would Eat That Shit Up

The use of Scripture-influenced practices and laws clearly highlights those choices. The most obvious is the euphemistic Ceremony based on the account in Genesis 30:1–3 ("Behold my maid Bilhah, go in unto her; and she shall bear upon my knees, that I may also have children by her."). But there's a whole assortment of selective sampling noted throughout the book and series that establishes this framework: control over the treatment of Handmaids by the Wives (Genesis 16:6); the head covering—or shaving (you're hilarious, Aunt Lydia)—required of Handmaids (1 Corinthians 11:3–9); the designation of "Marthas" as helpers in the house (Luke 10:38–42); the refusal of anesthetics for a painful childbirth (Genesis 3:16); the prohibition of reading among women and their subordination under men (Timothy 2:9–15); the death penalty for rape (Deuteronomy 22:23–29); legal cases against "gender treachery" (Romans 1:26); the removal of an eye or hand for transgressions (Matthew 5:29–30); and that insistence on remaining "meek" (Matthew 5:5).

It doesn't really seem, though, as if these passages and accounts were what led to the Gileadean ideology. Not exactly. It's more like the other way around. Atwood notes in the introduction to the book's latest edition that the story is not "anti-religion" (and that's clear enough from Offred's own thoughts and comments); it's against the *use* of religion for tyrannical purposes.

Aside from Scripture, we also witness that *use* during a flashback scene in "Jezebels"—when Commanders Waterford, Pryce, and Guthrie are discussing the formation of the Handmaid program: "There is Scriptural precedent" for it, Pryce points out, following Waterford's reminder that they need the support of the Wives or they won't succeed. Calling it a "ceremony" sounds "nice and Godly," Guthrie adds. "The Wives would eat that shit up." And apparently, they did—well, maybe some of the programs and policies more so than others: just ask Serena Joy how much she loves "traditional" forms of women's work like knitting (she "truly detests" it, we learn in "Women's Work"), having her own ideals twisted into her very subjugation, or a good whipping by her dear husband. I think we all know the answer to those last two as well.

Prayers and sermons aren't immune to this selective sampling either—even among Gilead's fearful subjects. Offred remixes the famed hymn "Amazing Grace," playing with words like "bound" and "free" to better reflect her condition (p. 54). And her own spin on the Lord's Prayer (pp. 194–95) is rich in ironic commentary and tongue-in-cheek remarks (even though I think we all prefer that more to-the-point version of this at the beginning of "June"). But in various scenes throughout the series, we see mashup more noticeably taking place.

A good example of this is when Jeanine hands over her baby (*their* baby, sorry) to Commander Putnam and his wife Naomi in "The Bridge": Putnam solemnly reads from his Bible during the ritualized scene. It sounds like a single passage, too. But it's not. He's explicitly mashed up Luke 1:48, Genesis 33:6, and 2 Samuel 2:6 to make a commentary fitting the occasion. Serena Joy's union ritual with Offred ("Other Women") does something similar with Job 5:9 and Matthew 19:14. And we see the same thing happening at the Prayvaganza (quite the creative title for a revamped "worship service" and display of piety, no?) when Commander Pryce is presiding over the group wedding ("Seeds"): his favorite passages for the occasion are apparently Genesis 2:18, Genesis 2:22, Genesis 3:16, and Genesis 2:24. The remix artist in him knows there's no need to stick to one passage in particular, its entirety, or order.

All We've Done Is Return Things to Nature's Norm

Another underlying theme throughout the tale is the idea that what is happening now in the former United States is a particular deviation from what had been a recognizable norm: there was some *thing* from which this *new* thing has emerged. For those in Offred's position, it's obviously an unwelcome change. "Every night when I go to bed I think, In the morning I will wake up in my own house and things will be back to the way they were," she tells us (p. 199).

But for people like Commander Waterford, it's been a corrective sort of reversal in society. The years before Gilead emerged? They "were just an anomaly, historically speaking . . . Just a fluke. All we've done is return things to Nature's norm" (p. 220). Either way, the idea is present in both camps: there is some sort of original or untarnished state with which Gilead is in dialogue. And Offred's understanding of Christianity in contrast to what Gilead is peddling demonstrates this as well: during her Lord's Prayer, she also states, "I don't believe for an instant that what's going on out there is what You meant" (p. 194).

The problem, though, and something remix theory directly engages, is that this romantic vision of an original, static form is as much a fairytale as the timeless stories influencing the title of Atwood's work itself: they don't exist. And remix theory helps us see through some of the issues with these types of assumptions. The gist is that ideas like sole authorship and creation from nothing (creation *ex nihilo*, if we want to be fancy) are troubling modern constructs that stifle creation in the contemporary world. Everything is *always* building upon what came before; influence and inspiration are seldom fully acknowledged (myself and my fellow contributors to this volume are doing it too—building upon a genre, stylistically). So this idea that Offred's former life was never in flux or that some pure state was tarnished and Gilead is a swift return to that Puritan state (recall the museum to Gilead's *actual* "ancestors" Offred and Ofglen point out to us in the book) is a problem on both sides.

What You Meant

For the first few centuries or so of the Common Era, there wasn't really something neatly separated that we'd call "Christianity," distinct from other ideologies in their respective areas. Places, people, events, varying beliefs and worldviews— all of these things necessarily lead to the creation and development of *new* cultural features. Religious traditions are no different, and it gets very hard to pinpoint precise moments of their creation since practices, concepts, and worldviews already in existence help shape the formation of new ones.

Gilead is no different either. Pieixoto tells us, "As we know from the study of history, no new system can impose itself upon a previous one without incorporating many of the elements to be found in the latter, as witness the pagan elements in medieval Christianity and the evolution of the Russian 'KGB' from the czarist secret service that preceded it; and Gilead was no exception to this rule" (p. 305).

The Item in Its Original Form

That "Historical Notes" section at the end of the book provides us with another great opportunity to engage remix theory. Not long into Pieixoto's "Problems of Authentication in Reference to *The Handmaid's Tale*," we realize that the text we just read was not actually a manuscript when Pieixoto and Professor Knotly Wade first encountered it: it was an unorganized collection of about thirty cassette tapes someone (Offred) had recorded, presumably *after* the events described had taken place. Pieixoto and Wade, ultimately deciding that the tapes weren't a forgery, simply assembled and transcribed the collection "in the order in which they appeared to go," which was based on approximate "guesswork." It wasn't a manuscript when it was discovered, it certainly didn't have a title (we can thank Professor Wade for seeing Atwood's Chaucer reference through), and it "is not the item in its original form." This all might sound a little familiar, too (if you aren't already thinking about Bibles and how *they* were assembled, you should be now). How *authentic* is this tale, then?

It's definitely a reconstruction. Offred even says so: "This is a reconstruction. All of it is a reconstruction" (p. 134). This is a recurring theme throughout the narrative, too. When she's relaying Moira's attempted escape, she tells us: "I can't remember exactly, because I had no way of writing it down. I've filled it out for her as much as I can: we didn't have much time so she just gave the outlines . . . I've tried to make it sound as much like her as I can." The same sort of thing takes place when she's describing her first encounter with Nick. After her first version, she notes, "I made that up. It didn't happen that way." Then after the second version, "It didn't happen that way either. I'm not sure how it happened; not exactly. All I can hope for is a reconstruction" (p. 263). So does that make the jumbled cassette tapes even less authentic than what actually happened, being an additional, reconstructive step removed? Well, it might not be that simple.

Always Already Reconstructed

The bigger question we're dealing with here is whether or not Gilead is *authentically* Christian. The French postmodern theorist Jean Baudrillard (1929–2007) can help us see why remix theorists might be troubled by even asking that sort of question. According to Baudrillard, our situation is one in which representation has become more *real* to us than what is *really real*. In *Symbolic Exchange and Death* (1976), he tells us that "the real is not only that which can be reproduced, but *that which is always already reproduced*." This *hyperreality* of ours is comprised of simulacra: representations that no longer refer to anything that *really* exist—signs without referents in the *real* world.

His most famous example demonstrating this in *Simulacra and Simulation* (1981) is Disneyland: from the pristine Main Street, U.S.A. to the coon-skinned caps Mickey Mouse innocently sports throughout Frontierland, Disneyland's version of history seems to make us believe (or want to believe) while we're there that it is more real to us than what *actually* happened. Mickey frolicking around with his cartoonish musket leaves little room for a mural depicting the decimation of indigenous populations. But leaving the park, we realize that what's outside is obviously more *real* than the sterilized images and representations across its threshold. Except, that's not really what's going on: Baudrillard tells us that "Disneyland exists in order to hide that it is the 'real' country, all of 'real' America that is Disneyland . . . Disneyland is presented as imaginary in order to make us believe that the rest is real, whereas all of Los Angeles and the America that surrounds it are no longer real, but belong to the hyperreal order and to the order of simulation" (*Simulacra and Simulation*, p. 12). It conceals that America is actually hyperreal itself: there's no longer any difference between image and reality. Bleak, huh?

We don't necessarily need to spend our lives dwelling on what we're to do now, knowing that *everything* is actually hyperreal, but we can use this insight to point out that the distinction between real and representation no longer matters as much as we might have initially thought—and that the question of authenticity might be somewhat misguided, if an "authentic" *anything* is no longer to be found. Baudrillard's interpretation of reality here can also help us realize something else about Gilead: we might think of it as existing not as a contrast to *real* Christianity, but in order to hide the fact that it *is* Christianity. Gilead isn't unique for us in this regard; it's *presented* as unique in order to make us believe it actually is.

It Was Not a Manuscript at All

We can apply Baudrillard's thinking in another way as well: remixed works (and what Pieixoto and Wade have done with Offred's cassette tapes is most certainly a remix) shouldn't be thought of as copying material from an "original"; they should be thought of as creating *new* originals from copies themselves. Remix scholars point out that music recordings, for instance, tend to be thought about as pure preservations—that they are actual *recordings* of things that were singularly performed. The truth is that they are typically made of bits and fragments pieced together by engineers and producers. The recording is already a copy, and most likely, already itself a remixed work.

So should we consider the Pieixoto and Wade manuscript—*The Handmaid's Tale*—a poor copy of guesswork assemblage? A copy of a copy based on a reconstructed account from Offred's memory? Is it more *real* to us than the cassette recordings, the reconstructed narrative she committed to memory, and what *actually* happened? Who's to say which version is *really* the most authentic in this situation? I told you this wasn't that simple.

But what if we change the way we're thinking about originals, copies, and simulacra? In "Plato and the Simulacrum" (1967), Gilles Deleuze (1925–1995) notes that copies and simulacra aren't exactly the same thing. Whereas a copy is always in response to an original, a simulacrum is copying the *appearance* of that original. With Baudrillard, we get this sort of implication that we're living an inauthentic representative reality of images without any *real* correspondence. But for Deleuze, the situation can become one of liberation: simulacra are no longer constrained to what an original requires as a guide towards the copying of it. "If we say of the simulacrum that it is a copy of a copy, an infinitely degraded icon, an infinitely loose resemblance, we then miss the essential, that is, the difference in nature between simulacrum and copy . . . The copy is an image endowed with resemblance, the simulacrum is an image without resemblance" (p. 257). It is *not* a "degraded" copy, following Deleuze; it is both free from the constraints of appealing to an "original" and from the sequential chain and hierarchy of resemblance that make it out to be mere imitation rather than *real* itself.

So, does freeing the Gileadean "copy" help make it more authentic as a Christian political movement, since an *original* "Christianity" doesn't really exist? Are the "spoken" prayers rolling out at Soul Scrolls less authentic and degraded copies of the prayers *originally* called in by Gilead's pious Wives? Or are they unique, performative demonstrations of loyalty and piety, actual content aside? There's not necessarily a clear answer here, and it might seem like we've just embarked on our own sort of Particicution in trying to make sense of how authentic both Offred's tale and the Republic of Gilead actually are. But in many ways, this is also the point of critical remix: a cognitive disruption that forces us to rethink things we normally take for granted—and power, hierarchy, and authority are all very important features of this.

It's Truly Amazing What We Could Get Used To

Framing the processes and practices of the Republic of Gilead as remix allows us to uniquely reconsider our own ways of thinking about concepts like originality and authenticity. It also helps us remember that the world revolves around change. And one of the other things *The Handmaid's Tale* reminds us is that change isn't always most effective when it's quick.

The Sons of Jacob worked thoughtfully and deliberately for Gilead, which allowed them to gradually infiltrate the deeper recesses of the United States government before the

President's Day Massacre, when the President was shot and Congress machine-gunned. In "Baggage," while cutting out old newspaper clippings during her stint at the abandoned *Boston Globe* building, Offred realizes something startling about this group: "You were there, all the time. But no one noticed you." Well, not exactly *no one*, she adds. People like her activist mother did.

She recalls her mother having once told her that it's "truly amazing what we could get used to." Granted, she was talking about women and their rights being slowly stripped away, but it's an important point regarding change in general, power, and the use of certain features in the creation of something new. "Nothing changes instantaneously," Offred points out early on in the novel. "In a gradually heating bathtub you'd be boiled to death before you knew it" (p. 56). And *that*, along with the way Gilead specifically uses its source material, is perhaps what's most haunting about this tale.

8
From the Handmaid's Tale to the Handmaids' Tale

Trip McCrossin

"*Job*," Offred exclaims, a little more than midway through Margaret Atwood's *The Handmaid's Tale*. "It's a funny word," she continues, in one of her many reminiscences of "the time before," discussing in particular how for her, for women of Gilead generally, it's "strange, now, to think about having a job."

It's also a pretty famous name. We may wonder, given the various scriptural references that punctuate the novel, and its overall moral and political outlook. We're put off at first, as she continues her having-a-job refrain, but then suddenly, the reference, set out in its very own paragraph, rises conspicuously from the page: "The Book of Job."

The Handmaid's Tale surely reflects the problem for which Job is the conventional touchstone: the problem of evil—the perniciously difficult to satisfy "need to find order within those appearances so unbearable that they threaten reason's ability to go on," as Susan Neiman has described it, as when (at times incomprehensibly) bad things happen to (at least relatively) good people, and (at least relatively) good things to (at times incomprehensibly) bad people.

I Want to Know What I Did to Deserve This

From its ancient origins in the Book of Job, or farther back even in the Babylonian *Poem of the Righteous Sufferer*, through the early decades of the Enlightenment, the problem of evil is primarily a theological problem. Human reason strains, in the above "find order" spirit, to reconcile conspicuous human suffering with faith in divine wisdom, power, and benevolence, which either makes or allows it to happen.

Midway through the Enlightenment, however, as Neiman proposes, the problem began to evolve to include also a more *secular* version. Here, while it's no longer in response to suffering's ostensibly divine origin, reason strains similarly nonetheless. In both versions, we worry that the strain may be sufficient to call into question reason's *ability* to make the order it so fervently desires.

The Handmaid's Tale, in the original and the reformulation, is unusual in this respect, concerned as it is with *both* versions of the problem. Notwithstanding its rich assortment of religious and theological references, the storyline is engaged with the secular version. What follows the above reference to the Book of Job is a detailed description of the shockingly sudden political rise of Gilead, which in the series spreads across various episodes.

Gilead ultimately falls, as the novel's "Historical Notes" reveals (following the model of the Appendix in Orwell's *Nineteen Eighty-four*, which reveals the fall of *that* dystopian regime). While the "Historical Notes" doesn't tell us just how Gilead meets its demise, we can expect that the TV show will do so.

Whatever Offred may think of the Commander's sermonizing in advance of the first Ceremony, she's also driven to a different, more private dialogue, which appears to be not only genuinely observant, but also, as such, channeling Job.

"I pray silently," she offers, "*Nolite te bastardes carborundorum*," a phrase her predecessor etched in her closet, which she'll learn the meaning of only later, from the Commander, in a rendezvous subsequent to the above ones. Still, "it will have to do," she adds, "because I don't know what else I can say to God." Faced with the unfathomable, what better response than the meaningless, which she emphasizes in repeating the gesture, but adding a question. "Oh God, I pray," and again, "*Nolite te bastardes carborundorum*," its meaning still elusive, but now, in that spirit, she asks, "Is this what you had in mind?"—as in unfathomable abuse, or partially meaningless prayers in response, or both?

We can't help but hear in Offred's prayer Job's memorable plea. The Accusing Angel torments him, as a result of God's wager that, as the most righteous of subjects, he can withstand whatever torment may come. He's unaware of their rivalry, however, let alone its point in this instance, and so, while he has no desire to "curse God," he wants a story as to why, given his righteousness, he's being allowed to suffer. "What have I done to you, Watcher of Men?," Job objects, "Why have you made me your target and burdened me with myself?"

And the echo of Job's plea is all the more palpable in the reformulation of Offred's prayer for television, moved to a moment alone before the onset of the first Ceremony, midway through the series premiere. As in the original, she descends from her room, enters the sitting room, alone for the time being, and kneels in the appointed place. As reformulated, however, we hear her ponder now, Job-like, "I want to know what I did to deserve this." And it's all the more provocative in relation to Offred's subsequent recollection of Janine's Testifying, and the manner in which it's presented to us.

As Offred thinks the above question, initially, the camera slowly pans in on the left side of her face, on her left eye in particular it seems, and, while the background music continues unabated, it cuts to what we first imagine to be a close-up of her left eye, with the camera panning slowly out now. As it does, and as a bandaged right eye becomes visible, the music begins to fade into a ticking clock, and we realize that this is no longer Offred, but Janine.

"The boys just kept coming," she begins then to describe, at Aunt Lydia's instigation, to Handmaids seated in a circle around her, her horrific pre-Gilead gang rape. Aunt Lydia's goal is a twisted sort of pedagogy. "And who led them on?," she asks Janine, "Who's fault was it?" When Janine says she doesn't know, Aunt Lydia asks the encircling Handmaids, who, on cue, raise their arms, point at Janine, and repeat, over and over, "Her fault!" Offred, newly arrived at the Center, and new to this ritual in particular, is slow to join in, and has her right ear boxed as a result. "And why did God allow such a terrible thing to happen?," Aunt Lydia asks in turn, and with Offred joining in, the Handmaids point again in unison and say over and over, "To teach her a lesson!"

As the echo of their repetition fades, finally, and with the background music again continuing unabated, the camera cuts back to Offred. She's back in the sitting room, having just asked her why-me question, Rita and Nick join her, and they "hurry up and wait."

The substance of Offred's reminiscence, Janine's Testifying, is evocative of the long middle section of the Book of Job. In its three successive "rounds," Job is confronted by and confronts in turn his three "comforters," friends who come from afar, having learned of his misfortune, to console him, but at the same time to "teach him a lesson." They pity Job, but are also incensed by his complaints. They insist, from a variety of apparently specious angles, that he end his unseemly, impious complaints, because God surely can't be held to account.

Over and over, Job hears that he must accept the blame for his own suffering, even while he can't fathom his imagined transgression, God, after all, being God, simply can't be mistaken in the reward-and-punishment business. "Can an innocent man be punished?," Eliphaz offers, early in the first round, "Can a good man die in distress?" And he, Bildad, and Zophar become ever more strident as the rounds go on. Job resists throughout, but afterward, not so much, or at least differently.

"I will never let you convict me," he says to Bildad, in the third round, "will hold tight to my innocence; my mind will never submit," and "if only God would hear me," in the summation to the three, "I would justify the least of my actions." When God turns up, though, as the famous Voice from the Whirlwind, Job does ultimately capitulate, to a degree at least. "Where were you when I planned the Earth?," God asks, poignantly, but also rhetorically, needless to say, and a divine onslaught ensues. "I will be quiet," Job concludes by the end of it, suitably awed, "comforted that I am dust." To a certain sensibility, however, he's still resistant.

There would seem to be two importantly different interpretations of Job's contrition. He *was* saying that he's owed an explanation. What he may be saying now, on the one hand, as conventional wisdom would have it, is that he chooses to refrain from saying so, as he no longer believes he's owed anything of the sort. What he may be saying instead, however, on the other hand, is that he's willing to refrain, while at the same time he believes that, even if he's not *owed* an explanation, still he *can't help but want one*. It seems the second gambit may well be Job's, and also at the heart of the storyline's blurring of the theological and secular perspectives on the problem of evil—the idea that even if we give up worrying about it from the former, we may, perhaps even we must, still worry about it from the latter. It seems the second gambit's Offred's as well, but the way there is not uncomplicated.

From Her Fault! To My Fault! To . . .

What makes the three-stage setting of the why-me scene particularly provocative is not only that it channels Job's struggle with the comforters, but that on either end a connection is forged between Offred and Janine, rendering Offred both comforter and comforted. As Job resists his comforters, Offred must resist hers, in this case herself as her own comforter—must move from, "I want to know what I did to deserve this?," to, "I want to know what could possibly make me deserve this?" The challenge is heightened by the effect that comforting has on Janine, in the original and in season one of the series, and what effect a different, less formal Testifying will have on Offred in season two.

Janine's Testifying in the series is the first of two described in the original, in which, instead of saying merely, "I don't know," in response to Aunt Lydia's question, she "burst into tears," and then worse. "None of us wanted to look like that, ever," Offred relays. "Even though we knew what was being done to her," she adds, with regret, though she mitigates it by making sure we know that this was "for a moment" only, "we despised her." "We meant it," she adds, of the "Crybaby" refrain that wells up, "which is the bad part." "I used to think well of myself," she concludes, but "didn't then," with an odd mix of verb tenses that leaves us wondering whether the disapproval is still with her, or was just in the moment. Nor do we know whether, if it's the latter, it's because the next "week Janine doesn't wait for us to jeer at her," but volunteers unassisted that "it was [her] fault," had "led them on," and so "deserve[s] the pain," heralding the persistent imbalance we see her experience in the original and series alike. It also heralds the forging of a later and more thorough, though fortunately also temporary, connection between Offred and Janine in season two's fourth episode.

When Offred steps into the black van, and gives herself over to "the darkness; or else the light," she can't be doing so ambivalently, but rather hoping for the latter, as the original's readership has long hoped, and series' audience must also have done in the ten months between season one's finale and season two's premiere. Given that we knew already a month before the former that a second season was to follow, at least some worry had to creep in. In this respect, the latter didn't disappoint.

Offred's van is one of sixteen, we learn, delivering the Handmaids to an abandoned Fenway Park, to a long three-section gallows in the center of the outfield, a noose set for each Handmaid who disobeyed Aunt Lydia's order during the Salvaging in season one's finale. Terror ensues, and Offred looks up, hands clasped, praying for her and her fellow Handmaids' salvation, only to find her prayers answered by the anticipated hanging being revealed as a mock hanging, meant to terrorize them.

Aunt Lydia emerges then, not out of left field, which, idiomatically, would paint her emergence as unexpected, but out of right field, offering an extended version of a familiar passage from the New Testament, Mark 12:30. "You will love the Lord, Thy God, with all your heart," she announces, as if an ersatz Voice from the Whirlwind, and, ad libbing now, "walk with," and "fear," and "cleave onto Him," and "obey His word and the word of His servants here on Earth," or else! What the longer passage from Mark makes clear, however, is that this is the first of God's *two* most important commandments, the second being to "love thy neighbor as thyself," which Aunt Lydia conveniently neglects to mention. Offred's having none of it. "Our Father, who art in heaven," she thinks, in palpably Job-like fashion, albeit more profanely than Job ever was, "Seriously! What the actual fuck!!

Aunt Lydia's elaborately cruel ruse is the first salvo in the "not small effort" she's devised to "bring Offred to heel," the last coming finally toward the end of episode four. "Such a selfish girl," Aunt Lydia berates, on a seemingly impromptu walk to the wall, after her tenuous reintegration into the Waterford household. The walk, not impromptu at all, is meant to confront her with a hanged man, alone on the wall—the bread delivery truck driver, who, risking all, took her in when, asked to deliver her to a Mayday safe-house from the Boston Airport hanger she'd been delivered to from her previous hide-out, the abandoned headquarters of *The Boston Globe*, the safe-house was unexpectedly compromised. She's understandably devastated, all the more to learn that his wife has been forced to "redeem herself" as a Handmaid, their son "placed with new parents." "Whose fault is it?," she asks, in the manner we recall from Janine's Testifying, "Who induced him to commit such a crime?," and "Why did God allow such a terrible thing to happen?" "My fault," she replies, and then "I did," and finally, "To teach me a lesson." "To teach *June* a lesson," Aunt Lydia deviously corrects, which is to sacrifice herself in order that Offred, who needn't "bear *June*'s guilt," may survive as a dutiful Handmaid.

Aunt Lydia again doing her best Voice from the Whirlwind impersonation, just as presumptuously, but more cleverly now, June concedes, as the only apparent end to her torment. Offred later debased and reintegrated into the Waterford household, we find her at night back in her closet, searching for her predecessor's now missing etching, repeating over and over to herself, "My fault." And in the morning we find her back in an earlier reminiscence, of the origins of her, Luke, and Hannah's life in the "time before," but drawing now a harsher conclusion, channeling Job's "I will be quiet, comforted that I am dust." "I have done something wrong," she thinks to herself, "so huge I can't even see it, something that's drowning me." "I am inadequate and stupid, without worth," she continues, "I might as well be dead," "Please, God, let Hannah forget me," she concludes, let "me forget me." And it would seem, for better or for worse, that hers is the Job of the *first* of the above two gambits, for the time being at least.

As we mourn June's absence throughout the following episode, as reflected in Nick's, Rita's, and Mrs. Waterford's growing consternation, she's cruelly devastated by Nick's forced marriage to Eden, and threatened that night by an apparent miscarriage. Slowly, ceremoniously, she closes her closet door, as if to say, "let the bastards grind me down," sits on the windowsill where we first met her, at the outset to the series premiere, and fades to unconsciousness. And when she's next in view, she's lying in the muck on the other side of a sewer grate, waiting to die. Yet again, this and what follows are presented not a little provocatively.

As carefully as we may look, that is, we find no tangible evidence as to how, unconscious when we left her, she's nonetheless whisked there from her room, from the house, in a rainstorm. Nor do we find, however carefully we look, any such evidence as to how Nick gleans that she's there, in order to save her ultimately. He just stops, in the pouring rain, and somehow knows to turn and precisely where then to look for her. In a damning depiction of a theocracy, in which the resistance is depicted as also faithful, at least in part, it seems that no effort's been spared to infuse this with mystery, divine or otherwise—the mystery not only of why bad things happen to good people, but why even good things happen to them.

Mysteries notwithstanding, Offred survives. She wakes in the hospital, surprised generally, and in particular that she didn't miscarry after all. "You're tough, aren't you?," she says to her future child. Pulling the covers over her head, to hide the remainder of her conversation from guards standing watch, she continues. Looking again at the production of the scene, we find that Offred—June once again, effectively—displays a telling mixture of four distinct gazes.

"Now, you listen to me," she begins, her gaze cast down. "I will not let you grow up in this place," her gaze back up again, focused on a vanishing point somewhere in the distance, as if steeling herself, "I won't do it." "Do you hear me?," gazing down again. "They do not own you," gazing up and into the distance again, "they do not own what you will become." "Do you hear me?, gazing down yet again, "I'm gonna get you out of here." "I'm gonna get us out of here," gazing up again, but *now* directed at *us*. "I promise you," with eyes shut, as if in prayer, and then reopening them, gazing up and at us still, she repeats, in a deeper, less motherly, more authoritative voice, "I promise." Cut to credits, rolling over, yes, hymnal refrains.

Offred's channeling Job's *second* gambit now, and is doing so, if we track her gaze and voice, not just on her and her unborn's behalf, but somehow more broadly. We're reminded of her reaction, in the original, to learning of Mayday from Ofglen, rejoicing to herself, "there is an *us* then, there's a *we*." And we're reminded as well, in this same spirit, of what she did and learned while holed up at the *Post*, in season two's second and third episodes, and wonder now how this may relate to her Job channeling, and to the problem of evil more generally.

The Gravel Path that Divides

When Atwood first began writing *The Handmaid's Tale* she entitled it simply *Offred*. Had she stuck with the choice, she would have joined legions of likeminded authors. A pair of titles stands out in particular, Voltaire's *Candide* and Rousseau's *Émile,* and indeed, remembering her connection to Orwell, she might even have chosen for *Offred* one or the other of their subtitles: *or Optimism* and *on Education* respectively (though in the latter case, she might have chosen instead *on Reeducation*, first at the Red Center, then by Mayday). Which leads us nicely to a second of Neiman's clarifying distinctions.

Having distinguished the theological and secular versions of the problem of evil, Neiman goes on to propose that, in response to both, primarily two competing perspectives arise during the Enlightenment, beginning with the public rivalry between Rousseau's and Voltaire's, the former insisting that "morality demands that we make evil intelligible," the latter that "morality demands that we don't." Our heroine would seem clearly to be cut from the former's mold, which, already evident in the original, is all the more so now in the reformulation.

"Humanity is so adaptable, my mother would say," Offred reminisces, having realized she's pregnant with her and Nick's child, and resisted Ofglen's entreaties to let Mayday help her to escape Gilead, wanting to remain near him. "Truly amazing," she continues, though less obviously recalling her mother's testimony than offering her own now, "what people can get used to, as long as there are a few compensations."

Reformulating the scene for the series, in "Baggage," Miller places June several months into her hide-out at the *Globe*, revisiting her shrine to fallen journalists, now greatly expanded, and shortly thereafter continuing her work piecing together the surprisingly long history of events leading to Gilead's rise. "You were there all the time," June thinks, staring at a wall covered in newspaper clippings revealing this hidden history, "but no one noticed you." "All right," she admits, wistfully, "not no one," recalling adolescence with her activist mom. "She knew," she later recalls telling Moira, reacting to a propaganda movie picturing her mom as forced labor in the Colonies, "she knew all along."

"I knew," she continues, as she pictures in her mind's eye her and her mom at a rally, "or should have known." She's referring, ostensibly, to the idea that her mom was taking her out at night not to feed the ducks, but to attend a *Take Back the Night* rally. Still, she seems also to be pointing to something else, something deeper, about what she, and others, should have known. And we feel this again when Nick relays to her that Mayday will soon be coming for her, but she insists that she "can't leave." Clearly she means primarily that she can't leave without Hannah, having just asked him whether he'd been able to locate her yet. Hearing her say this as she continues to clip articles, however, it also seems that she's reluctant to leave at least in part because she hasn't finished piecing together Gilead's prehistory.

Finally, though, without additional warning, the time comes to leave. "I left some stuff upstairs," she says, gesturing to her need to collect and take it with her, but is met with the driver's insistence that he'll "get rid of it" instead. As she stands and watches, distraught, the loading dock closing slowly from above, we can't help but think that she's suffering some variation on captivity syndrome. We also can't help but think, in light of the above, that she's experiencing palpable regret, in not being able to finish her prehistory project, or at least bring along what she'd so far pieced together. Salvation lies at least in part, that is, for Offred as for Rousseau, in deeper historical awareness of what and whom we seek to be saved from, and why.

Not Brave, But . . .

June's escape goes badly after leaving the *Globe*, as we learn in the remainder of the episode. Still, the help she gets along the way nicely clarifies the Rousseauian work she was doing there.

"Are you brave or stupid?" she asks the bread truck driver, the morning after her rescue, as he's leaving with his family for church. She's continuing, playfully, a theme he'd begun earlier. "I'm not brave," he answers, amused, "so there you go." She's also amused, though less obviously so, as if pondering his answer, as if to counter that she knows better. Granted, he's put not only himself at risk, but also his family, which his wife seems to think is stupid. And later she finds a Quran and prayer rug hidden away, which can't help but be risky, under the circumstances, and so perhaps also stupid, some might say. Clearly, though, as she opens it to view and spreads out the rug, she's not marveling at stupidity. Still, there no denying the care he takes to resist the bravery moniker, while not admitting to stupidity, as if to say that he has another motivation. And of course he does, being motivated, as he surely is, as we witnessed in his response to June's pleas for rescue, and so as she surely also knows, by *compassion*.

In this Offred reveals herself to be all the more Rousseauian. If salvation lies in deeper historical awareness of what and whom we seek to be saved from, and why, it arises, Rousseau thought, by making long flourishing evil newly intelligible. To do so, he thought, is to see it arise from our very long history of unwittingly promoting our natural instinct to *preserve and promote ourselves*, little by little across the ages, at the expense of a proportional degradation of what he understood to be our equally natural instinct to *act compassionately toward others*.

Offred is moved by the problem of evil, as a theological problem, but also a secular one, and responds as a Rousseauian. She's additionally so in the sense that the business of making evil intelligible isn't conducted for the sake of intelligibility alone, but to use it to mitigate, perhaps even eradicate it—to liberate herself, in other words, and her fellow handmaids.

The original's final chapter comes to a close in this spirit. Mrs. Waterford has discovered that Offred has accompanied the Commander to Jezebel's, and when the "black van" appears, she believes that she is to be hauled away to face some form of punishment, she knows not what. "It's all right," Nick whispers instead, it's "Mayday. Go with them. Trust me." And we see her do just that, trust him, recalling her thinking earlier, upon learning of Mayday from Ofglen, now dead, that "there is an *us* then, there's a *we*."

"And so I step up, into the darkness," we hear her conclude her tale, "or else the light." Notwithstanding that we learn in the appendix that no one knows of Offred's fate, Gilead falls, and we can't help but imagine that she's had a hand in this.

"Seriously! Guys, This is Insane" and Sixty-six "I'm sorry, Aunt Lydia"s

Offred's parting reference to "the darkness; or else the light" is not her first. We remember her earlier one, as part of a preparation in the original, in between her excursion to Jezebel's with the Commander and her preceding rendezvous with him, in which he translates for her finally, "Nolite te bastardes carborundorum," as, "Don't let the bastards grind you down." As she looks from her bedroom window out over a barren garden, preparing to recite and expound Job-like upon the Lord's Prayer, she refrains from closing her eyes. "Out there or inside my head, it's an equal darkness," she confides, or "light."

"My God," she begins, "Who art in the Kingdom of Heaven, which is within." "I wish I knew what You were up to," she pleads, but "whatever it is, help me to get through it, please," because "I don't believe for an instant that what's going on out there is what You meant." Heaven we may need God to make, she muses, but "Hell we can make for ourselves." "I wish You'd answer," she continues, again Job-like, "I feel so alone. . . . How can I keep on living?"

Offred was jubilant to learn that "there is an *us* then, there's a *we*." And indeed, as she comes again to give herself over to "the darkness; or else the light," she's presumably part of the *us*, the *we*. But she's still alone, as she has mostly been throughout, wondering whether she'll be saved, by Mayday, by God, or perhaps by both.

In the corresponding scene in the series, however, concluding Season One's finale, what we find is that she's giving herself over to "the darkness; or else the light" as a result of a very different set of circumstances. What precedes her entry into the black van is not being berated by Mrs. Waterford as a "slut," but a Salvaging, Janine's, which has gone not at all according to Aunt Lydia's plan, and the how and the why it hasn't paints a provocatively different picture.

"Three bells," Offred thinks as she wakes, "a death knell. There's a Salvaging today." She's lying on the floor, surrounded by a cache of letters from handmaids testifying to their capture, imprisonment, and abuse, which Moira retrieved for her from Jezebel's, so that she could get it to Mayday. When we last saw her, she was reading them, all of them, reveling in them, feeling consoled, as if, for at least these moments, she's not alone in her terrible trial. Leaving the Waterfords, though, meeting Ofglen at the gate as usual, she's dragged immediately back into their unhappy, in this instance seemingly childish, bickering— "Shut *up*! *You* shut up!"—immediately and, as it turns out, interestingly.

The Handmaids assemble—sixty-seven Handmaids, in two groups, each six columns by six rows, three missing from one back row, two from the other; kneeling on snow-covered ground; surrounded by twenty armed Guardians, four of them atop corner towers. Three wheelbarrows of fist-sized stones are delivered, between them and the stage, where Aunt Lydia addresses them, her "special girls," about the sin than which there's "no greater," which is endangering a child. Aunt Lydia calls on them to collect a stone and reassemble into a circle before the stage. Janine is brought into the middle of the circle and, for having committed this sin, they're commanded to stone her to death.

"*Seriously!*," Ofglen protests—the new Ofglen, that is— "Guys, this is *insane*." "No, I'm *not* going to do it," she resolves, "I'm *not* going to kill Janine," in response to which she is struck down by a Guardian and dragged away. "Girls, that is *enough!*," Aunt Lydia implores, "you *are* to *do* your *duty!*" Still they don't. Offred then steps forward into the circle, with quiet resolve, even while a Guardian threatens her, intending not to strike, but to shoot her.

Aunt Lydia descends from the stage, enters the circle, and faces Offred, who calmly raises her arm, stone in hand, and drops it ceremoniously, following this with, "I'm sorry Aunt Lydia." And then, another follows suit, again calmly raising her arm, stone in hand, dropping it ceremoniously, following again with, "I'm sorry Aunt Lydia." And then, the other sixty-four do likewise, repeating in quick succession the same gesture, the same phrase.

The scene is surely meant to be eerily reminiscent of Janine's Testifying. The latter scene's production led us to contemplate Offred, while forced to act as Janine's comforter, resisting being her own. Here she also resists being Janine's. That she does so, and also how she does so, raises a certain sort of question that seems to point in a certain sort of direction. They're in the spirit of Aunt Lydia's trivializing assertion that she would not have acted as she did, were she not pregnant, and so presumptively immune from punishment, at least direct bodily punishment. But Aunt Lydia can't know this, any more than we can. After all, even if this were a factor in Offred's decision, given that she was presumably already otherwise motivated not to help execute Janine, then *she* would have been first to refuse, not Ofglen.

In the same spirit, would Offred have acted as she did, had she not been consoled and inspired, earlier still, by the cache of handmaids' testimonials? We can't know, but she was, and she did. Would Offred have acted as she did, were it not for Ofglen's prior refusal? Again, we can't know, but their routine querulousness dissipated in the face of shared trauma, and the overwhelming need for solidarity. Would others have acted as they did, were it not for Ofglen and Offred's prior refusal? Yet again, we can't know, but their querulousness must have been common knowledge, and so their solidarity in spite of this can't help but have been moving.

All of this points to something genuinely new in the series, relative to the original, or at least newly emphasized, which is a heightened solidarity among the handmaids. And not only in the Salvaging scene, though it's perhaps the most conspicuous instance so far, but elsewhere as well.

Moira's daring escape from the Red Center in the original, in spite of June's attempts to warn her off, becomes, in "Nolite Te Bastardes Carborundorum," Moira and Offred's shared caper. At the mock mass hanging, two of the Handmaids manage to unbind their wrists and hold hands, leaving us to imagine that the others would do likewise, were they able. In "First Blood," the uncanny unison of the Handmaids fleeing the impending explosion at the inauguration of the new Red Center. And during the ensuing "We remember them" funeral ceremony, in the following episode, the surviving Handmaids' heartfelt grief for the thirty-one deceased, even in spite of admissions during the ride home afterward that individually they "didn't even know most of them," found this or that one to be "kind of a jerk," and so on. And later in the episode, finally, in Loaves and Fishes, inspired by Emily's and Janine's return from the Colonies, the Handmaids' joyously disobedient exchange of banned names.

In the original, when Offred learns from Ofglen that "there is an *us* then, there's a *we*," before she had Mayday as a name to put to it even, her joy appears to be more a function of what the revelation means to her, than what she may mean to what's been revealed. In the series, on the other hand, while Offred experiences her share of cold feet, as the post-Salvaging storyline has progressed, it appears now that the order has been reversed. At least as important to her now, as what Mayday means to her in particular—her prospects for escaping Gilead, reuniting with Luke and Moira, with her and Nick's newborn, Holly, liberated with Ofglen as Season Two comes to a close, and liberating Hannah finally—is what she may mean *to it*, in order that it may mean more to her fellow handmaids in turn, and to Gilead's downtrodden more generally.

Liberation, for Offred and her fellow handmaids, as for Rousseau, comes with revolutionary political realignment—when the wills we express individually are governed by laws that reflect the general wills of the bodies politic they constitute—of those of Gilead's elite, on the one hand, and its non-elite, including handmaids, on the other—*and* the general wills of *these* bodies politic are governed by laws that reflect the general will of the body politic that *together* they constitute—of those of Gilead's elite *and* of its non-elite, including handmaids. Elites, in Gilead's case, as generally, typically have a better-honed purchase on their general will, and with power usurped, are predisposed to identify society's general will with their own.

The non-elite revolt in earnest when they hone *their* purchase on *their* general will, as no less a part of the overall general will than the elite's. Compassion, in the spirit of what drives Ofglen's and Offred's and then their fellow Handmaids' boycott of Janine's Salvaging, not to mention the bit of Mark that Aunt Lydia elides, is the beginning. It's what leads to solidarity, and from solidarity to liberation—what transforms, in other words, *The Handmaid's Tale* into *The Handmaids' Tale*.

Is Offred, who more and more we want to refer to as June, even while captive—is *June Osborne*, then, to Gilead what Katniss Everdeen is to Panem, or Beatrice Potter is to New Chicago: a reluctant, unassuming heroine who brings down a dystopian government in order to build something new in its place? Or will it be Hannah or Holly, brought up inside or outside Gilead's crushing reign? Or, better yet, will they team up? Or, better still, with their mom? Or . . . ? Whatever may be, it begins with a *shared* moral compass that won't be denied, and an ensuing compulsion to make evil intelligible. Needless to say, *this* makes June's developing story also *ours*.[1]

---

[1] I'm grateful to Susan Neiman, as always, for my interest in, understanding of, and attachment to the problem of evil, to Sue Zemka for her infectious enthusiasm for Atwood's storyline and what Miller and company are accomplishing by extending it, and to the volume's editor for the opportunity to bring them together. Finally, to Deborah Johnson, to whom I'm grateful for so much else: I took far too much for granted in writing this, far too much in general, and I am forever sorry.

Part III

Dying of Too Much Choice

9
A Rose by Any Other Brand

CARI CALLIS

"What's in a name?" asks Juliet about Romeo, and immediately gives her own answer: "That which we call a rose, by any other name would smell as sweet."

This response has often been taken to imply that the names of things are not all that important, but Juliet didn't make that mistake. The naming of people and things matters very much, as the citizens of Gilead also understand. Words have power. The Sons of Jacob who first seized control and created Gilead used marketing and branding to create a political philosophy designed to rule over others with absolute power.

The Sons seized power in a time of political chaos. In this rapidly changing world, the citizens were unprepared for the carefully orchestrated reign of terror the Sons of Jacob would inflict upon them. This was no last-minute coup, but a carefully crafted marketing campaign.

The Philosophy of Branding

The way we think about marketing and branding is, to this day, influenced by the ancient philosophers of Greece. There are four great thinkers we can call upon to understand how branding works and what factors influence whether or not a brand will be successful. In his book *The Philosophy of*

Branding, Thom Braun draws on thoughts from Heraclitus, Socrates, Plato and Aristotle to provide "a base for the way a 'philosophy of branding' was to evolve."

The Handmaid's Tale is a cautionary story about relying on computers. How did Atwood imagine thirty years ago the invention of the Compubank and predict how we could all be controlled by a computer? Her prophecy was and remains a warning to us all. (iPod, iPad, iPhone, Under His Eye—get it?)

But the story also teaches us how political ideals can be marketed to achieve a very specific set of goals. Braun's philosophy can help to explain how and why Gilead ultimately failed and why it could *never succeed.* The Sons of Jacob's marketing team didn't follow the principles for branding the great thinkers outlined. Braun brings the insights of philosophers to the of the world of branding by highlighting the following key thoughts:

1. The changing nature of the world in which brands have to exist.

2. The importance of rigorously questioning everything about a brand.

3. The relationship between a brand's superficial qualities and its deeper, more lasting nature.

4. The need to maintain a focus on the functional elements of a brand (what it *does*). (*The Philosophy of Branding,* p. 16)

Braun begins with Heraclitus, whose ideas have survived mostly in fragments and from quotations provided by later philosophers. Heraclitus said, "There is nothing permanent except for change." This was a radical idea to have come up with before quarks and subatomic particles were discovered, and science eventually proved it to be true. Every single thing is in a constant state of motion and always fluctuating, not only around us, but also within us. Heraclitus compared every thing that *exists*, past, present, and future, to a flame that has substance but is always in state of transition.

Branding and marketing must acknowledge this flux because these endeavors count on the value and association of what is being represented to the consumer. Trust and familiarity is crucial. In the face of dramatic upheaval and change, like the time when the Sons of Jacob faked the terrorist attack to take over the government, people looked for signs of stability, even if this stability turns out to be an illusion. If everything is always changing, as Heraclitus tells us, then nothing, including a brand can ever be truly stable. The brand exists only in our heads as potential consumers. The more fear and distrust a society in turmoil experiences, the more they will seek stability.

Braun says:

> Brand marketers are used to talking about brands as things that provide reference points for consumers in an ever-changing world . . . The rate of change and innovation is so great, and the number of conflicting media messages about what is good for us so overwhelming, that we need a kind of shorthand to help us tell the good from the not-so-good. Brands help us to do that. They act as signposts in a busy marketplace, clustering values and characteristics together in recognizable packages that we regard with different levels of trust or approval. Brands stand for something—and, as we all know, what they stand for often goes much further than superficial product or service attributes. (p. 20)

The Sons of Jacob are experts at this, and they do it with *people* as well as ideas and things. They established The Republic of Gilead to disempower anyone who is "other," and they accomplished it by immediately branding women, gays, poets, priests, professors, disobedient handmaids or wives, and anyone unwilling to assimilate. Homosexuals are branded as gender betrayers or *traitors* and hung on the wall as a visual reminder to all who question male authority—public executions are a marketing tool for compliance. Individual freedom is destroyed through the power of representation because every person hanging on that wall represents what can happen to anyone who resists.

There Is a Balm in Gilead

The most important brand-name choice is the name of the regime, the Republic of Gilead. Gilead was a mountainous place in the Bible. The word means "rocky hill of testimony." As a brand name, it is immediately associated with what fundamentalist Christians hold to be the most valuable moral compass in their lives. The Bible is used to justify all manner of prejudice, oppression and punishment in Gilead. The Sons of Jacob ignored the New Testament and pulled their rhetoric mainly from the Old Testament to appeal to their base audience—the conservative Christian religious right.

The name "Gilead" recalls the famous spiritual hymn "There is a Balm in Gilead."

> There is a balm in Gilead
> To make the wounded whole.
> There is a balm in Gilead
> To heal the sin-sick soul.

Heraclitus said, "A hidden connection is stronger than an obvious one." The "hidden" association with the well- known song suggests Gilead is a place where "sinners"—anyone outside of the norm or who resists—can be healed of their "sickness." It's not clear whether the healing is going to be for the nation in the midst of the Second Civil War, or the healing of the personal injuries inflicted on those citizens who have been mutilated as punishment, by having their little finger, a hand, or an eye removed. Or perhaps the not so hidden message is that while they might be delivering Old Testament punishment for sinners, there is a balm for redemption in Gilead.

Commander Waterford tells June in "Faithful" that Gilead allows women to finally fulfill their "biological destiny" in peace. When June questions this, he says "Children. What else is there to live for?" After a long pause June replies, "Love." He laughs and says, "Love isn't real. It was never anything more than lust with a good marketing campaign." And here is the foreshadowing of the Shakespearean downfall of Commander Waterford and of Gilead. Gilead's brand, with its fixed ideals, didn't adapt to the world it created. Once the shock and fear subsided, every character in the series, including Aunt Lydia, Commander Waterford, and Serena has a moment when they realize the patriarchal product they're trying to sell is inherently flawed and that without an understanding of the human capacity for love, the campaign is doomed to fail.

Speaking of love, another association with the name Gilead is as a sweet perfume called *The Balm of Gilead*, rumored to cure anything and everything. This may be the most seductive branding of all. Consider our current branding of perfume—ads tantalize with suggestions of allure, sexual pleasure, and romance. June understands that love is what gives people the will to live. She sees in the Commander what he doesn't recognize in himself, which is his desire to find "love" and romantic connection to his previous Handmaid and now with herself.

Love is the only "balm" for this society, and June finds it with Nick. June and Nick discover through their relationship that love can heal them. It can heal them sexually through their lovemaking. It can heal them physically, as when June conceives a child. It can even heal them spiritually, like when June is reunited with her daughter through Nick. In Gilead, the branding message is that it offers a cure for all of society's uncertainty. It offers a prescription for indoctrinated Christianity that provides a clear and "structured" resolution to infertility and redemption for the sins that caused it.

Re-branding, Logos, and Slogans

We learn at the conference in the last chapter of the novel that it was likely Waterford who conceived "Prayvaganza's" —and "Salvaging." The latter is a term for an execution. To salvage is to rescue, suggesting Gilead will be somehow saved from the person being executed. Fred Waterford must have been a very good spin doctor before he became

Commander Waterford. He also came up with Soul Scrolls, the franchise which allows the pious and faithful to order up prayers by Compuphone which are then spit out by machines called Holy Rollers, proving he thinks he has a sense of humor. Each machine has the branded logo of an eye painted in gold, flanked by two small golden wings. The Eye of God, but also the logo of the secret police. Gold, the color of money, the color of God watching you.

The naming and re-branding of people, places, events, and things is consistently repeated in the Hulu TV series and in the novel. Revealing their given names becomes the way the handmaids hang on to their individuality as well as their group loyalty. In Season One, when June begins her affair with Nick, she tells him that her name is June to establish intimacy and trust and to maintain her identity with him. She also reveals her name to Ofglen, her shopping partner and friend, who tells her about the underground group Mayday. Each Handmaid's given patronymic, composed of the possessive preposition and the first name of the commander they are given to for breeding, is a re-branding of their identity.

The power dynamics of creating ownership through a re-branding in the form of being given a name that is possessive, ultimately has a deeper purpose than the superficial naming of a person. It's intended to destroy the ability for women to self-identify. Once self-identity is destroyed, all of the qualities, beliefs, and unique aspects of individuality that affect the way you see yourself are extinguished as well. Heraclitus's flame does flicker. Self-esteem is directly related to how we see ourselves, relate to others, and behave in stressful situations. Resisting the brand name by using their own names became the way the rebels finally overcame and defeated the regime of Gilead. "My name is June—and I will survive."

So, what's in a name? Our names may be handed down or bestowed upon us by our parents at birth where they're recorded as public record. When we're registered at birth, we're assigned a birth certificate. That certificate assigns us a specific gender identity, race, parentage, and origin of birth. At least initially, this document defines our individual roles in society. That identity is registered with the government. Most countries have laws and statutes that require births to be registered. The reason for this is so that our government can tax us and then provide us access to public services, such as schools, fire and police, passports, and social security.

We create elaborate rituals, baptisms that initiate someone into a church society or weddings to change our name when we marry to create a new partnership identity. Our names define us as individuals but they are also a legal tool by which we're identified and treated in the society in which we live. When June has the opportunity to tell the truth about herself to the Mexican Ambassador, in Season One, she tells her that she is a *prisoner*, her renaming as Offred is the same as replacing a name with a number in any prison system, the intent is to remove all individuality from the prisoner.

Knowing that You Know Nothing

Braun applies the thoughts of Socrates to his next directive for creating a successful brand by saying that a lasting brand must question every aspect of itself, its consumer base, its associations and the society in which it exists. Socrates relentlessly asked questions to pursue the "truth." When its citizens begin to do the same, Gilead starts to fall apart. Its marketing team didn't apply Heraclitus's warning that all things, including brands, markets, and political climates, are constantly changing.

The Republic of Gilead failed, despite the strong associations for the brand and its aggressive terrorist-marketing, because it didn't question how the brand would continue to function in the long term. The American government in Washington was destroyed by "fake news" terrorists. The entire coup was actually orchestrated by the Sons of Jacob, who blamed the whole thing on "Muslim fanatics." American citizens were shock-branded into a hierarchal order before they realized what was happening.

But there was no "truth" in what the regime represented, and perhaps no one realizes this more profoundly than Nick, who started out embracing the mentorship of Commander Andrew Pryce. Nick learns through his love for June and their baby, that without gender equality, happiness doesn't exist. Atwood herself recently commented on this in *Forbes* magazine. She asks us to consider Iceland, which ranks first in the World Economic Forum's Global Gender Gap Index and is always in the top five in the World Happiness Reports. "Does it make for a happier society on the whole if women have more equality? That does seem to be the case. Does it make for a more prosperous economy if women are engaged in the workplace and in decision making around the economy? That too seems to be the case," says Atwood.

The citizens of Gilead didn't have the option to engage in Socratic dialogue, that rigorous process of asking questions and examining different answers, because they were forced into accepting religious "signposts for stability." Women were so quickly classified as beings with a single purpose—to solve the fertility crisis—that no one on the marketing team questioned their assumption that all women live for is to reproduce and have children. Clearly that didn't appeal to all women.

Plato, the student of Socrates and his biggest fan, built on what Heraclitus was saying about things being in a constant state of change and took it a step further. As Braun says, Plato made it clear that "a brand *as we experience it*, should never be seen as something that is, but rather something that is always *becoming*" (p. 40). A brand manager must always be thinking about what the brand will be in the future for consumers, and not focus only on what it currently is. Branding must have two natures. On one level, it should be always in the process of becoming something else—this will make it appear fresh and receptive to the needs of the moment. At a deeper level, however it must have values that don't change over time.

As the women are rounded up and classified in a hierarchical rank as Wives, packaged in blue, the soothing and virginal color of Mother Mary; Aunts, in a uniform of paper bag brown looking like a cross between a prison warden and a Catholic nun with a cattle prod instead of a rosary; Marthas as domestic servants packaged in green with an apron associating them with the biblical Martha, the sister of Lazarus known for her obsession with housework; and Econowives, the lowest class, fulfilling the role of Martha, Wife, and Handmaid and packaged in red, blue, and green striped dresses signifying they fulfill all of the roles, it might have appeared that they were following the ideas of Plato by *becoming* something else but the core value, what stands behind the brand and what the women were experiencing in the here and now could never endure or be sustained.

The brand of Gilead built its assumptions on the single fact that women's prime goal and function in the world is to breed. Waterford and his team effectively forced the brand attributes upon women through violence, but the value behind the brand was based upon an assumption about women that is false. The term "Unwomen" was thrust upon the sterile, political dissidents, lesbians, nuns, and any women unwilling to assimilate, who are sent to the Colonies to die. Killing the consumers because they don't buy your brand is not an option for success.

The Four Causes of Branding

Our final example of philosophers consulting on successful branding comes from perhaps the greatest thinker to have ever existed, our beloved Aristotle. Application of Aristotle's thinking suggests that we should examine the brand in terms of what it actually does.

What the regime *does* is to subjugate women and what it is *for* is to promote an elite group of Commanders to rank above all others and to package with normalcy an elaborate ritual of rape, "justified" by the biblical story of Rachel and Leah. The Rachel and Leah Center is used to brainwash women into accepting this. One way to ensure temporary success is to simply eliminate the competitive market, which is exactly what they did.

Braun applies Aristotelean ideas to theories of branding and comes up with what he calls the four Causes of Branding (pp. 52–55). The first is The Material Cause, which is what the brand is physically. Gilead is a totalitarian regime that occupies roughly half of what was once known as the United States of America. It is a brutal and violent society.

The second is The Efficient Cause—in this case, what (or who) brings the brand into being. The Republic of Gilead brand is brought to you by the Sons of Jacob, a group of men who created chapters around the country and worked to overthrow the government of the United States to enforce religious propaganda that they themselves never believed and simply used to justify their fascism.

Commander Fred Waterford is a noteworthy component of the efficient cause. He is one of the primary architects of Gilead, and we learn that he possessed a background in market research. He was responsible for the design of the Handmaids' costumes, borrowed from the uniforms of the German prisoners of war in Canadian POW camps of the Second World War era. He's also most likely responsible for designing the hierarchical structure imposed on women, making use of name branding and color coding. The Rachel and Leah Center is also his design.

The Third is Formal Cause—the structural component that makes a thing one thing rather than any other thing it could be. What is it about the brand that makes it distinct from other products on the market with which it might be confused? The design features that stand out about Gilead are that it is a theocratic, patriarchal system in which women are reduced to their wombs and those wombs are used as a resource. Toward that end, its citizens are oppressed.

This is something that the Mexican Ambassador grasps when she meets the Wives and Handmaids at a banquet honoring the birth of their children. Even as she admires the children, a rare occurrence in this new world, she's also aware of the restrictions that are placed on women. For example, she mentions that Serena's book can no longer even be read by women. The Ambassador recognizes both structural elements of Gilead's brand.

The last is the Final Cause which is a brand's reason for existing. It's clear that the reason for the brand of Gilead to exist is to find a solution for infertility and to use scripture to subjugate women. Here's the major flaw—the brand management team of Gilead didn't account for the fact that other countries or markets which maintain the equality of women offer more benefits than Gilead could ever do with its prescribed relationships for men and women.

And yet the irony behind all of this branding of the women is that the Aunts are the ones dealing out the punishment, holding the cattle prods up high. Without the complicity of women none of it would have been possible. There is no clear functional reason why any woman would "buy" into any of their branding. And yet they did. The Wives and the Aunts are complicit in delivering punishment to other women to make them conform, in effect participating in their own subjugation. They betray their gender to align and connect with power in the only way that is open to them.

Any Questions?

So why do this novel and the television series seem so relevant now, perhaps even more so than thirty years ago when the novel was first published? Perhaps because we're living in a world where "Grab them by the Pussy" is president and reproductive rights are being challenged daily, people of color are being killed by police who are getting away with it and immigrant families are being separated from their children who are being put into cages. We use branding to give us a false sense of security, in a world of likes and emojis, opinions provided by Russian bots, fake news from a myriad of sources and lying "poli-tricksters." The more we bombard ourselves with screens and information the more we search for meaning in branding. It becomes something we believe we can trust. It is something that is consistent in the chaos. Make America Great Again. Those bright red hats are enabling hatred, racism, violence, misogyny, and cruelty.

Hatred and distrust between classes, races, and genders are not that difficult to grow if you plant the seeds or manipulate social media. Tell a lie enough times and people will believe it.

I first read Margaret Atwood's *The Handmaid's Tale* over thirty years ago when I was the age of Offred and her friends. But even as I squirmed with anger for Offred and her situation, there was a small, smug part of me that believed this would never happen in America. Not in my town. Not in my country. I no longer feel that way. We have all been "branded" and conditioned by branding—through our jobs, shopping habits, both online and in person, by billboards, commercials, even down to our choice of how we communicate or travel.

Branding changed the politics of this country. The women living Atwood's dystopian fictional future, are not so very different from us now. Just as Offred and her sisters secretly exchanged the names that defined them as "individuals," to preserve their identity women have now taken to the streets with posters and slogans in hand to protest a racist, sexist, homophobic, misogynistic political party whose lies grow more outrageous every day—while they still can.

10
Babies and Pleasures

SAMANTHA WESCH

The Handmaid's Tale is, frankly, creepy. The story is set in the near future in the Republic of Gilead, a newly-renamed part of the former United States of America. Here we meet Offred, the protagonist who has been forced into a kind of reproductive labor in the wake of the mass infertility experienced in her culture.

Her name has been changed to reflect the man she serves ("Of-Fred"). She has been torn away from her husband, her daughter, and the entire life she lived before Gilead. Offred is trapped in the home of a wealthy Commander and his wife, Serena Joy, for the purposes of conceiving the Commander's child. In this new world, high-ranking men are assigned "Handmaids" like Offred to produce their children when their wives cannot. They are also assigned women called "Marthas," who are in charge of domestic labor. If lower status men are allowed access to women at all, they have "econo-wives" who must fulfill the roles of Wives, Handmaids, and Marthas.

Rat in a Maze Is Free to Go Anywhere, as Long as It Stays Inside the Maze

Gilead functions through a strict sex division of labor and tightly-maintained gender roles. Everyone is monitored, regulated, and indoctrinated into a cult-like political regime. The leaders of the regime, Commanders like Fred and other high-ranking older men, try to legitimize Gilead's power through ultra-conservative readings from the Old Testament about men, women, childbearing, premarital sex, and homosexuality.

Sex for pleasure is outlawed (at least for women and low-status men) and women are confined to the home. They are not allowed to have jobs, own property, read, or write. Their bodies have become property of the state—anyone who defies their "ordained" sex roles is accused of "gender treachery" and punished accordingly. Gilead is a totalitarian state. It engages in surveillance of all of its citizen's behaviors, even down to the hormonal cycles and basic bodily functions of women. The government exercises total control over sexuality and reproduction. No one is free and everyone is constantly watching and judging those around them, on guard for a gender traitor or some other enemy of the state.

Atwood's chilling speculative fiction has got her called a "prophet of dystopia," but, perhaps, Gilead is not simply a dark vision of the future. In fact, Atwood herself expressed that her writing is "always about now," and is not meant to be taken as offering predictions for what's to come. Even though *The Handmaid's Tale* is *set* in the future, the characters are grappling with the problems of the here and now.

Atwood identifies what she does as *speculative* fiction, rather than *science* fiction. For Atwood, science fiction is based in impossible technologies and fantasies about aliens, other planets, time travel and things that could never be. It's more fantasy than reality. But speculative fiction concerns events that could *really happen*. Although speculative fiction presents us with new and different worlds, they are worlds that ours *could* be.

The Handmaid's Tale has no space battles or dimension jumping, but is based in a world like yours and mine. However, science fiction and speculative fiction share an outward-facing interest, and a fascination with the future of humanity. On speculative fiction, author Neil Gaiman writes:

People think—wrongly—that speculative fiction is about predicting the future, but it isn't; Or if it is, it tends to do a rotten job of it . . . What speculative fiction is really good at is not the future but the present—taking an aspect of it that troubles or is dangerous, and extending or extrapolating that aspect into something that allows the people of that time to see what they are doing from a different angle and from a different place. It's cautionary. (Introduction to *Fahrenheit 451*, p. xii)

Speculative fiction, then, is *not* about fantasizing or guessing at what's to come, but, instead, thinking about the world we live in. All good speculative fiction uses elements of the real world, our social problems, power dynamics, political conflicts and upheavals, and explores them in a new setting.

How different is Offred's life from the lives of women today? Sure, the exact details are different, but look closer. The government's interest in women's bodies and reproduction, along with the tactics of surveillance and punishment, aren't too distant from contemporary events. Perhaps the reason that reading the book or watching the show is so eerie is because we recognize ourselves and the conditions under which we are made complacent in the lives of Offred, Serena Joy, and the other Wives, Handmaids, and Marthas.

When Power Is Scarce, a Little Is Tempting

Particularly spooky is how the characters themselves become accustomed to these cultural changes, and, at times, even participate in the sick tools of power and control used against fellow citizens. Despite her personal strength and disgust with how she and other women are treated, Offred has moments in which her thoughts and behaviors follow from the logic of the new regime.

When she and her shopping buddy and fellow Handmaid Ofglen run into some foreign tourists, Offred judges the clothes of the women, the kind of clothes she herself wore a few years ago, as revealing and indecent. After the incident, she observes, "It has taken so little time to change our minds" (Emblem edition, p. 32). In even more disturbing instances, Offered and the other Handmaids engage in a cruel victim-blaming ritual called "testifying" in which they collectively shame one another for past sexual assaults and transgressions against the values of the regime, pointing and shrieking "Her fault!", "Teach her a lesson!", and "Crybaby!" at the Handmaid currently receiving the emotional beating (p. 82). Offred even reflects on how even she believed the Handmaid deserved it, and how she hated the women during the testifying. Offred thinks; "For a moment, even though we knew what was being done to her, we despised her . . . We meant it, which is the bad part."

The Handmaids even go so far as to participate in the ceremonial torture and murder of an accused (but not guilty) rapist. The ceremony is called a "Particicution," during which the women go into a frenzy and tear the victim limb from limb. When fed a lie that the woman the man supposedly raped was pregnant and the baby died, Offred thinks that "despite myself I feel my hands clench . . . It's true, there is a bloodlust; I want to tear, gouge, rend . . . There's a surge forward, like a crowd at a rock concert in the former time, when the doors opened, that urgency coming like a wave through us" (pp. 321–22).

How could these women, who led normal lives like you and I, so quickly fall into the clutches of the regime? How is it strong women like Offred are swept up in its power and punishment? Michel Foucault's most famous book *Discipline and Punish* (a title so appropriate it could have been a subtitle to *The Handmaid's Tale*) focuses on what Foucault called "biopower," or "power over life."

Foucault was deeply interested in "power," or the ways in which people are controlled and control other people. He offered a unique view, in which power is not "possessed" by one person and wielded over others, but, rather, we are all enacting power on each other at all times. Power is not top-down, with one person controlling everyone else, but instead, every person is constantly contributing to the control of others, and being controlled themselves. Foucault writes:

In short, this power is exercised rather than possessed; it is not the "privilege" acquired or preserved, of the dominant class, but the overall effect of its strategic positions—an effect that is manifested and sometimes extended by the position of those who are dominated. Furthermore, this power is not exercised simply as an obligation or prohibition on those who "do not have it"; it invests them, is transmitted by them and through them; it exerts pressure upon them, just as they themselves, in their struggle against it, resist the grip it has on them. (*Discipline and Punish*, pp. 25–27)

Offred reflects on something her mother, a badass raging feminist, once said, observing how it is; "truly amazing, what people can get used to, as long as there are a few compensations."

Where I Am Is Not a Prison but a Privilege

In *The Handmaid's Tale*, everyone thrives on exercising the small bit of power they can get their hands on. Serena Joy dominates the household, her assigned domain; Rita bosses around Cora and Offred in the kitchen. Ofwarren, another Handmaid Offred despises, proudly displays her pregnancy and revels in being the object of the other Handmaids' jealousy. Even Offred buys into Gilead's regime when she gets a chance to think she's better than other women, bully another Handmaid, or desecrate an enemy of the regime. When on her way to the grocery store with Ofglen, Offred expresses her enjoyment of taunting the young hormonal desires of celibate Guardians:

> As we walk away I know they're watching, these two men who aren't yet permitted to touch women. They touch with their eyes instead and I move my hips a little, feeling the full red skirt sway around me . . . I enjoy the power; power of a dog bone, passive but there. I hope they get hard at the sight of us and have to rub themselves on painted barriers, surreptitiously. (p. 25)

Power, for Foucault, is constantly moving between individuals as they are dominated, dominate others, and push against how these power relations effect them. Every character copes with their situation by also becoming part of the dominating machine of Gilead. While each is also monitored and controlled, they, in turn, find some solace in wielding over power over others. In asking *how* seemingly normal people could so quickly and easily become servants of Gilead, understanding the "perpetual spirals of power" which define the complicated relationships of submission and control between individuals shows how tempting and corrupting power is.

Biopower works through enacting power *internally,* not externally. Biopower can produce ideas, thoughts, and behaviors in its subjects as a means of control. How does Gilead change the ways in which its citizens think, feel, and act? Rather than working through the fear of violence or punishment in the way that public executions and torture worked in the far past, biopower operates through altering the behaviors, thoughts, and attitudes of individuals. It, in Foucault's words, has power over the "soul."

Offred recalls something Aunt Lydia once said: "The Republic of Gilead . . . knows no bounds. Gilead is within you" (p. 26). Foucault would very much agree:

> It would be wrong to say that the soul is an illusion, or an ideological effect. On the contrary, it exists, it has reality, it is produced permanently around, on, within the body by the functioning of power that is exercised on those punished—and, in a more general way, on those one supervises, trains, and corrects. (*Discipline and Punish*, p. 29)

Foucault discusses numerous "technologies" (tools of operation) through which biopower is able to control its citizens. Though many of these appear in *The Handmaid's Tale,* we're going to look at just a few: splitting populations, surveillance, and investment in reproduction.

Better Never Means Better for Everyone. It Always Means Worse, for Some

Biopower is first and foremost concerned with its population. It seizes power and maintains its control over the population by presenting itself as "benevolent," and claims to work in the best interests of the collective. Operations of biopower are made possible through claims that it can best protect the population through controlling it. Aunt Lydia, one of another class of women whose job it is to train Handmaids for reproductive labor, urges the Handmaids to see that they're better off in their captivity than they were before Gilead. Offred remembers her training classes with Aunt Lydia:

> Sometimes the movie she showed would be an old porno film from the seventies or eighties. Some kneeling, sucking penises or guns, women tied up or chained with dog collars around their necks, women hanging from trees or upside-down, with their legs held apart, women being raped, beaten-up, killed. Once we had to watch a woman being slowly cut into pieces, her fingers and breasts snipped off with garden shears, her stomach split open and her intestines pulled out . . . Consider the alternatives, said Aunt Lydia. You see what things used to be like? That was what they thought of women, then. (p. 137)

It is essential for the workings of biopower that citizens *believe* that these tactics and organizations are best for them. Biopower works subtle and silently, aimed at controlling people without their notice. Aunt Lydia is quick to remind the Handmaids that they are, in fact, free: "There is more than one kind of freedom, said Aunt Lydia. Freedom to and freedom from. In the days of anarchy, it was freedom to. Now you are being give freedom from. Don't underrate it" (p. 28).

Though there are public executions in *The Handmaid's Tale,* these are not Gilead's primary tactics for getting its way. Pay attention to the *attitudes* of the characters. Sure, all the characters are afraid of being executed or sent to the Colonies to slowly die while cleaning up radioactive waste. But there's more than just the fear of death that gives Gilead control over its citizens. It's the combination of splitting populations, surveillance, and control of reproduction that makes the characters shockingly quickly and easily conform to Gilead's laws. Well, at least the population that "matters."

Biopower is "power over life," its power directed at growing some groups of people and eliminating others. It works through establishing and maintaining a "dualistic system" that places people on either side of binary, mutually-exclusive pairs. First, biopower identifies groups as desirable and others as undesirable. Biopower operates through dividing populations into groups like men/women, white/black, straight/gay, and so on. These divisions are arbitrary; though they may map onto "real" differences in some respects (men and women *really do* have different reproductive organs) they are arbitrary in the sense that these small differences, like gender, skin color, sexual preference and so on, don't make us different *kinds* of things. Foucault writes:

> Generally speaking, all the authorities exercising individual control function according to a double mode; that of binary division and branding (mad/sane; dangerous/harmless; normal/abnormal) and that of coercive assignment, of differentiated distribution (who he is; where he must be; how he is to be characterized; how he is to be recognized; how a constant surveillance is exercised over him in an individual way, etc.) . . . The constant division between the normal and the abnormal, to which every individual is subjected. (*Discipline and Punish*, p. 199)

Foucault's point is, qualities like "women" or "man," and "gay" or "straight" are equally as useful for grouping people together as qualities like brown eyes, or blonde hair for determining whether or not these people are "really" different. In each of these binary pairs, one is "normal" and the other is "abnormal." Sovereign power's slogan is "let live and make die," through brutal and horrifying executions. However, biopower uses these false dichotomies to figure out how to control the population further.

Under His Eye

The Eyes are the secret police of Gilead; everyone knows they are around, but nobody knows exactly who or where they are. Anyone could be an Eye; Offred often worries that Nick, the Commander's flirtatious chauffeur, might be keeping an eye on everything she's up to, waiting to report back about her indiscretions. But it's not just the Eyes who keep everyone in check; Offred knows that Serena Joy, and the Marthas, Rita and Cora are watching her as well. Everyone has eyes on everyone else, keeping a clutch on the small amount of power afforded by the ability to watch and snitch on others.

In the work of Foucault, eyes also have a special significance. In French the word for the verb "to see," *voir,* is a part of the word for "power," *pouvoir.* Foucault believes this is significant, a key means by which power is enacted is through observing and monitoring. Eyes also have a special part in *The Handmaid's Tale;* they are the secret police hiding out in Gilead, waiting for a misstep, a runaway Handmaid, or an enemy of the regime.

Foucault called the disciplinary power of knowing there is always a possibility that one is being watched "Panopiticism." Philosopher Jeremy Bentham developed what he thought was the "perfect prison" in which all prisoners would be on their best behavior, and called it the Panopticon. Foucault describes the prison as a "marvelous machine" in which the cells were entered around a single watchtower, where the inmates were each in their own cell that they could not see out of but knew could be seen into, and which prisoners always knew there was the possibility someone was watching. Never having privacy, and always at risk of being found out and punished, Foucault observed, has a particular effect on the human psyche:

> Hence the major effect of the Panopticon: to induce in the inmate a state of conscious and permanent visibility that assures the automatic functioning of power. So to arrange things that the surveillance is permanent in its effects, even if it discontinues its action; that the perfection of power should tend to render its actual exercise unnecessary. (p. 201)

We act differently when we know we are, or could be, watched. For Foucault, Bentham's literal Panopticon is a metaphor for contemporary social organization. Foucault thinks we're constantly watching, observing, and waiting to tattle on one another. This practice has the same effects as Bentham's prison.

Before Offred gets to know Ofglenn better, they both hold tight to the rules they have been taught and convincingly appear to each other to be believers in the ideology of Gilead; "The truth is that she is my spy, as I am hers" (p. 21). This never-ending observation keeps everyone on their best behavior at all times, reminding them they are never alone. When Offred and Ofglen are asked by the foreign tourists if they are happy, they don't hesitate to say that they are. They know they *could* be being watched, and this is enough for Gilead to maintain tight control over Offred's thoughts, feelings, and behaviors.

Everyone in Gilead is a kind of Eye, watching everyone else and being watched themselves. Gilead is itself a Panopticon; without the constant awareness and fear of being watched, Gilead would not be such a tight ship. Gilead cannot always be watching, but, if the citizens believe there's always the possibility that an Eye is among them, or, even better, that they cannot trust each other, its power is always present and controlling each person's every move.

Blessed Be the Fruit

Gilead strictly controls the sexuality of women and lower status men. Reproduction is at the forefront of its interest. Well, the reproduction of *some,* that is—only the wealthy. Because biopower works through creating and maintaining certain groups of people and marginalizing and attempting to eliminate others, it invests its energy in making some live, while neglecting and ignoring the group it has deemed "abnormal."

In *The Handmaid's Tale,* women are first split up into "Legitimate Women" and "Unwomen." Unwomen are "abnormal," and are comprised of women who Gilead thinks of as sinful or undesirable. They are unmarried women who've had premarital sex, feminists, nuns, widows, lesbians, and those who opposed the regime. If a Handmaid doesn't conceive after three two-year assignments, and fails to fulfill her "normal" duty as a childbearing machine, then she is shipped off to join the Unwomen. Unwomen are not valued by Gilead, and, though they are not executed directly, the regime "allows them to die" through forced labor in "the Colonies," where the women are exposed to the deadly pollution which has caused the mass infertility. Cleaning up the radioactive mess leaves the Unwomen covered in tumors, many of them passing away quickly from the toxic exposure, and never reproducing.

Just as there are "Unwomen," there are "Unbabies," children born with disabilities or genetic deformities, likely because of the exposure of the population to pollution. In Gilead, not all babies are made equal. Though Offred doesn't know what happens to Unbabies after they are born, their disturbing nickname, "shredders," suggests they are "allowed to die" along with the Unwomen. Gilead is concerned with the dropping population due to infertility, but it's particular groups in the population that it is invested in promoting and protecting.

Gilead treats the "Legitimate Women," in particular, the Handmaids, in the exact opposite way. The health of the Handmaids is tightly regulated to ensure they secure the best chances for the best babies. As biopower is preoccupied with promoting "desirable" populations and extinguishing "undesirable populations" the reproduction of fertile, well-behaved women with high status men is central to its purpose. Biopower's ability to change the way individuals think and feel is centered on individuals believing they are or are not part of the desirable populations, and understanding and buying into their scripted role in the regime. Even Offred begins to believe her only purpose is child bearing:

> I used to think of my body as an instrument, of pleasure, or a means of transportation, or an implement for the accomplishment of my will . . . Now the flesh arranges itself differently. I'm a cloud,

133

congealed around a central object, the shape of a pear, which is hard and more real than I am and glows red within its translucent wrapping. (p. 84)

The regime even explicitly "makes live" the Handmaids by being hyperconscious of the Handmaids' temptation to escape their situation through suicide. Offred observes the lengths Gilead has gone to in order to make sure the handmaids stay alive:

I know why there is no glass in front of the watercolor picture of blue irises, and why the window only opens partly and why the glass in it is shatterproof. It isn't running away they're afraid of. We wouldn't get far. It's those other escapes, the one's you can open in yourself, given a cutting edge. (p. 8)

Offred knows that the regime values her for her ability to reproduce the desirable, high-status population, and therefore, that she *must* be kept alive.

The Handmaids participate in another kind of "making live" as well. Gilead also "makes live" through the forced reproduction of Handmaids with high-status men. This is Gilead's interest in keeping the Handmaids alive and well in the first place; it is connected to a greater desire to control the form of the population generally. Gilead actively monitors which men do and do not have access to fertile women. It is the Handmaids who are blamed then relocated when they fail to conceive the children of older men, who, a doctor tells Offred, are likely the one's who are sterile.

Gilead isn't concerned with making as many babies as possible by any means possible, but, rather, making sure some populations, specifically powerful, high status men, carry on. First, it's considered shameful for any woman who can reproduce to resist her duty. Offred recalls that, while at the Red Center, Aunt Lydia called women who used birth control "lazy sluts" (p. 130) and accused them of being selfish in not continuing the population. Abortion doctors from the time before are retroactively punished for "killing babies" in the past and birth control is partially blamed for Gilead's current infertility.

Though Gilead presents itself as concerned about *babies* and the carrying on of the world, in reality, it is worried about maintaining its "desirable" population. As Offred observes, in a state concerned with producing and "making live" certain kinds of individuals, she needs to have children. She knows that she and the other Handmaids are "not to be wasted" (p. 7).

Nolite te Bastardes Carborundorum

Foucault's political work isn't completely doom and gloom; he believes that it is "bodies and pleasures" which are a means of resisting oppressive biopolitics. Pleasure, in eating, in sharing secrets in the bathroom with Moira, and in her love making with Nick, are Offred's means of resistance. It is in these moments, where she imagines the foods she used to eat, or shares a moment of illegal passion with her lover, in which she doesn't let "the bastards grind her down." Offred resists the domination of her body by Gilead, her forced sex with the Commander, the tight medical surveillance of her body, and her restricted rights, through her pleasurable sexual relationship with Nick. Offred recalls their first kiss, illegal and in the middle of the commander's house late at night:

> He puts his hand on my arm, pulls me against him, his mouth on mine, what else comes from such denial? Without a word. Both of us shaking, how I'd like to. In Serena's parlour, with the dried flowers, on the Chinese carpet, his thin body. A man entirely unknown. It would be like shouting, it would be like shooting someone. My hand goes down, how about that, I could unbutton, and then. But it's too dangerous, he knows it, we push each other away, not far. (p. 113)

Her sexual passion with Nick is, in effect, her wiggling her middle finger at the regime, refusing to allow them to claim ownership of her body. In having wanted sex purely for pleasure, Offred reclaims her body. She reinforces her identity as a woman, and reproduces herself (her "soul") outside the grasps of biopower. Foucault writes about the liberating qualities of sexual pleasure on one's own terms, "The rallying point for the counterattack against the deployment of sexuality ought not be sex-desire, but bodies and pleasures" (*History of Sexuality, Volume 1*, p. 57). What is important about these moments of resistance, moments when the control of the regime is thwarted, and characters forget what they have been made to believe, is that they are spaces for the possibilities of a new, better, world. After making long and meaningful eye contact with a guard, a small but forbidden act, Offered thinks, "a small defiance of rule, so small as to be undetectable . . . Such moments are possibilities, tiny peepholes" (p. 24).

Moments of resistance, refusals to let "the bastards win," are enjoyed by many different characters in different ways throughout Atwood's story. The power in *The Handmaid's Tale* is not in conjuring up a new world, or predicting the consequences of the sexism and misogyny that exist in and structure our social world. Rather, she shows us a world of unimaginable horror, which, the more we read, the more we realize looks a lot like our own.

But, more importantly, she provides us with the possibility to resist domination through resilience and pleasure.

11
What about the Men?

TIM JONES

It's natural and right to look at the sexual abuse and marginalization faced by the show's female characters, but what about the men?

Nick, for one, is coerced into sex almost as surely as June. It's not as if he has the authority to turn down Serena's orders that they sleep together in "Faithful," so an opportunity for genuine, meaningful consent is denied him as much as it is her. So why is there so little interest in how hard life in Gilead can be for its menfolk?

What if it's because there's something about this story that makes this question a little . . . inappropriate? It's an adaption of a female-authored novel, examining the sexual subjugation of women not just in Gilead, but in Atwood's own society too. Perhaps it's just not supposed to be *about* men. And perhaps part of escaping the horrific possibilities it envisages for women's futures comes from male viewers or readers recognizing that it's not about men and learning to be okay with this—recognizing that women's issues and experiences can occupy center stage and not looking to bend the conversation to their own interests instead.

This might be a little difficult, given that much of culture and society tells us we should do the opposite and make it all about the men, all the time.

Choice and Agency

It's not that we couldn't make *The Handmaid's Tale* all about the men if we wanted to. Just look at the situation Nick finds himself in when Serena becomes so desperate for a child that she demands he and June sleep together.

Throughout the previous episodes, we've seen June subjected to the Ceremony. We never see her physically or verbally resist this in a way that would make it absolutely clear that her consent is denied, until the graphic sequence in "The Last Ceremony." But this isn't the point; her lack of overt resistance up to that moment doesn't stop this in any way from being rape, because any resistance would only put her in greater danger. If she disobeys the regime's orders, she could find herself mutilated like Janine, or sent to the colonies like Emily—or worse.

She isn't capable of consenting to the Ceremony, then, because having these consequences hanging over her means that she isn't given the free option of saying 'no' to it. And if you can't refuse consent, then consent is meaningless, since you're compelled to pick one outcome over the other for your own safety, rather than getting to decide between consent and refusal for yourself. Any "sex" that takes place in those circumstances is just as surely rape as it obviously is in "The Last Ceremony," when she's kicking and screaming.

This applies as much to Nick as it does to June. Though the regime is obviously and deeply misogynist on every level, it's just as ready to punish men as it is women. Warren has his hand cut off in "Night" for having sex with Janine outside of the Ceremony; the guy who shelters June in "Baggage" is seen to have been executed in the very next episode. These guys might have certain privileges (like being allowed to read and write . . .), but this definitely doesn't extend to being able to break Gilead's rules with impunity.

So when ordered by Serena to sleep with June, what can Nick do, exactly? Probably very little, other than exactly what Serena wants him to. Given the influence that Serena has over him via the Commander, and given what she could have happen to him if he refuses, then he's no freer to refuse her demands than June is free to turn down Fred during the Ceremony.

Sure, he's an Eye, so he clearly has contacts and options that Gilead's average male citizen does not, but this doesn't mean he can do what he likes. This is proven in Season Two when Fred lands him with a wife he doesn't want, just to keep him away from June.

Which brings me to the moment in "First Blood" when he finally consummates his marriage with Eden. Much like his first sexual encounter with June, this act is another one beyond his agency, given the consequences of refusing the regime's demands that man and woman work dutifully to produce offspring. Abstaining would be especially dangerous, given the initial suspicions that Eden voices to June about Nick being a Gender Traitor.

We've seen through Emily's story how barbarically Gilead treats gay people. Once again, then, Nick lacks the option of choosing not to have sex, and so even though we see him willingly engage, this willingness is coerced, and so it's not really all that willing at all. It shouldn't be controversial to call unwilling "sex" rape, regardless of whether it's a man or a woman who's being compelled.

One scene in "First Blood" is especially ironic. To maintain her own safety, June is completely fine with ordering Nick to ignore his lack of physical attraction and moral qualms and sleep with his wife, even if he has no wish to do so. The regime compels June to have sex against her will and we see how much this makes her suffer, emotionally, mentally, and physically, yet she has no qualms at all about compelling Nick to do likewise. It's not even that she lacks the means to enforce her demands—to give them the weight that they'd need to have any coercive power, should she choose to use it. A simple DNA test would reveal that Nick is the real father of her baby, and we're shown in the very first episode what happens to a man accused of raping a Handmaid. We see in "The Last Ceremony," when he denies to Eden that he fancies June, that he knows how dangerous such an accusation would be.

Nick might be pretty sure that June wouldn't be able to make an accusation stick, or that Serena and the Commander would together ensure that the DNA test didn't happen, to keep the household together around their new baby. He might even be sure that her love for him means that she'd never even make such a threat, yet alone go through with it. But given this possible means of holding power over him and the possible consequences of her exercising it, can he really take that risk?

My point here is that there's a definite case to be made that Nick is put under the same pressures as June; just as she can't be said to be consenting to sex with Fred, neither can *he* be consenting the first time he sleeps with either June or Eden. Sure, in neither of these cases is it the female character who's forcing herself on him, like Fred is on June, but the same institutional pressures are there to ensure that he has no more control over what he does with his body than they do. You might even say they have it as bad as each other.

Arguments that focus on the suffering of the show's female characters just don't seem that bothered about how much the entire *other* half of Gilead's population suffers too.

Who Gets to Speak

But regardless of whether or not you *could* focus on the men and the women of Gilead both having it bad, *should* you?

I'm not so sure—principally because the cultural and political context outside the text ensures that making such an argument runs the risk of drowning out a critical and emotional focus on the female characters. It runs the risk of ensuring that an analysis of how Gilead affects the lives of its male citizens becomes the *main* argument that people are interested in, which runs counter to everything that I reckon the book and show both want to achieve.

To understand why this risk exists, we can look at *who* gets to speak in society outside the pages of the book and consider what influence the answer to this question has on *what* exactly gets spoken about. Look at the political makeup of the USA in terms of gender. The 115th Congress, sworn in on January 2017, is the best yet for gender diversity—which sounds great, until you look into it a little more and see that the 104 women with seats across the House and the Senate comprise only 19 percent of the country's total lawmakers. This is in a country where women make up just over 50 percent of the total population, further highlighting how badly women are represented amongst the political decision makers. June's mother Holly would definitely not approve. These stats are a considerable improvement over Gilead for sure, but it could be lots better—and I'm not sure that that's the best basis for a comparison in the first place!

It doesn't seem possible that this discrepancy wouldn't affect the sorts of ideas that get put forward to Congress and get discussed there—and, by consequence, the sorts of ideas that are considered part of the regular discourse outside Congress too. Men and women hold lots of interests in common, because at the heart of it we're all people, but there are lots of important issues that the majority of men are going to struggle to get the same handle on, simply because those issues won't ever form part of their day-to-day lived experience.

Breast-feeding in public; the need for access to free contraception, or abortion; how safe it is to walk home at night without fearing sexual violence . . . It's unlikely that these issues will ever be discussed—by the bodies who have the power to legislate to make a difference—as openly, or considered of such importance, as they might be were the gender balance to be tipped the other way, or, heaven forbid, levelled out somewhere around fifty fifty.

And it's not just politics that's affected by this gender imbalance. Look at the wider media too. How many of your favorite TV shows are written by men? How many of their episodes have male directors? How many have male main characters? As for movies, a study undertaken by Dr. Stacey Smith as part of her Media, Diversity, and Social Change initiative at UCS discovered that across the 1,300 top-grossing films released between 2002 and 2014, only 4.1 percent of them were directed by women.

Before anyone insists that women just don't like making films, bless them, female film graduates number 50 percent of *all* film graduates, yet only 5 percent of these women end up working on major film projects.

Just like in politics, it's men who get to speak, despite an equal number of women clamoring for the same voice. So it's men's experiences of the outside world that tend to get spoken about, with the issues that are apparent to men occupying the majority of the discourse.

When It's Not about You

What this means is that men are very used to the narrative that male issues are the ones that need addressing and are worth discussing, while the rarer nature of work that specifically addresses women's own lived experience of the world continues to see these interests cast as strange aberrations that belong on the margins—even though they're the experiences of the majority of the population.

This corresponds with feminist blogs (such as feministing.com, for one pretty accessible example) that describe how male readers react to the discourse on these blogs. This is discourse that, naturally, does not put men's interests first—it's discourse that explores the issues raised by women's experiences and considers these issue's effects on women's daily lives.

The blogs' description of common male reactions to their content has given me the title of this chapter—"What about the Men?" The phrase pokes fun at the idea that men are so acclimatized to seeing their own life experiences at the front and center of every discussion, they find it hard to imagine anything different. And so when men come across an article that doesn't fit with this, which prioritizes women's experiences and needs instead, they seek to make it about them, just like the majority of popular culture is . . . even when the material under consideration absolutely doesn't warrant it.

The Handmaid's Tale adaptation might be show-run by a man, but the world that it describes is one envisaged by a woman. It's a world characterized by a lack of female influence, where women exist at the beck and call of men, to service their needs in the home and in the bedroom. It's a world characterized by a twisted sexual politics that asks its audience to consider how much it reflects the sexual politics of the real world. Saying that June's plight is just like that of the women in our society might sound a bit of a stretch, but given the massive spread of the #metoo movement in highlighting the ubiquity of women's experiences of sexual violence, I don't think seeing parallels between the two requires as much of a leap as you might think.

During one of my days writing this chapter, America was listed as the tenth most dangerous place to be a woman, narrowly beating such bastions of women's rights as Saudi Arabia (where until 2018 it was illegal for women to drive), Pakistan, India, and the Congo. The survey, carried out by Thomson's Reuters Foundation, polled 550 experts on women's issues on the likelihood of women across the world experiencing sexual violence, forced trafficking, or domestic slavery . . . basically the sorts of things faced by characters like June, Emily, and Janine in the show.

Now, I have problems seeing that women in the USA could possibly have it that bad. But then again, I'm not one of them, so I'd have no way of knowing one way or the other... Except by listening to those female experts that are telling me that they do. Whoa.

The Handmaid's Tale is a show that strikes against the general failure of media in making women's experiences of the world its main subject matter. This is why it's important that men know when to step back—when to let a rare text like this speak its rarely made point, even when that point might not correspond with the sorts of points they see elsewhere in the media, or with the experiences of their own lives.

When men don't step back, even female-led discussions about women's lived experiences can become dominated by male voices around which the discussion ends up molding itself, such is the power of patriarchal conditioning in insisting that women prioritize male needs over their own. The original point the discussion was trying to make then gets lost and the discussion becomes indistinguishable from the rest of what we see in the media, missing entirely what that discussion was trying to accomplish through its unapologetic focus on women's issues marking such a departure from the norm.

Men don't have the fear of sexual violence as part of their day to day lives hanging over them with the same ubiquity as women. Much of popular culture is formed by men, so this possibility isn't usually its focus, simply because these men don't know that it's there. When a rare piece of popular culture does make this possibility apparent, then, men have two options. The first is to listen to it and see what they can learn about the day-to-day experiences of the other half of the population, from which popular culture usually keeps them sheltered. The other is to block it out, because it doesn't correspond with what they see or hear most of the time, and to make it about men instead.

Don't Be This Guy

Margaret Atwood's novel knows this risk and closes by sounding a warning. June's narrative finishes in the book at the exact same point as the show's Season One finale, with June urged by Nick to trust him as she makes her way into the waiting van outside her household, wondering if she's stepping up into "darkness. . . or else the light." The novel then switches to an academic conference in Canada, around two hundred years in the future, where an analysis of June's narrative is being delivered by a male speaker.

His main interests involve making flirty jokes about the racial identity of the conference's Chairperson; punning on the possible sexual innuendo behind the narrative having been called *The Handmaid's* Tale (look up the Latin connotations of "tail"); and discovering the true identity of the novel's otherwise unnamed Commander. For reasons the academic can only guess at, Book Offred is frustratingly vague on who he really is.

It's a bit of a shame that she was too busy being ritualistically raped every month to give a damn about the motivations a male academic, two centuries in the future, might have for looking at her narrative. These motivations of his don't concern the emotional content, or the ways in which the narrative might help him understand the experiences faced by women in his own culture—he just wishes the historical facts were a little less woolly, since that way it'd be of far more use to his own research into Gilead and, therefore, his academic career.

The speaker's motivations make June's narrative all about him and his own interests, like the men called out by feminist bloggers for interrupting their conversations with demands that those conversations cater to the male experience of the world, rather than allowing it to remain about *her*, or the wider experiences of her gender. I have a feeling he'd love the first half of this chapter, but be a little less engaged by the second.

The challenge faced by a male reader of the book, or a male viewer of the show, is to be a better audience than the conference speaker in the "Historical Notes" section of the novel—and, by doing so, hopefully avoid prioritizing the sort of male-centered analysis with which I began this chapter. The challenge is to let it remain primarily of relevance to women's lived experiences, rather than reacting to a perceived need that it speak to men too—or even to men instead.

I don't want to suggest there's no place at all for an analysis of how a man like Nick might be coerced into sex, either through institutional factors over which he has too little influence to resist, or even through physical force. Men *are* raped and that obviously needs addressing. But when a text like *The Handmaid's Tale* places women's experiences at the front and center, and when this is such a rare sight, you might want to have a think about the appropriateness of this being the question in which you're most interested.

12
Gilead as Palimpsest

CHRISTOPHER KETCHAM

Palimpsest. n. A piece of written material where the original writing has been erased and something new written over it, but where traces of the original may be discerned.

Offred lives a holocaust existence. Granted she does not experience the brute violence, physical deprivation, or continuous threat of imminent death of the Nazi death camps. However, she has had her given name excised and a new one tattooed on her body in as much indelible ink as was writ upon Jewish forearms.

Atwood's tale suggests that we are always under threat of holocaust by degree in the form of cultural destruction to serve the needs of ideologues who are ever-present in society, hovering like vultures, waiting for the right moment to pounce and rid people of their past, their identity, and, as the Nazis did, their future. It is the generation that exists through the holocaust event that witnesses the palimpsest of a new world order being written over the past, proclaiming the glorious future for the deserved few:

"You are a transitional generation, said Aunt Lydia. It is the hardest for you. We know the sacrifices you are being expected to make . . . She did not say: because they will have no memories, of any other way. She said: because they won't want things they can't have" (*The Handmaid's Tale*, p. 117).

Offred cannot forget what she cannot have—her past, particularly her husband and her child. Their ink bleeds through the new manuscript writ over her prior existence. She exists in a W.E.B. Dubois twoness, a double consciousness of existence that cannot let the past expire while it struggles to endure what has been forced upon her as truth and order. Atwood types a stark tale of cultural change wrapped in the guise of legality, security, and societal need based upon the object of its futurity—its ability to procreate.

The fertile woman is both oppressed into involuntary submission and servitude to alpha males, but at the same time she is elevated to the status of necessity in an environment where cruel genetic deviancy has become the norm. In this tale, Atwood shows us how the abnormal breeds the new norm and how those who lurk in the shadows and wait for such abnormality can emerge vociferously like a bolt of lightning—as those who endure are lulled into a false sense of security, huddled for warmth against the gathering storm's violence, oblivious to its destructive power.

In one of her many moments of reflection, Offred explains this passivity: "We were the people who were not in the papers. We lived in the blank white spaces at the edge of print. It gave us more freedom. We lived in the gaps between stories" (p. 57). Atwood's dystopian tale is about the extremes, the abrupt writing over of culture as the result of near-extinction events. However, she, through Offred, is suggesting that we, even those of us who are not individually the subject of the news, must not ignore the goings on that do not yet affect our freedom, but ultimately will.

Atwood reminds us that there are those in our own society who have objectives, desires, and an ethic that will deny our freedom in favor of their superiority, whether that be through brute power, religious fundamentalism, a return to a former mythological greatness, or greed. They simply are waiting for the right amount of suffering to initiate their scourge upon what society has conceived as the good.

In other words, power emerges through the cracks in culture that form when a people deal with significant events of change in their existence—suffering, useless suffering. Given the chance to mitigate the suffering that results, the ideologues resolve to do this through highly focused mythology that meets the narrowest of needs of a select few, but is expressed to the many as the salve, the cure, even a divine intervention couched in the guise of a superhuman, whether this be the Aryan eugenics of the Nazis or the repressive hetheonomy in the *Handmaid's Tale*.

In the blank white space of pain, the ideologue who answers the sufferer's pain is at the bedside of society, offering cures that provide momentary relief to the sufferer, a moment of gratitude towards the healer, but long-term hell for those who survive the ordeal. What then can we learn from Offred's ordeal to prepare ourselves for the cultural crises that are emerging even as you read this chapter?

Under Erasure

The writ of culture is always ~~under erasure~~. Offred's personal world in *The Handmaid's Tale* is bifurcated into the past and the present, both which compete for her attention and her soul. Her past is *sous rature*, ~~under erasure~~.

Martin Heidegger first used the convention of writing a word and then crossing it out. Gayatri Spivak in her introduction to Jacques Derrida's *Of Grammatology* explains the convention, "Since the word is inaccurate it is crossed out. Since it is necessary it remains legible" (p. xiv).

For Offred, her past is a necessity because it binds to her as something real that cannot be taken from her even as the world of Gilead has taken all that once mattered to her. She knows she cannot express in this new world who she was without becoming a pariah, or worse, hung like putrid meat in the town square. Therefore, her memories of the real are inaccurate and crossed out in this new order of existence.

Margaret Attwood spares us the gore of the revolution that created Gilead; but we're suspicious of how a culture and a way of existence could be wiped away as quickly as chalk, leaving only white dust motes in the air to hint at its prior existence. Let us not forget the rapid cultural turns to Fascism in Italy and Germany during the World War II era, and Fidel's brand of Communism in 1960s Cuba.

Ideologues like Hitler, Mussolini, and Castro persuaded vulnerable populations that they were the salvation of the people and the culture. Each demonized a people or their beliefs: Hitler—Jews; Mussolini—Communists; Castro—Batista and his corrupt cronies. In the world of Offred, the culprit is anyone who does not adhere to the rigid restrictions of a strict interpretation of the bible as construed by its leaders. This form of he-theonomy we know today as ISIS and the Taliban.

Therefore, we must understand that the fragility of culture and norms is real and that *sous rature* is a process people live through. Think of *sous rature* like a living bridge that connects the past and the present cultures and its people who have been put under erasure all the while they have been reconstructed to conform to the new norm. The pain of silence, the suffering in silence, is a price we pay when the past is erased by others but retained by those who live through it.

Passivity

However, humans are resilient creatures. Offred develops methods of coping in the new he-theonomy by becoming passive. It is a passivity that Emmanuel Levinas explains is more passive than receptive; an ordeal "more passive than experience" ("Useless Suffering," p. 157).

This pathological passivity is suffering. When overwhelmed, one response is hiding, another is running, a third is fighting. Offred at first hides in the anonymity of being outside of that which makes news, the silent majority Richard Nixon once called his own. Then she runs with her husband and daughter but they all incur the wrath of the he-theonomy that by this point in her existence has become dominant and omnipresent.

Offred has been forcibly deprived of her now unlawful marriage and her now illegitimate daughter and put into sexual bondage. It is her freedom that has been put ~~under erasure~~. Certainly, she is as free as she can be given her caste and place in this new society of Gilead, but the freedom that she once had in her prior existence is now not possible. She has become passive, hiding once again in the required cloak and mantle of her servitude, living in two worlds at once. The past gives her both succor and pain as she strains to continue the stories of a daughter and husband she fears that she will never see again. She copes and endures . . . But does she?

Useless Suffering

Levinas called suffering inflicted on the other—useless. Therefore, Offred and all the other women whose freedom has been shredded into definable chunks of required behavior, exist in a state of useless suffering. Even those who once railed against the progressive norm of the prior society realize the pinch of useless suffering as the restriction of freedom.

Offred comments about the former activist and her master's wife, Serena Joy, "She doesn't make speeches anymore. She has become speechless. She stays in her home, but it doesn't seem to agree with her. How furious she must be, now she has been taken at her word." Serena Joy has no one to blame but herself for it was her words about the place of women that helped lead to the suffering that is now Gilead.

For Levinas the beneficial passivity that is more passive than any other is in service to the other, being responsible for and to the other: "Responsibility for the other, in its antecedence to my freedom, its antecedence to the present and to representation, is a passivity more passive than all passivity, an exposure to the other without this exposure being assumed, an exposure without holding back, exposure of exposed-ness, expression, saying" (*Otherwise than Being*, p. 15).

However, because I hold nothing back in this service, I am exposing myself to suffering at the hands of the other. The

151

passivity of substituting oneself for another, to be responsible to the other, not only serves the other, but Levinas sees it as the location for where my freedom begins. My freedom is not the inward dwelling "I" who is comfortable just being me, my freedom is in the cause of freedom, responsibility. This form of non-useless suffering is what is missing in the he-theonomy.

In Levinas's freedom each person is unique, different, and this difference is worth celebrating and preserving through responsibility. In Offred's world, the individual is an object, a category of person bent not to serve the other but the he-theonomy at the expense of individuality and otherness. Thus, the passivity that Offred enters is not one towards responsibility to the other, but a passivity that seeks to preserve her once and responsible self at the expense of the other—the he-theonomy.

The Destructive Force of Useless Suffering

In the he-theonomy of Gilead, we are introduced to passivity that is not in service to responsibility and that is the overwhelming experience that produces the passivity when a person suffers uselessly. This passivity is a form of cocooning against the experience of pain and evil, a regression into oneself, which means that the one who suffers uselessly is in no condition to be available to be responsible for the other. Useless suffering produces a separation and segregation of the individual into a space where the oppressor can continue to rule with impunity because the oppressive place has become a personal prison that the afflicted cannot escape, even by force of will.

However, there will be those who try as did Moira, who escaped in the habit of Aunt Elizabeth. "Nevertheless, Moira was our fantasy," Offred says (p. 133). This suffering in silence, gaining succor by fantasy, Levinas describes as evil, "It is not, to tell the truth, through passivity that evil is described, but through evil that suffering is understood. Suffering is a pure undergoing." It is the undergoing of being put ~~under erasure~~ by others.

Levinas recognizes that most useless suffering is not caused by physical blows. It is the oppressive nature of the he-theonomy that Offred and the other women endure in their cruel patriarchy deemed necessary by ideologues, who emerged from the scourge wrought by the former leaders who spawned disastrous genetic mutations. Levinas says, "The not of evil is negative right up to non-sense. All evil refers to suffering." We can also say that all useless suffering is evil. Offred uselessly suffers.

Yet, Offred reveals the kernel of her being with her fantasy of escape, both with her husband and daughter in search of life in Canada, and again with knowing that Moira has run away. However, as the story unfolds, Offred cannot yet discover a means to escape. She fantasizes three versions of Luke and his fate and asks whether he can hope, giving us the notion that she has put her faith in this once and still precious other to rescue her. As she cannot yet find a way to free herself she says, "But I believe all of them, all three versions of Luke, at one and the same time. This contradictory way of believing seems to me, right now, the only way I can believe anything. Whatever the truth is I will be ready. This is also a belief of mine. This also may be untrue" (p. 105). It is then that she reveals the depth of her useless suffering when she recalls the tombstone that has on it "In Hope. In Hope."

She says, "Why did they put that above a dead person? Was it the corpse hoping or those still alive?" In this Offred discloses that she is both the corpse and the survivor, but instead of giving herself hope, she projects this onto Luke, "Does Luke hope?" (p. 106). What if he cannot hope? Does this mean that Offred is condemned to suffer uselessly in a state that resembles purgatory where the suffering souls are made to repeat over and over again the substance of their lives while enduring unrelenting pain? It ends as we feared it would; even during her Mayday escape, Offred remains ambivalent. At the end of the book, Offred says, "Whether this is my end or a new beginning, I have no way of knowing: I have given myself over to the hands of strangers because it can't be helped. And so I step up, into the darkness within; or else the light." Useless suffering's grip remains strong; helplessness hovers over her passivity even as she is rescued. She knows not whether the future is more of the same or a new beginning. Even so, she is to carry what she has become, a palimpsest of the past and the future into an uncertain tomorrow . . . A holocaust survivor today still knows the number tattooed on her forearm and what it means to her.

Even before her rescue revelation, we can see the seeds of the erasure under which Offred suffers uselessly. She sees a dishtowel and realizes it is no different than the dishtowels from her prior life. She says to herself, "Sometimes these flashes of normality come at me from the side, like ambushes" (p. 48). These ambushes are symptomatic of post-traumatic stress disorder where everyday things can trigger flashbacks.

Gilead

Atwood's Gilead is an ancient place and a modern place. It is the call of a Biblical time before any notion of the modern. It is a call to erase the modern that came before the new Gilead and replace it with a biblical notion of being that comes from a new New Testament as proposed by the postmodern but equally regressive he-theonomy that calls itself progressive.

So, how can all this happen? How can a society write over with impunity the prior society and even societies that precede it? What is it that produces the palimpsest where even the most strident efforts of erasure never completely erase the experience of existence for those who have experienced that other world?

The palimpsest of culture is not unlike Ernest Hemingway's *Old Man and the Sea*, a fisherman who has caught the fish of his lifetime, only to have it be devoured by hungry sharks. The fishhooks of his dream seem to maintain their grip of resistance in the marlin even when the fisherman's line goes slack. He retains the memory of the dream, but reality has intervened. His new reality cannot always forget what has been. A bit of both remain: that which is put ~~under erasure~~ and that which is imagined to replace what has been erased.

The palimpsest of the he-theonomy includes the weaving of the fabric of passivity's cocoon Offred and other women wear in their useless suffering. We have seen this same fabric of passivity woven before in crisp black uniforms and yellow Stars of David pinned onto striped pajamas. The Germans suffered hyperinflation in the 1920s. Hitler rose to prominence by promising a cure to the people's useless suffering. He promised prosperity by damning the countries that forced Germany to pay reparations after the armistice that ended the violent hostilities of World War I, but where resentment continued to fester in the German people. Then he turned on his own citizens, the Jews, to make them the personal scapegoats of German suffering.

Hitler's form of eugenics elevated some and condemned others to death. In Gilead, the suffering of war also caused the rise of the he-theonomy that elevated the true believers of the fundamentalist faith where the 'he' is ascendant over 'she.' Those perceived to be the cause of the mutations, the former politicians, scientists, and learned folk are hung from hooks for all to see like so much diseased meat. Books, knowledge, fake news, are all blamed for the suffering that the people have endured and that which has been writ over these now disappearing tomes is a new order constructed from the ashes of the prior troubles. Those in the cognitive borderlands, they who have memories of the old that are being forcibly erased by the new, enter a phase of useless suffering far more intrusive than the suffering that caused the rise of the he-theonomy.

If we can take from Atwood just one lesson, it is that the passivity caused by suffering is not just useless, it is dangerous. If we accede to the passivity trap of suffering by becoming cocooned against the gathering storm, we have only ourselves to blame when this suffering becomes even more oppressive and we are forced to abandon what is good for all, to what is good for a select few who now maintain our suffering in a new and even more decidedly passive form. For this passivity is the palimpsest of putting our very being ~~under erasure~~; to mold a new but beaten down being that (not who) serves the ideologue. In fact, the face of the other is put ~~under erasure~~ and is replaced with a dogma the no longer resembles the human face . . . It is the image of Big Brother in George Orwell's *Nineteen Eighty-Four*, or the Commanders in the world of Gilead.

It is our duty to resist and even overcome the passivity into which useless suffering plunges us, and together rise for the other, any and all others, and reject solutions that replace one useless suffering for another. Hitler and the he-theonomy never lift their people from useless suffering. Both maintain the people in that dank passivity even as they proclaimed an end to suffering.

Beware then the ideologue who promises the good but demonically erases what is good in society, all in the cause of ending suffering.

Part IV

How Easy It Is to Invent a Humanity, for Anyone at All

13
Gilead vs. the Self

ERICA A. HOLBERG

The Handmaid's Tale explores how extreme oppression as a political ruling system can establish and maintain itself. The state of Gilead arises through the exploitation of a crisis concerning biological reproductive failure.

As a novel form of social organization, Gilead makes possible the seizure and redistribution of this desperately desired good, children, for those who have power within the new social order. But Gilead's guiding ambition is not merely the reallocation of existing children, but to control reproduction for society in general, so as to preserve and project its social hierarchy into the future. Sustaining such an extreme, authoritarian social arrangement presents many difficulties.

According to the ethical theory of Immanuel Kant, an oppressive system like Gilead must struggle to maintain itself, for, in demanding that large segments of the population be treated as non-persons, as resources to be used to attain the social aim of producing and distributing children, the central organizing principle of this society is morally incoherent.

The Handmaids are explicitly characterized as vessels, objects for use, lacking any agency, but in fact, all the women and most of the men are treated as instruments for achieving what is decreed to be the benefit of the whole society. Most people are thus denied the possibility of thinking for

159

themselves and acting according to what the individual agent reasons to be good. So many lose so much for the benefit of so few.

Further, because reproduction and sexual intimacy are central to a person's understanding of herself in pursuit of her own conception of the good life, the implementation and maintenance of such an oppressive political regime will always be under immense pressure; my commitment to my wife or my child is not something I can simply get over because ordered to, at least not without losing something essential to who I am and am striving to be.

To sustain itself, Gilead must disrupt each person's recognition of her own intrinsic value and equal status in relation to all other agents: Gilead must prevent reason's self-recognition of its activity and its value. Feminists who use Kant's moral framework to think through the nature and persistence of sexist oppression, see the social subordination of women to men within patriarchy as similarly requiring societal structures to stunt women's growth into moral agency, with the resultant unequal social positioning and powers defended as the natural, morally good, order.

For Kantian feminists, the systemic attack upon the self-respect of individuals of a certain group is key for explaining social oppression; of all the various harms that oppression inflicts (and there are many), the most insidious is this encompassing, sustained attack on an individual's sense of self-worth. For the damage inflicted deliberately aims to debase the individual agent in her own eyes, incapacitating her own judgment and agency, thereby making her less fit as a moral agent, less able to resist unjust external demands, and so over time, more and more into a hollowed-out thing to be used by others.

In his *Groundwork for the Metaphysics of Morals* (1785), Immanuel Kant proposed that each person, simply through her possession of reason, has infinite, intrinsic value and also self-awareness of her agency and its inherent value. According to Kant, the intrinsic value each of us has is apparent to all other persons through our shared participation in reason.

Morally wrong actions violate another's inherent dignity and integrity as a person, because the other person is treated as an object, or mere means, to getting something wanted without regard for her agency.

Because it concerns a patriarchal, authoritarian society first establishing and then struggling to enforce its power upon its subjects, *The Handmaid's Tale* can, as a refracted image of sexist oppression, provide insight into how a society erases an individual's sense of herself as deserving of respect, and so transforms a person into a thing for others' use. What makes self-respect vulnerable to such external harms is that, although self-respect is natural to us through our experience of ourselves as rational agents, freely choosing and so responsible for what we will, we must develop rational agency as an ability and we do this through exercising it in relation to others. If others around us regularly thwart our efforts to think and will freely, our rational, agential abilities cannot develop and function in the ways that these powers, by their very nature, aim to do. Reason wants to be free and self-determining, but we need modeling, practice with, and reinforcement from others to get there.

In its narrative, *The Handmaid's Tale* shows the systemic attack on self-respect to occur through deploying two temporalities of oppressive force: oppression as a quick onslaught that radically remakes the ordinary and is achieved through the manipulation of fear, and oppression as a slow grind that consists in having to live with the new ordinary and is achieved through the manipulation of shame. Fear and shame are used in tandem to undermine self-respect, but also the sense of being or having a stable self at all. Fear of pain and death produces the abasement of the self and the severing of connectedness to others (for the agent may betray those she loves in her fear, or her loved ones are not there or not able to help in this moment of terror). The fear experienced causes her shame in the internalization of this experience of herself as a weak, isolated, groveling thing vulnerable to terrorizing force. This new shameful relation to herself means she feel less worthy of the help and care of those around her and so more isolated, more fearful of the force that can be used against her, and less able to prevent or manage such threats.

Oppression as Quick Onslaught of Fear

The first temporal mode of oppressive force, quickness, is deployed to create uncontrollable fear. In *Rhetoric*, his book on persuasion and propaganda, Aristotle defines fear as the painful feeling that destruction or pain is imminent (Book II, Chapter 4). The speed with which Gilead inflicts pain or death is part of its effectiveness, for it breaks down the subject's ability to predict what will happen, and so her ability to respond to this terrible power, and more minimally, to effectively manage her fear.

If I cannot predict what harms are imminent because harms come quickly, unexpectedly and without warning or any clear logic, then harm is always imminent and fear is always justified. The jarring abruptness and the incomprehensibility of the harms inflicted makes Gilead's power more effective. For example, the unrealness of losing your job because you're a woman is incredibly disorienting and offers no possibility for reasonable response:

> . . . there were two men standing there, in uniforms, with machine guns. This was too theatrical to be true, yet there they were: sudden apparitions, like Martians. . . .
>
> Since none of us understood what had happened, there was nothing much we could say. We looked at one another's faces and saw dismay, and a certain shame, as if we'd be caught doing something we shouldn't.
>
> It's outrageous, one woman said, but without belief. What was it about this that made us feel we deserved it? (*The Handmaid's Tale*, p. 177)

By violating the up-until-then shared common sense that this is not a possible thing that could happen, Gilead uses swift violence to disrupt each individual subject's ability to judge what she should fear and how to avoid fearsome harms. The bewildering quickness with which a subject is violated is meant to produce hasty and total submission by instilling the terrifying fear that there are no rational nor moral constraints to what those exercising this power will do to you.

Even as these harms defy any clear logic or predictability, the speed with which they are inflicted conveys an underlying meaning. What the TV show makes especially vivid is that Gilead is a possible near future of our present day; Gilead is continuous with our world. The continuity of Gilead with our world implicates us: the "moral" principles structuring Gilead are intelligible because they are refractions of values and norms of our world. After the devastating loss of her job and bank account, June (her name is not disclosed in the written narrative) reflects upon how the meaning of such violations is clear, and reverberates through her, infecting her relationship with Luke, who now must play the role of patriarchal protector:

> But something had shifted, some balance. I felt shrunken, so that when he put his arms around me, gathering me up, I was small as a doll. I felt love going forward without me.
>
> He doesn't mind this, I thought. He doesn't mind it at all. Maybe he even likes it. We are not each other's, anymore. Instead, I am his. (p. 182)

Everyone immediately knows what these harms mean, even if such harms were unthinkable up until the moment they occur. By conveying meaning without making sense, these swift exercises of force use fear to produce acquiescence to certain power relations. The novel culminates in a momentary total loss of self in the fear of death for conspiring with Ofglen:

> I don't want pain. I don't want to be a dancer, my feet in the air, my head a faceless oblong of white cloth. I don't want to be a doll hung up on the Wall, I don't want to be a wingless angel. I want to keep

on living, in any form. I resign my body freely, to the uses of others. They can do what they like to me. I am abject.
    I feel, for the first time, their true power. (p. 286)

Living continuously with this terrifying fear wears away the narrator's resistance to the ultimate meaning of the violence, that one must submit.

Oppression as the Slow Grind of Shame

The second temporal mode of oppressive force, slowness, is deployed to create debilitating shame. A handmaid has no future to look forward to, and memories of the past are painful, leaving her suspended in a hellish now.

There's time to spare. This is one of the things I wasn't prepared for—the amount of unfilled time, the long parentheses of nothing. Time as white sound. . . . I remember . . . paintings of harems . . . Studies of sedentary flesh . . . These pictures were supposed to be erotic, and I thought they were, at the time; but I see now what they were really about. They were paintings of suspended animation; about waiting, about objects not in use. They were paintings of boredom.

But maybe boredom is erotic, when women do it, for men. (p. 69)

By imprisoning and isolating the Handmaids and then overwhelming them with time they have no power to fill, these women are transformed into objects. A person's understanding of herself as thinking or acting is destroyed if large expanses of time with no external changes prove her activities can go nowhere and produce no results.

Besides undermining the subject's agency, a crucial effect of the passage of time is to make this new social order seem ordinary. "Ordinary, said Aunt Lydia, is what you are used to" (p. 33). Gilead aims to make its subjects conform to this new ordinary without active thought or participation in doing so, as with the stock phrases that structure basic social interactions. The self is not engaged, but kept hidden, isolated, and so somewhat safe amongst others in murmuring, "Praise be."

Within this drawn-out experience of suspension, June continually circles around the idea of suicide. The self-annihilation of suicide appeals as an escape, but also as an affirmation of her agency in refusing this new now. But June mistakenly seems to think that in not choosing suicide, she is choosing her present situation. Because of our need as rational, moral agents to engage in sense-making, and so too to see the world as in any way responsive to our own agency, June construes her actions and inactions to embody more meaning, more choice, than they are capable of having in these circumstances. For example, June narrates, "Whatever is going on is as usual. Even this is as usual, now. We lived, as usual, by ignoring. Ignoring isn't the same as ignorance, you have to work at it" (p. 56).

She's right that Gilead requires a certain amount of work on her part to simply make it through the day (as June puts it, "They force you to kill, within yourself"). She's mistaken that this work on her part makes her complicit with this new order. What Gilead, as oppressive, authoritarian force, is able to do is make it seem to June that her efforts at self-protection compromise her moral integrity, so that she does not deserve better. In other words, Gilead is able to produce a veneer of consent. June tells us:

> . . . the Commander is fucking. What he is fucking is the lower part of my body. I do not say making love, because that is not what he's doing. Copulating too would be inaccurate, because it would imply two people and only one is involved. Nor does rape cover it: nothing is going on here that I haven't signed up for. There wasn't a lot of choice but there was some, and this is what I chose. (p. 94)

Similarly, in describing the Salvaging, she states:

> I've leaned forward to touch the rope in front of me, in time with the others, the rope hairy, sticky with tar in the hot sun, then placed

my hand on my heart to show my unity with the Salvagers and my consent, and my complicity in the death of this woman. (p. 276)

Repeatedly June thinks of herself as blameworthy for behavior that someone with more sound moral judgment would excuse as coerced. June even accurately diagnoses this taking on of blame as the desperate desire for meaning, for agency:

It's like Janine, though, to take it upon herself, to decide the baby's flaws were due to her alone. But people will do anything rather than admit that their lives have no meaning. No use, that is. No plot. (p. 215)

A plot requires an agent, someone who can affect the world around her. From her need to understand herself as acting in this world, as consenting to this world, the badness of Gilead contaminates June's self-understanding, wearing away her self-respect through shame. But the story demonstrates consent is not necessary, submission will do, for there is shame too in being an object for another's will. Repeated submission grinds down the self over time, making the person less capable of resisting the injustices being done to her and to others.

The Vulnerability and Resilience of the Thinking, Acting Self

Yet the book somewhat, and the TV show more pronouncedly, lend support to Kant's claim that our grasp on ourselves as free, self-determining agents, because secured via reason, is difficult to fully extinguish. The bastards do grind people down, but don't often succeed in breaking a person's will completely.

As June tells us in describing Emily driving the car, "They didn't get everything. There was something inside her they couldn't take away. She looked invincible." While giving support to the Kantian idea that there is an innate drive within each person as rational agent to think for themselves, the tales also demonstrate that, as Kant implies and feminist accounts of relational autonomy explicitly argue, we learn how to think for ourselves with others.

For any person to see herself as an agent, actively affecting the world through her thoughts and actions, she needs to have her own rational judgment acknowledged by another. The possibilities for this sort of acknowledgment are structurally foreclosed to a Handmaid. A Handmaid's social role is to be fertile, to conceive and deliver a healthy baby. However well a Handmaid succeeds at this task, there's no room for her will in accomplishing it, which means there is no way for her judgment to be recognized in fulfilling her assigned task.

June signals her recognition of all that is lacking in her life in Gilead, in stating, "I want to be more than valuable. I repeat my former name, remind myself of what I once could do, how others saw me" (p. 97) and in her criticism of Gilead to the Commander as lacking love (p. 219). Love is the most basic, fundamental way we acknowledge another person as an individual, as more than what she does or can do for you, but as valued for herself. Moreover, in loving another, you distinguish yourself as an individual; for June, love "was the way you understood yourself" (p. 225). In her connectedness to other individuals, each individual can find her self.

Our need to reach out to other rational agents for affirmation makes us vulnerable to other people's indifference, cruelty, and manipulation. Gilead uses the need for affirmation and connectedness against its subjects, to produce compliant behavior. In the book, June stays home from the marches, trying to protect her family from harm by limiting her exposure to those she does not already trust (p. 180). But it's no use, for her family is betrayed to the authorities; her description of the betrayal shows Gilead has already succeeded in dissolving the basic trust necessary for openly thinking and acting amongst others.

Two of the most suspenseful exchanges in the tale are the delicate conversational dances June enters into in trying to reach out to Ofglen and new Ofglen; she is trying to see who each really is, but without exposing herself too much.

Perhaps the most devastating illustration of this vulnerability, though, comes in the "Historical Notes," which consist mainly in the short lecture of Professor Pieixoto, one of two original editors of the written tale. In his lecture, Professor Pieixoto condones Gileadean society, stating, "Our job is not to censure but to understand" (p. 302). This intellectualized distancing of himself and his audience from the narrative represents a moral failure to acknowledge what this story is striving to be. Through her words, June is trying to reach out to another person, to give herself, her life, integrity through the affirmation of her judgment by another. She says:

> I wish this story were different. . . . I wish it showed me in a better light, if not happier, then at least more active, less hesitant, less distracted by trivia. . . . I'm sorry there is so much pain in this story. I'm sorry it's in fragments, like a body caught in crossfire or pulled apart by force. But there is nothing I can do to change it. . . . By telling you anything at all I'm at least believing in you, I believe you are there, I believe you into being. Because I'm telling you this story I will your existence. I tell, therefore you are. . . . After all you've been through, you deserve whatever I have left, which is not much but includes the truth. (pp. 267–68)

She's reaching out to the reader, pointing towards a truth she cannot accomplish alone. In believing in the reader, she is finding a way to believe in herself, to reassemble herself despite the forces working to nullify her self. But because of what she has suffered, she cannot adequately convey the true nature of the harms done to her. She pushes her story forward to us: the one-directionality of what should be a reciprocal relation of acknowledgment expresses just how constrained, how damaging, her circumstances are.

This missive from another world places upon us the moral responsibility to affirm, not particular judgments, but that her capacity for judgment functions soundly enough to convey some truth, that there is an individual here deserving of love and respect, and that a monstrous moral wrong has been done to her.

Despite failed attempts to reach out to another for acknowledgment and validation, the tales present several crucial examples of how connectedness to another provides the self the integrity and strength necessary to resist some harm being done to it, for instance, Emily's driving follows upon her telling June her real name. Pivotal instances of self-empowerment through another happen not through some immediate, in-person connection, but through the imaginative invocation of another, loved individual as morally better and stronger than the agent currently understands herself to be.

June finds the strength to get off the floor and try to use the Commander to better her situation by telling herself, "Moira would never stand for this shit." Moira is able to find the strength to break out of Jezebel's, deliver the package, and find sanctuary in Canada through the exhortations of June. In these acts of resistance, self-respect is re-established through the re-establishment of hope.

The hope is not that all will turn out well for yourself, but hope that the world can become better for the people whom you love. This hope for a better possible future world in turn nourishes the hope that the agent herself can succeed in taking a step in the right direction, even if she ultimately fails. The attempt itself is perceived as meaningful, because of what it may mean to those who care for her and follow her. Season One and the narrative conclude with one last attempt to project the self forward through reaching out to another:

> Whether this is my end or a new beginning I have no way of knowing: I have given myself over into the hands of strangers, because it can't be helped.
> And so I step up, into the darkness within; or else the light.

June's story shows that it is the nature of our thinking and our acting to need a lift from others to go aright. Gilead uses reason's dependency upon others against its subjects, so as to strip persons of their agency and self-respect.

But June manages to challenge the authoritarian assumption that dependency negates the self. Instead, June's recognition of her dependence upon others and the inescapability of the need to trust others are inseparable from her insistence upon the power and dignity of herself as an active agent.

14
The Value of a Handmaid

EDWARDO PÉREZ

... you are special girls. Fertility is a gift directly from God. He left you intact for a Biblical purpose. Like Bilhah served Rachel, you girls will serve the Leaders of the Faithful and their barren wives. You will bear children for them. Oh! You are so lucky! So privileged!

—*The Handmaid's Tale*, "Offred"

Aunt Lydia's observation presents an insightful look at the value of a Handmaid in Hulu's pitch-perfect adaptation of Margaret Atwood's dystopian classic: namely, that a Handmaid's value is calculated through her body, not necessarily in the traditional physical appeal of a woman's form (though that happens, especially at Jezebel's), but in the ability to conceive and carry children.

Indeed, while most of the women are shocked at Aunt Lydia's twisted reasoning (especially Janine, who pays a horrific price for mocking Aunt Lydia), the look on their faces reveals the undeniable reality women throughout history have struggled against—from the tradition of a Pater Familias in Ancient Rome, to the practice of Purdah in South Asian peoples, to the current abortion debate in America, and many other oppressive, patriarchal systems in between—their body is not their own. It belongs to men, to children, to society, to laws, to customs, to traditions, to history, to the present, and to the future.

Still, if Aunt Lydia is correct, if Handmaids are gifts from God, then why are they treated so abhorrently? What value do Handmaids really have if they can be esteemed on one hand and dehumanized on the other? What is their fertility worth? What are their lives worth? Are they a means to an end? Are they commodities?

To help us understand a Handmaid's value, let's examine Handmaids in three ways: through moral value, economic value, and cultural value.

I Didn't Choose This

Well, this is our fault. We gave women more than they could handle. They put so much focus on academic pursuits and professional ambition, we let them forget their real purpose. We won't let that happen again.

—"A Woman's Place"

Such is Warren Putnam's opinion about the roles of women in pre-Gilead American society, a position that articulates the rationale used to strip women of their rights and subjugate them into involuntary servitude—which includes ritualized rape, forced pregnancy, and physical, emotional, and psychological torture. It also includes having to immediately surrender their baby upon birth, defer every judgment about their lives to the Commanders, Wives, Aunts, and Marthas, and surrender any sense of self that existed prior to Gilead— such as their names, their friendships, their knowledge and education, their professions, and their families (including any children and spouses they may have already had). What sort of value does this suggest?

Immanuel Kant (1724–1804) proposed that the rules we follow in our actions should be the kind of rules that could be made universal, binding on everyone (*Groundwork of the Metaphysics of Morals*, p. 52). An example would be the rule that we treat others as we want to be treated. Given the way women are treated in Atwood's dystopian narrative, especially the Handmaids, Gilead doesn't seem to be following Kant's advice.

While Mexico seems interested in emulating Gilead's methods ("A Woman's Place"), nothing Gilead does—at least by Kant's logic—could be deemed universally binding, let alone universally appealing. Indeed, Canada's actions—taking in refugees in "Little America" ("The Other Side") illustrate just how un-universal Gilead's laws are regarded. For example, there's a stark contrast between Moira being given a choice between the Jezebels and The Colonies in Gilead and being given food, clothing, a pre-paid cellphone, a medical insurance card, and start-up money at the consulate in Canada. Unless this ends up being an evil twist we don't see coming, Canada seems like the best place on Earth to be a woman in the TV adaption of Atwood's alternate universe.

By contrast, Offred's treatment by Mexico is heartbreaking—because just when you think she might have an ally who could do something to help her (and all the Handmaids), all she gets is some Mexican chocolate and an "I can't help you" response from Ambassador Castillo. To be fair, the Ambassador's assistant tells Offred that Luke is alive (which turns out to be true) and seems genuine in his desire to help her (which he does, as Luke is shown getting the note Offred wrote).

And, it's possible that Ambassador Castillo is playing a long-con on Commander Waterford and will eventually obtain Handmaids not to use them but to free them (which the Hulu adaptation may eventually reveal as it develops the narrative past Atwood's ambiguous conclusion). Still, in the moment, Ambassador Castillo's cold response and apparent resolve to help her own people at the expense of others echo Gilead's dehumanizing disposition toward the Handmaids, one that betrays Kant's imperative.

The Human Race Is at Risk

It's significant that Gilead and Mexico view Handmaids as necessary to the survival of humanity and, by their logic, Handmaids have a moral duty to bear children. In other words, they try to use a moral argument to justify their actions—the same argument Serena Joy formulates when she and Fred are shown crafting what will become Gileadean law.

As Serena Joy states it, reproduction is "a moral imperative" and fertility is a "natural resource" ("A Woman's Place"). So, they're trying to be ethical, right? Serena Joy's moral reasoning addresses the bigger picture of global infertility, doesn't it? After all, if no more children are born, what happens to the human race?

What Gilead and Mexico fail to see is that while children are indeed necessary for humanity to continue its existence, forcing women to have children (and enslaving women in the process) is not a moral way to go about it, fertility is not a natural resource that can be exploited as Serena Joy frames it ("A Woman's Place"). We're meant to understand the context of Gilead's response, but the perversion of religion and twisted logic negates the morality of Gilead's cause. Likewise, we're meant to see Ambassador Castillo's perspective.

But, as tragic as her situation is, her condoning of the Handmaids' treatment strips the Ambassador's argument of any moral weight or sympathy it may have had—if it had any at all. Perhaps we can be sympathetic to infertility when it reaches the scale it does in *The Handmaid's Tale*. Certainly, when Ambassador Castillo sees actual children running and laughing, it's slightly moving.

The logic Gilead and Mexico use is flawed, since it views Handmaids as a means to an end and not as an end unto themselves. As Kant explains: "In the realm of ends everything has either a *price* or a *dignity*" (*Groundwork*, pp. 52–53). If we have a price, then we can be equated with or traded for something. If we have dignity, then there is no equivalent, nothing could equal our worth. Accordingly, Kant divides price into two categories: a *market price*, which refers to "universal human inclinations;" and an *affective price*, which refers to the things we like that don't necessarily have a purpose (like really good Mexican chocolate).

In Gilead, women have a price, not a dignity. Most have a market price, like Handmaids, Wives, Aunts, Marthas, and

Unwomen—any of them could be exchanged based on inclinations and needs and they all serve a purpose. Handmaids seem to have the most value, as the trade deal between Gilead and Mexico illustrates. As Commander Waterford confesses to Serena Joy, Gilead needs to trade or Gilead will "fall off a cliff in six months" ("A Woman's Place"). And, as Ambassador Castillo confides to Offred, her city in Mexico hasn't seen a child born alive in six years. So, Gilead and Mexico each have needs that Handmaids can meet. It's easier for Gilead and Mexico to fulfill these needs when they don't see Handmaids as human beings, objectifying them makes them easier to exchange, an exchange that amounts to human trafficking and sex trafficking.

Jezebels, on the other hand, have both a market price and an affective price, as they fulfill a different sort of role in Gilead. Working at Jezebel's, a former hotel converted into a brothel/sex-club, Jezebels work as prostitutes on behalf of Gilead, servicing Commanders and foreign diplomats, unable to refuse any request, yet given certain freedoms forbidden in Gilead (such as alcohol, cigarettes, make-up, drugs, and books, and being able to have same-sex relationships). Clearly, there is a market for their services. As Commander Waterford explains to Offred when she asks who the women are who work at Jezebel's:

Oh, all women who couldn't assimilate. Some were working girls before. . . . We've got lawyers, a CEO, a few journalists. I'm told you can have quite a good conversation with some of them, if what you feel like is talking. We've got quite a collection. They prefer it here. ("Jezebels")

Of course, the Jezebels (like any women in Gilead) don't really have much of a choice—Handmaids forced to bear children, Unwomen forced to work in the Colonies, or prostitute at Jezebel's—and given the relative comforts and perks Jezebel's offers, it's easy to see why Moira made her choice.

It's a strange betrayal of Gilead's so-called "traditional values," which are supposedly based on Judeo-Christian biblical teachings. Or maybe the men of Gilead are simply following the examples of Abraham, Jacob, Isaac, David, and many other biblical men who engaged in polygamy, incest, and fornication on a regular basis. As with the Handmaids, the moral dignity of the Jezebels is never considered: they're dehumanized and objectified. But their value isn't just a *market price*, which as Commander Waterford notes, helps "to stimulate diplomacy and business," they also have an *affective price* for the men who patronize Jezebel's, who, as Commander Waterford explains to Offred, like a little variety. While the market and affective prices of the Jezebels seem to overlap, what's paramount is that despite all this value, Jezebels remain tradeable objects, used and trafficked for the sake of Gilead, just like the Handmaids.

Blessed Be the Fruit

Karl Marx defines a commodity as "an object outside us, a thing that by its properties satisfies human wants of some sort or another" (*Capital*, Volume 1, p. 27). This is how Offred and the Handmaids are treated, isn't it? Certainly, Handmaids have what Marx calls *use value*, a value based on their utility—they provide children to Commanders because the wives cannot, they provide companionship and friendship to each other (even though they're not supposed to, except if they're a Jezebel), they help create a structure for the Gileadean way of life, and they provide hope for the future of the human race.

Because of their usefulness (they're essentially the most useful women in the world), they also have what Marx calls *exchange value*. For Marx, *exchange value* is "a quantitative relation . . . constantly changing with time and place." As Marx explains, "when commodities are exchanged, their exchange value manifests itself as something totally independent of their use value" (p. 28). In other words, where a person's *use value* is based on their usefulness (like being able to bear a child), their *exchange value* is based on what that usefulness is worth (such as making sure humanity survives) or on what it can be traded for (like establishing an economic relationship with Mexico). What this means is that a Handmaid's *exchange value* is essentially greater than her *use value*.

Linking both types of value is the issue of fertility. Without it, a Handmaid has no value and this reveals an interesting paradox with regard to how Handmaids are treated. In one sense, a Handmaid is almost revered, as if they were magical creatures—such as when Serena Joy admonishes an Eye and Aunt Lydia when Serena Joy catches them torturing Offred with a cattle-prod, using "She's pregnant!" not just to save Offred, but to shame the Eye and Aunt Lydia, who visibly feels bad for having hurt Offred ("Late").

Offred wasn't pregnant—her late period simply caused Serena Joy to think she was and this illustrates the other side of a Handmaid's value. When Serena Joy learns the truth about Offred's non-pregnancy, Serena Joy severely punishes Offred by dragging her to her room, throwing her to the ground, and threatening her—and later, when Serena Joy finds out that Offred went to Jezebel's with Fred, Serena Joy strikes Offred with enough force to knock her to the ground.

Similarly, once Janine served her purpose for Commander Putnam, giving him a baby girl, Janine is reassigned to Commander Monroe and expected to simply get pregnant again. But, when Commander Monroe tries to have a Ceremony with Janine on the very day she's reassigned to him, Janine is unable to go through with it, causing her to kidnap the baby she'd had for Commander Putman and nearly jump off a bridge with the infant. Offred saves the baby but Janine jumps into a river anyway. Of course, she doesn't die. Rather, she is saved only to be brought before a circle of Handmaids who are expected to stone Janine to death for the crime of endangering a child. The novel's version of Janine's story is markedly different—the baby dies—but the outcome for Janine is similar: she loses her mind.

Thus, Janine had *use value* and *exchange value* so long as she was fertile and accepting of her role, but once she rebelled, Janine lost her value. Indeed, if Gilead is willing to kill an otherwise fertile woman, then perhaps fertility isn't as valuable as obedience. And, given Janine's crime, it's clear that Handmaids aren't as valuable as children.

Given the scope of the narrative, there are many more examples that illustrate Handmaids being simultaneously valued and devalued in every aspect of their lives—most notably, Emily (Ofglen, who undergoes a forced clitorectomy) and Moira (who becomes a Jezebel). Even when they are seemingly given a choice, Handmaids remain objects capable of being used, traded, and disposed of depending on the fluctuation of their *use value* and *exchange value*, which seems dependent on their obedience and adherence to Gilead's rules.

If women had realized how valuable they'd be before the government of Gilead had taken over America, they might've been able to capitalize on their significance, charging for the use of their womb and being extremely selective with the men they coupled with (because shouldn't the men be worthy of fertilizing the last viable eggs on Earth?). After all, they'd be the mothers of the world, why not profit from that status? Isn't that what capitalism and consumerism are all about?

Marxism views capitalism as being dependent on consumerism, on the selling, buying, and trading of goods at the market—it's how a capitalist society relates to the world at large and it's why things like Handmaids are commodified. Gilead is not really a capitalist society—it's a strange mixture of communism, authoritarianism, imperialism, and theocracy. Yet, the capitalist need for a market, the need for consumers to feel good (or to feel insecure enough to motivate them to pursue consumer goods), and the need for things to have value remains part of Gilead's social fabric (even if its thread is hidden beneath layers of oppression and subjugation). Women play the most important roles in stitching this social fabric together, roles that give them value and power. This brings us to an interesting conception of value and power as types of capital.

Now I'm Awake in the World

Pierre Bourdieu outlines three main ways to conceive of capital: *economic capital* (money), *social capital* (relationships), and *cultural capital* (knowledge and skills). He also divides *cultural capital* into *objectified capital* (objects of value) and *resistant capital* (knowledge needed to rebel). In essence, Bourdieu's point is to recognize that capital isn't just about money and neither is power. Indeed, when it comes to value, money might be the least valuable type of capital one can possess or obtain. So, where does a Handmaid fit in to all of this capital?

Given that women are not allowed to possess money, they have no *economic capital*. And, even if they did, money seems to be useless in Gilead—not just because Gilead's economy is unhealthy, but because the society is so strictly regulated a Handmaid wouldn't be able to buy anything without an Eye finding out. So, if money is worthless, how about friends?

Relationships are difficult to maintain as a Handmaid, especially when no one in Gilead seems trustworthy—everyone seems like an Eye. However, Offred can form relationships with several people who ultimately prove valuable, which in turn increases Offred's value. Certainly, Offred's prior relationship with Moira helps Offred cope with the Red Center, with learning how to be a Handmaid, and with "keeping her fucking shit together," as Moira recommends. Yet, Offred also forms relationships (to varying degrees) with Emily, Alma, Janine, Rita, Nick, Aunt Lydia, Serena Joy, and Commander Waterford.

As Bourdieu would recognize, this *social capital* increases Offred's value, as she's able to utilize these relationships to keep herself alive. Certainly, all of these relationships can be seen helping Offred at various times, giving Offred an advantage in Gilead, one money could never buy her. What makes this social capital even more valuable is its scarcity. Given the oppressive climate of Gilead, it's rare to see a Handmaid develop such a supportive network. Similarly, Offred's knowledge also brings her a great deal of value.

As Bourdieu explains, *cultural capital* consists not just of knowledge, but of skills, especially intangible skills that help you achieve social power. Handmaids are forbidden to read and learn, yet their ability to adapt to Gilead's harsh environment coupled with whatever knowledge and skills they already possessed endows them with value—to survive and to potentially rebel, which relates to Bourdieu's conception of *resistant cultural capital* or the knowledge you need to be able to fight back.

Unlike Janine, Offred learns how to quickly adapt to the Handmaid way of life, which is admirable, given that her daughter was literally ripped out of her hands after her husband was shot while they were trying to escape. She should be as messed up as Janine (and she could've easily given up like Moira did at Jezebel's), but Offred's *cultural capital*, her ability to instinctively know what to do to survive the situation she's in (with Aunt Lydia, Serena Joy, Fred, Nick, Jezebel's, and so on) endows her value and power.

As Elizabeth Moss plays her, Offred isn't afraid to push back as often as she can, whether with a well-timed (and typically sardonic) facial expression, verbal quip, blunt admission, or pointed accusation. In this sense, Offred is showing *resistant cultural capital*, which, at times, is just as valuable as her *cultural capital*, if not more so, as the incident with Janine's stoning illustrates. This brings us to the third type of cultural capital Bourdieu observes—*objectified cultural capital*.

While Handmaids like Offred can have *cultural capital* and *resistant cultural capital*—they can possess knowledge and skills and education—they can't possess things (other than a closet full of red dresses and white hats). Serena Joy may give Offred a music box, Fred may give her a sequined dress, and Moira may have found a way to get Alma's package for Offred to hold, but Handmaids don't really have any objects of value—there's really nothing they can use or trade, not even anything sentimental or personal. And yet, for the Wives, Handmaids (especially obedient ones) and babies represent clear *objectified cultural capital*.

As we've seen, Handmaids and their fertility are valuable, they're objects possessing use value and exchange value. For any given house, a Handmaid essentially functions like a status symbol, especially if the Handmaid was fruitful—then the baby becomes the ultimate status symbol, which is what happens with Janine and the Putnams. This is what capitalism does, doesn't it? It creates commodities that we tell ourselves we need, we assign prices, and then we set about obtaining them—not because the object itself is necessarily worth anything, but because we equate our self-worth with the objects we possess.

Is this how Handmaids were created? Is *objectified cultural capital* the extent of their value? Do Handmaids only exist to make Commanders and their Wives feel worthy? Doesn't Gilead's interpretation of religion equate worthiness with fertility? And, how should we really regard Gilead's treatment of Handmaids? Should we condemn Gilead for the way they value and devalue Handmaids (and women as a whole) or should we try to understand that Gilead's methods are simply part of their culture?

We'll Be Having Intercourse with the Men between the Wives' Legs?

Bourdieu's thoughts on *cultural capital* reflect the way knowledge and objects have value that isn't necessarily monetary. But, as *cultural relativism* observes, what's valued in one culture isn't necessarily valued in another. What makes Gilead interesting is that it used to be part of the United States of America—it used to be a land that generally sought to expand freedom and equality, not curtail it.

So, Gilead is a society built upon a former society with a deep history of fighting for rights. In fact, this is what makes things difficult in Gilead, as everyone is part of a culture in transition, a culture that is trying to shift its values—and the new ones aren't any fun. It's a significant moment when Ambassador Castillo asks Offred if she's happy. As Offred ponders her answer, it's notable that everyone the camera cuts to (Fred, Serena Joy, and Nick) looks as if they're being asked the same question (perhaps they even want Offred to tell the truth).

Offred's answer, "I've found happiness," may have been a lie (and the only answer she could safely give), yet, it nevertheless reveals an important truth about Gilead and its value system: everyone's had to find a way to adapt. Happiness is relative. So, too, are Gilead's values.

Alison Dundes Renteln, who understands culture as the value systems that inform our ways of life, traces the seeds of *cultural relativism* back to Herodotus (484–425 B.C.), who recognized that, if given a choice between cultures, we'll always choose our own because we're convinced our ways are better. In a sense, this is how the Republic of Gilead was formed when the Sons of Jacob felt their way of life was morally superior to the American way of life.

Defending a version of *ethical relativism* which asserts that value judgements are culturally specific, Renteln suggests that concepts such as human needs, social imperatives, rationality, and human nature are not universal, they're "culturally determined" ("Relativism and the Search for Human Rights"). As Renteln maintains, "culture shapes the identity of individuals, influencing their reasoning, perceptions, and behavior" (*The Cultural Defense*).

We might want to say that forcing women to accept their fertility as a natural resource that can be systematically and methodically plundered is based on flawed logic and is morally wrong, as our examination through Kant's categorical imperative suggested. But, by making this observation we're appealing to the conception of morality our culture taught us, which is not universal and which doesn't necessarily apply to Gilead. We may not like it or condone it, but Gilead's culture belongs to Gilead.

Thus, in terms of value, *cultural relativism* shows that it's not the Handmaids or the children that actually have value in Gilead. Rather, it's the culture itself that has value. Perhaps Aunt Lydia is the best example of this as she seems to embody Gilead's culture in every aspect of her life—though, to be fair, we don't really know a lot about her pre-Gilead life. She may appear cruel in her treatment of the Handmaids but she's not completely heartless, even seeming to mother Janine throughout the season, being viscerally heartbroken at Janine's jump from the bridge.

As played by Ann Dowd, Aunt Lydia seems to be the only person in Gilead who actually cares about the Handmaids, because as stern as she is, she's actually helping them adapt to their new culture. As Aunt Lydia explains to the Handmaids in a motherly tone, "I know this must feel so strange, but ordinary is just what you're used to. This may not be ordinary to you now, but after a time it will. This will become ordinary," later adding, "The world can be an ugly place. But we cannot wish that ugliness away. We cannot hide from that ugliness" ("Offred"). Given America's history with slavery, it's not much of a stretch to imagine that Aunt Lydia might be right. If allowed to continue, Handmaids would eventually seem ordinary.

In Ann Dowd's conception, Aunt Lydia "loves those girls . . . she knows that if she does not get that job done, that they don't realize that this is what is expected of you and you had better get it, they're not going to survive." In fact, Aunt Lydia might be more dedicated to Gilead's culture than anyone else, which is interesting considering she doesn't directly benefit from the Handmaids' fertility, nor does she seem to obtain any wealth or power beyond her station as an Aunt. Thus, for Aunt Lydia, it's about the culture she's trying to help create and cultivate, a culture that happens to view the enslavement of fertile women as a directive from God.

Still, it's one thing to believe whatever you believe because that's the way you were raised. But, it's an entirely different thing to force those beliefs on others (who were raised differently) against their will. What makes Gilead problematic with regard to its cultural values is that no one has really been enculturated yet, not even Aunt Lydia—they're all just pretending that their illegitimate culture is legitimate. As Offred queries Nick, "Is this it? Is this enough for you, this bullshit life? Is this what you want?" ("Jezebels").

Offred's observation resonates beyond Nick, as it doesn't really seem as if anyone wants to live the Gileadean way. It's not just a matter of enculturation, it's the recognition that Gilead didn't naturally evolve. So, Gilead is relative in the sense that it has its ways, but these ways are not really acceptable given that they were constructed (sometimes improvised in the back of a limousine) and forced upon a population that didn't desire to change its way of life. And, even if Gilead continued to the point that everyone in the society had been enculturated, the artificial origin of Gilead would negate its claim to relativism.

This distinction is necessary in understanding that *cultural relativism* (and relativism in general) isn't merely a do-whatever-the-hell-you-want philosophy. Rather, it's the position that what's natural to one group might not be natural to another. Cultures and values change all the time. But, the point is that what's natural and what changes is more acceptable when they occur through a society's natural evolution, not a forced one. For example, if fertile women had decided to offer their wombs to society in order to save the human race, then we could accept (and maybe even respect) their cultural values (as Ambassador Castillo initially did when she thought the Handmaids were freely making a sacrifice) even if these values don't reflect our own.

Blessed Are the Meek

Can I tell you a secret? I can do anything I want. I had a baby. A good one. I had a good one! So they don't care. I can do anything I want. I can have ice cream. It's only vanilla, but I can have it. Do you want some?

—"Birth"

So, what is the value of a Handmaid? Do they have dignity? Are they commodities? Do they have power? Can they really do anything they want? Are they an army? It's interesting to note how Hulu's adaptation captures the vagueness of Atwood's novel, not just in the open-to-many-interpretations ending, but in the way Offred's narration of the story seems both candidly reliable and frustratingly unreliable, drawing us in, yet keeping us at a distance.

While future seasons will erase some of the uncertainty and speculation as to what happens to Offred and the rest of the Handmaids as it fills in various narrative gaps, one thing seems certain: there's value, there's power, and there's hierarchy among the women of Gilead and the Handmaids seem to be at the bottom of all this, but, as the Handmaids show when they refuse to stone Janine, maybe they're more valuable and powerful than anyone wants to admit.

As Offred observes, "It's their fault. They should've never given us uniforms if they didn't want us to be an army" ("Night").

Nolite te bastardes carborundorum.

15
June the Stoic?

GUILLAUME LEQUIEN

The Handmaid's Tale takes us on a bleak journey, far away from our modern democracies, to a nightmare world that denies women any freedom of choice. We can't help feeling sympathy for the female victims and anger at the religious totalitarian state. Every new episode of cruelty or oppression adds to the injustice we see and feel.

Most characters within the story, however, don't seem to show any emotions at all; they yield and accept whatever they have to endure, knowing any act of rebellion is doomed to fail. We feel bad about June's ordeal all along, and as soon as her tale is over, we enjoy the real world we live in a little more. While we enjoy our freedom, Handmaids want to be free to conduct their lives, choose their sexual partners, and embrace their own path to happiness. These are all things available to us but denied to them. How might June and the other oppressed citizens of Gilead respond to their bleak circumstances? What philosophical outlook might help them?

Under His Eye

Citizens of Gilead are governed by a totalitarian regime that affects their everyday lives in countless ways. Citizens conduct their lives under strict surveillance; the social structure is remniscent, at least metaphorically, of a *panopticon*, an architectural project designed by utilitarian philosopher Jeremy Bentham. The architecture allows for a single surveillance cabin to see all cells in a prison at once, resulting in the impression that prisoners are being watched by an invisible guard they can't even see for themselves.

In *The Handmaid's Tale*, the panopticon is manifested in everyday clothing and relationships. Every Handmaid has to wear a white wing to hide her facial expressions from observers. No eye-to-eye contact may happen. Every social interaction gets ritualized with set mottos and everyone has to repeat the same empty phrases that mean nothing in particular.

Handmaids are allowed to go out only in pairs. Everyone considers everyone else a potential "Eye"—a spy who might report their slightest missteps or lack of faith. No one knows what other people really think or feel about what they are going through. Not knowing who is a spy, everyone distrusts one another.

In *The Myth of Sisyphus,* Albert Camus wrote, "There is only one really serious philosophical question, and that is suicide." In the horrific world of Gilead, is that response right for June? If your life has no meaning and contains unimaginable suffering and little joy, is suicide the only way out? Gilead obviously recognizes this as a problem and takes steps to prevent Handmaids from committing suicide. They have to report any abnormal behavior or conversations, and any metal or sharp objects are kept out of their reach. In the absence of freedom or happiness should June just kill herself?

According to many philosophical theories, a meaningful human life involves, primarily, the pursuit of happiness. A noteworthy example of a philosophical theory of this type is utilitarianism. According to this theory, the right action to perform is the one that produces the greatest happiness for the greatest number. One thing is perfectly clear—The Sons of Jacob aren't utilitarians.

Utilitarianism would be a difficult philosophical worldview for June to adopt. Under a totalitarian government, happiness is a secondary concern. First comes survival, second perhaps the quest for individual freedom—happiness hardly matters anymore. When foreign ambassadors ask June if Handmaids are happy with their condition, we can't help distrusting her answer: "We are very happy." She has to look happy, to pretend that everything is alright and that she consents to the life into which they've forced her. How else might she answer? She does not feel free, and she has no happiness left to hope for.

Behave Like a Sister

Fortunately, there are other philosophical approaches the Handmaids might adopt. In 1993 American philosopher Joan Tronto advocated a new ethical theory, known as "care ethics." Tronto's approach grounded ethics in the importance of caring for others as social and political necessity. Tronto argues that giving care has been ignored in western societies while a stronger emphasis has been placed on modern individualism. We tend to relegate the importance of caring to private life rather than public life—we have traditionally conceived of care as taking place in domains historically populated by women (such as the home).

Tronto argues for applying the moral concept of care for others to an extended domain. She pleads for more caring politics, and for society to conceive of care as something in which everyone should be engaged, not simply those who have taken on traditional care work. Gilead has much to learn from Tronto. In the dystopia of the story, not only is real care for others undervalued by the state, but women are also deprived of the ability to care for others. Adequate care is always based on need, and Gilead isn't much concerned with the needs of its citizens.

There is always the possibility that the Handmaids can demonstrate care for one another. They share a similar fate and, as a result, they understand one another. This practice of providing supportive care for one another could assist in giving some meaning to their lives. Unfortunately, there seems to be very little "sorority" between them. Gilead has structured itself in a way that actively discourages sisterhood. The rules aim at neutralizing any expression of empathy, which is crucial to understanding the needs of the other.

For instance, when Serena Joy can't help crying during the Ceremony, everyone is aware of her sadness, yet nobody seems to care :

> Serena has begun to cry. I can hear her, behind my back. It isn't the first time. She always does this, the night of the Ceremony. She's trying not to make a noise. She's trying to preserve her dignity, in front of us. . . . The smell of her crying spreads over us and we pretend to ignore it.

Any outward sign of emotion needs to be concealed, as if it didn't matter at all, as if the emotion wasn't real. Everyone has to cope on their own, you can't expect help from anyone. Just as women can't have any power in this man-controlled world, the need to care for each other now seems irrelevant.

To Want Is to Have a Weakness

How might June and the other Handmaids respond to their situation? Are they doomed to lives of meaningless suffering, robbed of the freedom to even *feel* on their own? Stoicism provides one worldview that might reduce their suffering.

Emotions are quite diverse. Some are somewhat easy to hide. For example, you may feel anxiety for a long time, not knowing precisely why. It can linger on indefinitely. Other emotions are caused by external objects and are more difficult to control; you may fear a harmless spider and you might demonstrate that fear with uncontrolled gestures and cries for help. Anger can take both forms. It can simmer inside undetected, or it can explode unmistakably forward into action.

In a free world, we're allowed to let our emotions burst forth, as long as we don't hurt anyone. In the dystopian state of Gilead, the demonstration of emotion is prohibited. Feelings have to stay within, concealed. June explores her feelings in her diary, but hides them from outside observers. She feels disgust at having sex with the Commander, but can't let it show. Emotions can only be summoned in ways authorized by the state. For example, during the birth ceremony, Handmaids and Wives gather to express joy at the miracle of birth in a barren world in which a healthy child is rarely born. Nevertheless, June's account of such events reveals mixed reactions, the collective joy gets confused with jealousy of other barren Wives and the envy of the unsuccessful Handmaids.

Something similar happens during the hate ceremony, when the Handmaids are offered a male rapist to judge and lynch to death. The outburst of collective rage reminds us of the "Two Minutes Hate" in George Orwell's *Nineteen Eighty-Four*, where everyone gathers to express their hatred toward a political scapegoat, Emmanuel Goldstein. In *The Handmaid's Tale*, women who are not ordinarily allowed to express their uneasiness can at last unleash all the frustrations with the deprivations they have had to endure. Aunt Lydia's whistle is the symbol of the carnival of freedom. For a few minutes the authorities close their eyes until order is restored. By killing the traitor, the Handmaids release their fear and anger.

Aunt Lydia is one of the only characters in the novel who seems to be able to safely display outward emotion. While teaching at the Red Center, she preaches against any words of distrust or misplaced emotion. At the same time, she seems to enjoy expressing emotion herself. She often laughs when she advocates cruel principles, she demonstrates sadness when explaining how most women were cursed with barren wombs, and she orders Handmaids to lynch rapists with the utmost cruelty. How can she be allowed the very emotions every Handmaid is forbidden to express? Perhaps because her emotions are so reliably in the service of Gilead's interests.

Ancient Stoic philosophers were fatalists: they believed that earthly events are deterministic. In Gilead, God plays this deterministic role. Although no one knows why a sudden epidemic caused female bodies to be infertile, the citizens of Gilead have faith (or at least pretend to have faith) that somehow this demonstrates God's will—infertility was a mandate for a change of regime. The Handmaid who can conceive a child will be promoted. The others have to accept their fate as well, even if this means they will be relegated to the status of "Unwomen."

I Resign My Body Freely

Not unlike the Handmaids in our tale, the Greek Stoic philosopher Epictetus was a slave. His philosophy might prove useful to someone in June's situation. He wrote in his *Enchiridion*:

> Some things are in our control and others not. Things in our control are opinion, pursuit, desire, aversion, and, in a word, whatever are our own actions. Things not in our control are body, property, reputation, command, and, in one word, whatever are not our own actions.

Stoics maintain that freedom, such as it is, lies within the mind, in our thoughts and desires, as long as we can control them. Since we have no real power over the external events of the world, or over other people's thoughts and actions, we must learn not to care about them, and suffer whatever may happen with utmost resolution. A true Stoic wouldn't rebel in a totalitarian state, for she knows that any attempt would be pointless. June might do well to adopt this approach.

Epictetus points out that even our bodies are not exactly under our control, since we are exposed to unwanted sickness and injuries. June is subjected to countless degradations and humiliations and there is not much she can do about it. She must treat her own body as someone else's property. It's now the instrument of the religious state. She's viewed as no more than a "two-legged womb."

There is no better example of this phenomenon in *The Handmaid's Tale* than the Ceremony. During one of the most memorable scenes in the whole novel, June has forced sexual intercourse with her Commander. This is rape condoned by the state. The rape happens several times a month, when she's supposed to be most fertile, to increase the chances of future pregnancy, during a bleak ceremony, attended by both Commander and his wife. However, June learns to detach herself from her own body.

> What he is fucking is the lower part of my body. I do not say making love, because this is not what he's doing. Copulating too would be inaccurate, because it would imply two people and only one is involved.

In Stoic fashion, June detaches from her own body. The fact that she can disengage from her body in this way does not make the sick practices instituted by the Sons of Jacob morally okay. Instead, it illustrates that, whatever policies they implement, they can never *fully* control June, or anyone really.

Even her former name is erased. As "Offred," she is indistinguishable from the Handmaid who came before her. Perhaps the only hope, if there is hope at all, is mastery of her own internal states. Her body may not be her own, but she can control how she reacts to her circumstances.

A Stoic must also abandon any sense of property: whatever you now own, you're bound to lose one day, for it will be consumed or lost. If you value material things, you already know you'll end up disappointed and sad when the time comes to lose them. Not only should you give up all hope for wealth and comfort, you also refrain from conceiving of any object as your own. In Stoic fashion, June refuses to consider the room she sleeps in as her own. Her relationship to the space she occupies and to objects in that space is transitory. It is healthier for her to internalize the impermanence of her situation. Of course, June could be a better Stoic in this regard—she often longs for the material comforts of earlier times.

For the Stoics, the same principles apply to personal relationships. Epictetus believed that we shouldn't consider our relatives as "ours." Instead, we should recognize the mortality of others, so that their loss won't affect us any more than the loss of a material object. This is a difficult lesson for June to learn. Her husband and her daughter Hannah were forcibly ripped from her. In the TV series, she is permitted to see Hannah once more, provided she won't view her as her own.

Viewing family units as transitory and fleeting is essential for psychological health as a Handmaid. After all, Handmaids are forced to switch households whenever their society views such a move as appropriate. What's worse, the few lucky ones who give birth to a healthy baby are commanded to give it up to the house they serve, and never to consider themselves as "mothers." They are not allowed to have any friends or real families anymore, and any sign of inappropriate desire has to be banned. These are elements of their lives over which Handmaids have no control. They do have control over their mental attitudes toward those relationships.

Epictetus claims that a true stoic can be free even in the most enduring situation of physical torture. Stoics' minds can detach themselves from the utmost physical pain and from the fear of death. This is freedom of the most valuable sort. Even deprived of everything that makes life worth living, June can prove to herself that she is still a free woman in the midst of the cruelest totalitarian state.

When she stumbles upon the jokey Latin phrase "Nolite Te Bastardes Carborundorum," she uses it as an inner mantra that she repeats to herself when circumstances get darker and darker: "Don't let the bastards grind you down!"

She resists the bastards by controlling her own internal states—by demonstating mastery of her response to torture, she has, in a sense, achieved a victory even the Sons of Jacob can't take away from her.

16
Who Is the Meanest of Them All?

MIHAELA FRUNZĂ AND IULIA GRAD

> Is that how we lived, then? But we lived as usual. Everyone does, most of the time. Whatever is going on is as usual. Even this is as usual, now.
>
> —*The Handmaid's Tale*

Of all the words in the world—and Margaret Atwood surely has a way with words—why does Offred give the description, "too banal" to refer to her time spent alone with the Commander?

You know, when they play Scrabble and he gives her an old, dusty issue of *Vogue*? When she finds her courage and asks him why he does not play Scrabble with his wife, and he replies that his wife doesn't understand him? Of all the ways she could have characterized the exchange, she thinks to herself (privately, she knows better than to speak): "That's what I was there for, then. The same old thing. It was too banal to be true" (*The Handmaid's Tale*, p. 158).

Of course, the main theme of the story is that she is not there for anything we would consider "that same old thing." Her presence is not a solace for the poor Commander. Her mission in his home is to produce a child, without her explicit consent, that she will not be allowed to keep. If she isn't successful in this mission, she will disappear. She will become an Unwoman or will be executed in a bloody ceremony. This

195

is the farthest thing possible from being "banal." But surely, Atwood chose the word carefully. Why?

Some fifty years or so before *The Handmaid's Tale* hit the shelves, another woman used the word "banal" in an equally unexpected context. It was Hannah Arendt, a Jewish philosopher who was hired by *The New Yorker* to cover the trial of a famous war criminal: Adolf Eichmann. Eichmann supervised and co-ordinated the execution of several million Jews during the Second World War. When writing about him, in what finally became a book, *Eichmann in Jerusalem*, Hannah Arendt coined a phrase that made her both famous and infamous: "the banality of evil."

"So, does this mean evil can be banal?!" her fellow readers exclaimed. How can a Jewish woman claim that the murdering of a couple millions Jews is even remotely banal?!

Confusion like this happens when a philosopher's technical phrase becomes a catchy headline. Whatever they meant, both Atwood and Arendt used the "B" word. This can't be a coincidence. How can a better understanding of the banality of evil illuminate the content of a masterpiece such as *The Handmaid's Tale*?

Not Iago, Not Macbeth

When we think of evil, we tend to conjure the image of a super-villain, a supreme bad guy, a combination of Voldemort, Darth Vader, and Professor Moriarty: a dark, bold character dressed in all black, a tragic hero with wickedness seeping through his or her pores. We equate evil characters with pure negativity and good characters with pure positivity. But guess what? Life is more complex than that; so are good books.

During Eichmann's trial, Arendt was struck by the absence of anything heroic or tragic in the defendant, "He was not Iago, not Macbeth," she writes; "one cannot extract any diabolical or demonic profundity from Eichmann." A psychiatrist described Eichmann as "normal" and his minister, as "a man with very positive ideas." He was kind to his family and friends. He was neither stupid, nor a lunatic, and not even malefic: he was just an ordinary guy.

Perhaps Eichmann is just as ordinary as Atwood's Commander—whose secret fantasy is to dress Offred as a prostitute with cheap make-up and revealing clothes—exploitative, yes, but common. Can such a man really be evil? When Offred describes him, she hesitates frequently; and uses words such as "sheepish." We find from the epilogue of the book that the Commander (Fred Waterford) was the designer of several of the most terrifying elements that make Gilead what it is: from female costumes, to Particicution, Salvaging, and the collective rape ceremony. And yet, he is almost sweet, shyly asking Offred to kiss him "as if it was for real." He too could be "a man with very positive ideas."

When we browse through the characters of *The Handmaid's Tale*, we have difficulty finding "the meanest" of them all. Perhaps the Wives are the worst? Serena certainly seems to enjoy making things difficult for Offred—until she decides to help her conceive the required offspring with the driver. What about the Aunts? They're despicable, that's granted, yet their power is not absolute: a clever woman such as Moira manages to escape twice from their ward. The Guards? They're powerless in the face of a black car—after all, this is the manner in which Offred finally makes her way out. In the dystopian world of Gilead nobody has the monopoly on evil. Each of the characters is simply too banal for that.

If They Do Think

Another thing Hannah Arendt wrote when reviewing her notes from the trial was that Eichmann "never realized what he was doing" (*Eichmann in Jerusalem*). Again, we are not speaking of stupidity, nor of madness: his actions denote *thoughtlessness*. In plain English: he never considered the consequences of his acts. He couldn't care less, so long as he was satisfying his job description.

Thinking can be a dangerous game, not only in 1940s Germany, but also in Gilead. Sometimes it's better not to think, or at least not to look as if you were thinking, writes Offred. The scene that "looks like a normal life" behind the doors of the Commander's office evokes to Offred the memory of a documentary she saw when she was a child. It presented the mistress of a man that supervised one of the concentration camps in World War II. What made an impression on Offred, apart from the woman's makeup, was what she had to say about her lover: "He was not a monster. People said he was a monster, but he was not one." Offred adds: "What could she have been thinking about? Not much, I guess; not back then, not at the time. *She was thinking about how not to think.* The times were abnormal" (p. 145). With this kind of comment, Offred points to the core element of the banality of evil (in Arendt's terms).

Most of the current characters don't seem to think too much, they just play their part in the daily drama. When she meets the Guards, Offred thinks, "*If* they do think; you can't tell by looking at them." Many Marthas also attempt to avoid thinking. Why bother to think when you can distract yourself by cooking a fresh chicken?

When a Commander and his Wife request a Handmaid, they never think of her as a person: how could one truly think of someone else as a mere receptacle for an offspring? Gilead goes so far as to ban certain forms of thinking: for instance, reading is a crime.

The Commander, Too, Is Doing His Duty

What does it mean to do your duty? Appeal to a sense of "duty" seems to be the perfect excuse for all sorts of totalitarian freaks, from the various Commanders and Aunts, to the decision makers of the Third Reich. Thus, reports Arendt, Eichmann claimed he was not guilty of the genocide charge, as he did nothing to directly kill Jews. "I never killed a Jew," he testified. His lawyer added, "he could be accused only of "aiding and abetting" the annihilation of the Jews." In other words, he merely did his duty. But did he?

Well, those who take the time to think philosophically will not buy that. At least, not those who have heard of a philosopher named Immanuel Kant. To do your duty, in Kantian terms, means to do whatever all the other rational persons would do. You have to think first, in order to be qualified as a "rational person"; and second, you have to think not only for yourself, but to position the rule you follow as a universal law for everybody else. And beware: if the consequences of your actions lead to killing others (yourself included), that action is *never* morally permissible.

However, the term "duty" is used and abused by all the categories of citizens in Gilead, especially the Aunts, who are supposed to be the exemplars—duty personified. Offred thinks of Aunt Lydia as "the voice of those whose duty is to tell us unpleasant things for our own good." This characterization of duty mimics, to some extent, the way the concept is used in Arendt and Kant. However, it only mimics it. The difference? When we see the way the Aunts treat the Handmaids, the closest approximation is the re-education camps in totalitarian regimes.

Whatever the Aunts do, they are treating the Handmaids as (Kant would say) means for an end, not ends-in-themselves. Arendt would say that they are being treated as citizens deprived of their rights. Duty cannot be a pretext for mistreating others. Doing one's duty is something much more than mechanically obeying orders. There are far too few Kantians in Gilead, unfortunately.

This Is How You Can Get Lost, in a Sea of Names

If there are no demonic characters and everybody is just doing what they perceive to be their duty (in an Eichmann understanding of "duty"), what exactly goes wrong in the society of Gilead? Why is resistance so scarce? Why do all Handmaids behave exactly as educated by the Aunts? Why do all Marthas accept their subservient places in the houses of their masters?

If Hannah Arendt were to read this novel, she would say that many categories of protagonists (Handmaids being the most telling example) are deprived of their basic human rights. In another of her brilliant books, *The Origins of Totalitarianism*, she explains that those deprived of human rights do not belong to a community. For them, there is no law; their existence is merely tolerated by the others, who establish the limits of their behavior. Whatever the others grant to them is a matter of external decision; it has no connection to them. "Privileges in some cases, injustices in most, blessings and doom are meted out to them according to accident and without any relation whatsoever to what they do, did, or may do." This passage accurately describes the situation of Handmaids. They enjoy what seem like privileges: they are well fed, they enjoy special freedoms, and they may kill people during certain ceremonies; yet they aren't worthy of a proper identity.

When, one morning, Offred finds a new Ofglen, ready for shopping time, she naively asks: What happened to Ofglen? When the other woman proclaims her identity as Ofglen, Offred chides herself: "And of course she is, the new one, and Ofglen, wherever she is, is no longer Ofglen. I never did know her real name" (p. 283).

The Handmaids don't even have proper names, a practice that denies their uniqueness as human beings. Apart from that, they must conform to rules they have not chosen in all aspects of their lives: they have to wear special clothes; they can only walk in designated areas and in special company, they are subject to forced medical check ups, and they are continually sexually abused. They are not deprived of the freedom of thinking (this would be difficult if not impossible to ban completely) but what they can *say* is severely restricted. Both Arendt and Atwood would probably agree that the biggest limitation consists in the way their existence is expendable; they do not matter as persons. They are viewed as merely walking wombs.

As Offred puts it, "We are two-legged wombs, that's all: sacred vessels, ambulatory chalices" (p. 136). They are little more than objects that can be replaced; someone's property, valuable not in themselves, but in what they can grow. When the deeds of a class of persons are irrelevant for the fate of those persons, the society is seriously failing its members.

When Power Is Scarce, a Little of It Is Tempting

Can a society such as Gilead change itself for the better? Can it become democratic again? History shows us that totalitarian regimes end up in bloodshed and are overturned via rebellions or wars. This happens because, as Hannah Arendt shows, totalitarian regimes construct a web of guilty complicities among all the actors, "where all, or most all, are guilty, nobody is." The main tool for this mechanism is bureaucracy. A society where everybody mechanically follows orders is a society where everyone is deprived of individuality: each person is a small part of a bigger system, a part of a rolling mechanism. Even if one individual rebels, she is quickly annihilated and the system goes on. Arendt picks the idea of personal responsibility, noting that there is an "abyss between the actuality of what you did and the potentiality of what others might have done." The only criterion for objective judgment should remain the acts and not the "the possible noncriminal nature of your inner life and of your motives." To sum up: "in politics obedience and support are the same."

In Gilead, as in totalitarian regimes, power is distributed respecting a strict system of casts. Each member gains power over the others, and it's very tempting to abuse it. For instance, the doctor tells Offred he can help her conceive a child, and she has trouble refusing him in a polite way, "None of this has been said, but the knowledge of his power hangs nevertheless in the air as he pats my thigh, withdrew himself behind the hanging sheet" (p. 61). The doctor could lie in his records; has the power to change her destiny; and is regularly checking her health, which gives him access to her in ways that are not accessible to others. Offred herself abuses her power of showing off, of projecting a desirable apparition for the young guards: "I'm ashamed of myself for doing it, because none of this is the fault of these men, they're too young. Then I find I'm not ashamed after all. I enjoy the power; power of a dog bone, passive but there" (p. 22). In the Gilead system, very often, the criminal acts are carried through by the victims (and the terrifying scene of Particicution is the most telling example).

The dynamic of power between Offred and the Commander is even more fluid. At the beginning of their private encounters, he holds the power, and she can only attempt to find flaws in his wall: "But to refuse to see him could be worse. There's no doubt about who holds the real power. But there must be something he wants, from me. To want is to have a weakness. It's this weakness, whatever it is, that entices me" (p. 136). Yet, in the scene where she leaves the Commander's house, escorted by two men, the situation changes. When she looks down the stairs, she sees the Commander, who looks worried and helpless, with his hair very grey. She says: "I am above him, looking down; he is shrinking" (p. 294).

However, the last resort of power in the novel seems to lie ahead, in the future; and more precisely, in shaping that future through the act of narrating it. "The pen between my fingers is sensuous, alive almost, I can feel its power, the power of the words it contains." As we discover in the Historical Notes, it is the text that gains the ultimate power, because it's the only thing that can survive the passing of time.

How Easy It Is to Invent a Humanity, for Anyone at All

What is the end result of the banality of evil theory? It helps us better understand why and how a society may erase individuals' wills and values with little to no resistance from the victims involved. It can explain why evil can become ordinary and even banal; how can we get used to outrageous things and letting them become new habits.

In Nazi Germany, humanity was equated with the characteristics of a totally invented race (the Aryan), at the expense of exterminating millions of real Jews. In Gilead, humanity is reserved to those classes who are deemed worthy (Commanders, Wives, Angels), at the expense of abuses and instrumentalization of all the others. In the end, we lose the criteria for telling what's good from what's evil, and what lies in-between.

We are facing Offred's choice, when she finally exits the Commander's house: "And so I step up, into the darkness within; or else the light."

Part V

I Tell, Therefore You Are

17
The Red and the Black

MARIANA ZÁRATE, FERNANDO GABRIEL
PAGNONI BERNS, AND EMILIANO AGUILAR

"What color is the dress?" was a polemical social media disagreement triggered by a photograph of a dress that went viral in February 2015. To the great bewilderment of many, viewers disagreed over whether the colors of the dress depicted in the photograph was black and blue or white and gold. The controversy revealed differences in human color discernment and underscored one of the most important questions of philosophy: Should we believe our eyes?

Colors and philosophy are actually good companions. In addition to questions about color perception, philosophy is interested in how color and society intermingle and how color is codified through culture.

Colors exist by convention; human thought has given different colors different meanings. *The Handmaid's Tale* makes excellent, and quite nuanced, use of those conventions.

Philosophical Coloring Books

One of the first philosophers to call attention to philosophical questions pertaining to color was Aristotle in his *Peri Khromaton*, or, *On Colors*. (We're not certain of who wrote ancient documents, and some people say this was written by a different philosopher, Theophrastus.) Whoever he was, the author proposed that the potential of color in matter is activated by light (In doing so, he anticipated by many centuries a solution to the problem of the now famous dress).

Aristotle (we're assuming it's him) maintained that all colors are derived from mixtures of black and white. He also said that colors are associated with a deeper meaning, a symbolic content. Aristotle connects white with fire and air, while black is connected with water and earth. Colors were *signifiers of something else*, something that is beyond the notion of the colors themselves. What Aristotle was saying without saying it, is that color will be associated, through conventions, with external ideas.

The names of the different colors are just words. The convention by which colors come to signify things is largely a language game as well. We classify with words, and words are the expression of a culture, a social construction. There is no real correspondence between, say, white and purity or red and passion or blue and coldness. These parallelisms are produced, artificially, within the social and cultural context and may vary from society to society and from time to time.

The nightmare world depicted in *The Handmaid's Tale* relies heavily on colors and their social and cultural meanings. The colors that first pop out to any viewer, even those who haven't thought about questions related to color, are red and white. The pilot ("Offred") begins with a black screen. We can hear the sounds of police sirens. Rather than blue and red, the expected colors, the screen bursts with red and white. The show's title, *The Handmaid's Tale*, is depicted in red (the word "Handmaid's") and white ("The" and "Tale"). Even the words displayed before the main title ("Hulu presents" and "An MGM and Hulu production") are written in white and red letters, highlighting the importance of both colors in the show. Viewers will soon learn that the dystopian society they are about to enter is divided by colored classes, and that the Handmaids wear red and white dresses.

"Offred" signals the importance of red and white, beginning in the first scene. The show opens with June/Offred running away from the authorities. It appears that her husband has been killed and she's alone with her young daughter, who wears a red buttoned coat and a light grey hood. She passionately clutches a little white teddy bear. The color choices in this scene appear to be intentional. At this stage the connotations of these colors are innocent enough, but Offred's fate and, perhaps, by extension, that of her daughter is a destiny of red dresses and white bonnets as markers of sexual servitude. Further, if light waves are essential to the perception of colors to the point that these are inseparable, it may be significant that the first scene featuring Offred as slave (as a woman wearing red and white) shows her sitting at the frame of the window of her bedroom/prison, the light flooding her room, her silhouette and color palate in sharp contrast with the pure, blinding light.

We can see already that, in social contexts, colors are far from "innocent" of meaning. Aristotle was just one of the first philosophers to argue that there's more to study about color than just optics. Colors appear to us as a complex mix of the optical and the symbolic.

Teal Goethe

Some forms in art clearly refer to or represent something (such as a house or a person). Color is unique. Color is, by itself just . . . color. For colors to signify anything, meanings must be imposed on them. Over time, the language and use of color can become moralistic and political.

Johann Goethe's *Theory of Colors*, published in 1810, still provides the inspiration for many color theorists today. Goethe's theory combined physics with aesthetics. As well as trying to analyze physical facts about colors, Goethe had ideas about how color contributes to human experience. He pointed out that colors affect our state of mind and influence our moods. Positive colors (yellow, orange, scarlet red) and negative colors (blue, pinkish blue, bluish red, and green) are endowed with a certain character that affects whoever perceives them.

The scarlet red that identifies the Handmaids is, according to Goethe, a positive color. Red allows the mind to be agile, focused and, above all, to stay awake. Awakening is paramount for Offred. She goes through moments of extreme denial to moments of total awakening when she becomes aware of her situation and the need to fight in sisterhood with the others in red (the other Handmaids).

For Goethe (who illustrated his theory in a diagram known as "the circle of color"), the color red gives us an idea of gravity and dignity. This is consistent with the social role that is attributed to the Handmaids outside of the bedroom; in practice, however, they function as sexual slaves deprived of their free will, one of the most undignified roles imaginable. At the same time, Goethe highlights in red the ability to provoke grace and attraction. In *The Handmaid's Tale*, however, attraction has been suppressed in an attempt to center sex solely on the reproductive function. Thus, the story *mutilates* historical meanings to replace them with others which, in turn, ironically play with previous meanings (the Handmaids used as sex slaves).

The color red also symbolizes passion. Many of the Handmaids represent revolutionary passion. This meaning may be external to the events of the show, flagging something for the viewer rather than for the players in Gilead. The red of the Handmaids represents a spark of passion: for escape, to organize themselves in an army, for freedom.

Unlike the pure red of the Handmaids, the Wives wear teal, a composite between two negative colors: green and blue. The mixing of color seems to be a prerogative of Wives in Gilead. The green of the Wives' clothing is not like the green of the walls of the Commander's office, moss green, but a vivid color that blends together the blue of the Virgin Mary with the soldiers' green. This imagery motivates us to conceive of the Wives as soldiers defending the household. They are the ones who actually sustain the regime with their blind obedience (the Handmaids are mostly obliged to comply). Further, in the first ritual/rape scene presented to audiences, Offred concentrates on the color blue, a reminder of the complicity of the Wife in her ordeal.

Choose Your Colors for a Dystopia

Ludwig Wittgenstein's interest in colors is influenced by Goethe's theory, which motivated Wittgenstein to examine the dynamics of our language and how they contribute to the complexity of our concepts of colors. Propositions about colors are true because they are part of our social and cultural grammar, not because they present some "essence" of our visual perception of colors themselves. There is nothing "blue" in the color blue.

Wittgenstein points out that our concepts of colors could be different from what they are. Consequently, the meanings we give them could also vary. The social use is, ultimately, the natural foundation of what is affirmed. In other words: colors and their conventional meanings are social constructions legitimized by use. The conceptions of color that we have come to employ have resulted from "language games" in which we have participated.

Wittgenstein argues that color is not a property of an object, but an "internal relation" that cannot refer to any physical characteristic of colors that we know by experience. He warns against associating meaning (what we say about a color as an ideal) with reference (a real, concrete hue of color). We should avoid understanding this association as something "natural." As Wittgenstein says, "looking does not teach us anything about the concepts of colors" (*Remarks on Colour*, p. 72) because colors are pure logic/language rather than features of things.

In *The Handmaid's Tale* the choice of each color surely has a semantic hold, but it is interesting to think about the arbitrariness of the costumes, especially the red and white of the Handmaids, and the teal of the Wives. If, according to Wittgenstein, it's the *use* we make of things—such as colors—in a given context that makes them what they are (rather than some observable "truth"), then we can affirm that the red of the robes worn by the sexually enslaved Handmaids is strongly anchored to the images of sex associated with red by convention—by *use*—while the white of their bonnets represents subordination from the religious point of view.

The color red almost does not appear in scenes that do not correspond to the environment of a Handmaid. In fact, red paralleling servitude is only "useful" or meaningful in the context of this totalitarian state. It could mean anything else in any other society because its meaning is a language game, a social action. When June escapes with the help of some dissidents at the beginning of Season Two ("June"), she immediately takes off her clothes and throws them into the incinerator. With the elimination of red, she regains her identity, even if she has to bleed for it. The episode ends with her covered in red again (her own blood, spilled when she pulls the label from her ear), but now red has acquired another meaning: freedom.

The Swiss artist Johannes Itten explains that in a composition, "a color is always to be seen in relation to its surroundings (*The Elements of Color*, p. 91). In this sense, the red of the Handmaids acquires its properties of carnal subordination from its insertion in that aesthetic environment in which there is almost no red in other objects. These use and practices of red within the logic of *The Handmaid's Tale* constitute a system and only inside that system does red acquires its meaning.

In his book *Color for Philosophers*, C.L. Hardin argues that "all a human being has to do to have the concept of green is to experience green in an appropriately reflective fashion" (p. 122). It is in this sense, which is congenial with what Wittgenstein says , that we should think of red, white, and green according to the context of their use in the story, because in *The Handmaid's Tale* those colors do not necessarily represent what they might represent elsewhere. On the other hand, those colors do not represent different things for different persons but just one thing: red is equal to sexual servitude, grey refers to Marthas, and so on. It is this rigid classificatory system that points to the lack of freedom shaping this dystopian landscape. Rather than having a range of possible meanings, colors are rigidly fixed in just one authorized meaning.

They Should Never Have Given Us Uniforms if They Didn't Want Us to Be an Army

Walter Benjamin's "A Child's View of Color" is one of his shorter works (just two pages) but is filled with rich ideas. For Benjamin, colors have a spiritual quality that is lost when confined through form, categories, or boundaries. The pure, subversive quality of color is particularly accessible to children. Colors are always treading on the edge of playfulness and rule: when you blend two colors together, there is not just a blur: there is another color. Greenish blue or, say, yellowish brown is, in the end, another color (teal, for example)

This subtle existence of colors is somehow downplayed, however, when a color gets a name, it becomes "real"—it has a tag, a purpose. A child may feel the force of saying "greenish blue" as they playfully mix two colors together. Colors lose this spiritual, ethereal property when "greenish blue" becomes a proper, fixed color to make crayons or to sell to construction workers to paint houses. For Benjamin, coloring is better than painting. Coloring does not respect borders. Painting respects borders, forms, schemes, and thus, colors become dull. In *The Handmaid's Tale*, teal, the mixing of two colors means many things but, obviously, not playfulness or freedom. Quite the contrary.

The use of colors in *The Handmaid's Tale* evokes Benjamin's thesis. The colors are, in theory, sharp, elegant and "joyful." The red worn by the Handmaids and the blue worn by the Wives are striking, but, rather than suggesting joy and a subversive nuance, as colors should do, they function as norms, rules, and the visible markers of difference. The hues in the show are all the same: every Wife wears the same teal, every Martha the same grey and so on. There is no playfulness. The severity of the color turns the plain dresses into uniforms while homogenizing disparate women into servitude and categories—and also, potential armies.

There is, however, some meaningful mixing of colors, such as in "Birth Day." This particular episode narrates two births, one taking place in Gilead and the other one, told in flashback, of Offred's daughter. The first mixing is that of Offred's daughter: since the woman is Caucasian and her husband African American, the girl is mixed race. The little girl and her hybrid blood/race/colors code her as a subversive subject living within the boundaries of a society marked by rigidity. In the flashback, the little mixed-race girl is covered by a blanket with strips of red and teal, uniting what will be separated in the future: categories of color. Returning to the present, Offred is invited to the banquet made to honor the new birth: there, the ladies of the house eat multicolored macarons; only the upper class can "access" a wider range of colors.

Fade to Black

In classical cinema, fading to black marks the end of the movie. Within the show, black is a color mostly used by men, both those belonging to the working class (such as Nick) and those wearing dark, upper-class suits. There are two operative meanings here: first, black can be interpreted as "no color," the rejection of the boundaries subjecting women. In the dark (complete blackness) there is no color, because there is no light. If the show begins with Offred showing her true colors thanks to the light flooding her bedroom, men resist codification and objectification. After all, men represent the patriarchal power subjugating women.

Second, black is, according Theodor Adorno, the color of contemporary nihilism, like that represented by the TV show. Color, for Adorno, is just a way of "selling" out to capitalism and commercialism. "Radical art today is synonymous with dark art; its primary color is black. Much contemporary production is irrelevant because it takes no note of this and childishly delights in color" (*Aesthetic Theory*, p. 50). The joyous surface of color, in *The Handmaid's Tale*, cloaks a very black heart of human servitude and masculine dominance.

Black is mourning and emptiness and, thus, is perfect for the creators (men) of a new society that is depriving women of their names, identities, and subjectivities, using color to rigidly define and constrain them. The chromophobia of the men of the TV show demonstrates that they are outside the norms and color codes of this society. The reason is obvious: they invent them.

The meanings of colors are highlighted through the character of Castillo, the Mexican Ambassador. She appears first dressed in yellow, the most luminous color according to Goethe; apparently, she is a sympathetic character who has come to dismantle the oppressive structure. Later, at the point at which the Handmaids finally understand that Castillo intends to use them as a reproductive work force for her country, the ambassador appears dressed in black, homologous with the male oppressors. Finally, she wears green, paralleling the Wives and thus becoming complicit with the structural oppression.

Colors, then, are far from innocent: they answer social codification that, in turn, is different in each society and culture. One of the most brutal acts of the society reflected in *The Handmaid's Tale* is to destroy the ability that colors have to evade all attempts to codify them. It is this attempt to turn the always-open-to-interpretation color into a univocal meaning that shows the true colors of this dystopian society.

18
Smoke and Mirrors in Gilead

Stephanie St. Martin

Better never means better for everyone.

—Commander Fred Waterford, *The Handmaid's Tale*

Humans prefer to organize people and things into groups and patterns. This can be a useful exercise. But some divisions that humans create are arguably, unnecessary, and even harmful. For example, our culture tends to divide colors into two categories. When I announced in the first grade that my favorite color was green, a group of seven-year-old girls promptly yelled at me for liking a "boys' color." It's not just little girls who claim to be the authorities on what's appropriate and what's not. We all have bias, and that bias affects our choices, and ethical decision making throughout our lifetime.

I start every Introduction to Ethics class with the same assignment—one designed to explore the concept of bias. When the students enter the room, I have already placed pieces of paper on their desks. They read:

> Come in and sit down. Take ten minutes and in as much detail as possible, please draw the following professionals. Do not talk or share your designs with anyone else. We will discuss the drawings together as a group.

- Nurse
- Police officer
- Elementary school teacher
- Accountant
- Construction site manager

As the students hurry to draw in their notebooks, I take stock of the room. Every so often, a student will look up and meet another set of eyes. They nervously exchange glances. Once they finish their drawings, I select a random student to describe the pictures they've drawn. Every time I do the assignment, the drawings are the same. The students draw nurses and elementary school teachers as women, and the police officers, accountants, and construction workers as men.

I prepare the statistics ahead of time. According to the *Boston Globe,* as of 2016:

- **10 percent of nurses are men**

- **18.3 percent of police officers are women**

- **21.5 percent of elementary school teachers are men**

- **61.3 percent of accountants are women**

- **7.4 percent of construction managers are women**

I then tell the class that not everyone fits neatly into boxes. We all have biases, and, in this class, they will have to challenge their assumptions and biases daily. This is something we should all be prepared to do. We all need to check ourselves. Are our assumptions concerning how society should be structured defensible? We try to set up our homes, families, and societies in a way that is consistent with the right answer to the million-dollar philosophical question "*What is the best way to live?*" Ideally, we constantly strive to make the world better. But better, as we know, never means better for everyone.

The Sons of Jacob from *The Handmaid's Tale* believe it is their duty to get the world back on track and once again be looked on favorably by God. Pollution is out of control; the air is full of chemicals and radiation. Women are blamed for this decline of well-being. Commander Putnam claims that women had "too many pressures put on them" by society, making things "too difficult for them." Aunt Lydia refers to "dirty women" and "sluts" who don't appreciate that they are fertile. In the eyes of Sons of Jacob, society needs to be restructured to conform to a newly constructed, superior set of values modeled on the Bible.

Aunt Lydia! C'mon. We Can't Do This!

In Plato's dialogue *Republic,* Socrates tries to arrive at some clarity regarding the nature of justice. In standard Socratic fashion, he asks his friends for their opinions. Thrasymachus provides this definition: Justice is that which is to the advantage of the stronger (line 338c).

We can assume that the people in power count as "the stronger" in the sense in which Thrasymachus means it. These people create laws that align with their self-interest—and, according to Thrasymachus, this is just. *Might makes right.* But if this is the case, what counts as "justice" is subject to change. Any given understanding of justice in this context is dependent on the mighty staying mighty.

To this end, we can imagine that the powerful will set up systems of "education" and indoctrination for their citizens. The education will ultimately serve *the rulers' own self-interests*, and not necessarily the interests of their subjects. We can imagine further that citizens might come to see that the emperor has no clothes. But what happens when one subject figures out the deception—that "justice" changes when the system of power changes? The whole system starts to crack.

In *The Handmaid's Tale*, we see the cracks begin to form at the end of Season One. Ofglen #2 (we later learn her name is Lily) steps forward and protests Janine's (Ofwarren's) execution, we see her realization: If Gilead executes one Handmaid they will execute another. She's compelled to step forward:

"Aunt Lydia! C'mon. We can't do this," Ofglen cries, only to be told to get back to her place. "Seriously? Guys, this is insane" ("Night").

Of course, we know her punishment is to never speak out of turn again. That's how these rulers stay in power—through fear. The mighty are able to stay mighty and, therefore, set the standard for justice, because people fear harsh consequences. Thrasymachus probably inspired the Sons of Jacob.

Gilead makes excessive use of fear and punishment. Janine loses an eye for saying "Fuck you" to Aunt Lydia at the Red Center. The aunts whip June's feet as punishment for running away. Emily (Ofglen #1) sees her lover hanged and undergoes a clitoridectomy to help her stay in line "as things will be so much easier" for her now. We see people hanging on The Wall, executed for more serious crimes. The severity of the consequences make it very risky to rebel.

That seems simple enough: if the people of Gilead stay in line and follow the rules, they will live in peace. Gilead dishes out harsh consequences for rules violations, but they also reward blind, unquestioning compliance with the rules. For example, in "A Woman's Place," the Mexican ambassador pays a visit to Gilead. The commanders and their wives host a reception to charm their foreign guests.

Before the party, Serena Joy inspects all the Handmaids and asks Aunt Lydia to "remove the damaged ones" as she wants Gilead to make its best impression. When Aunt Lydia reluctantly asks Janine and others to step forward, thus disinviting them from the celebration, Janine's confused. "I didn't do anything wrong," Janine pleads. "I just want to go to the party." In her eyes—well, eye—her appropriate behavior justifies her presence at the party. "It's not fair," she continues to cry to Aunt Lydia. "You're absolutely right," Aunt Lydia agrees. "But sometimes we have to do what is best for everyone, not what is fair." She promises Janine a whole tray of dessert and Janine, with this reward for her obedience, follows Aunt Dylan to the van.

Janine's right. She's done nothing wrong and should go to the party, and yet, she doesn't get to go. She and the other "damaged" Handmaids, whose injuries were punishments for *past crimes*, suffer additional, undeserved consequences. In their traumatized state, however, they are often easily pacified by simple rewards. In *Republic*, Socrates's friend Glaucon claims, "It is best is to do injustice without paying the penalty; the worst is to suffer it without being able to take revenge" (359). The Sons of Jacob regularly engage in actions that are intuitively unjust without facing any penalty. The Handmaids constantly suffer injustice without the ability to seek revenge.

Justice can't work this way. Thrasymachus must be wrong. Justice is a moral concept, and there is nothing ethical about a system where might makes right. In a system like that, the interests of the weak are trampled upon by the selfishness of the strong. That way of thinking about justice creates republics like Gilead.

Red, Teal, Brown, and Green

Working from a clean slate, in Book II of *Republic*, Socrates tries to build the perfect city, or *kallipolis*, from the ground up. He starts with humans' basic needs: food, shelter, clothes, and so forth. Professionals need to provide the citizens with all the goods they will need in the city. To get eggs, the city needs a farmer; for shoes, a cobbler; for medicine, a doctor; for pastries, a baker. Socrates argues that each member of society should do all and only their respective jobs. No hobbies, no side hustles. He says, ". . . more plentiful and better-quality goods are more easily produced if each person does one thing for which he is naturally suited, does it at the right time, and is released from having to do any of the others" (370c).

As Socrates sees it, when each person is focused on their proper role, then and only then can they understand the nature of right and wrong. If a baker is doing what he ought to do by baking a cake, society can't punish him for doing what he ought to do by trade. He's also acting in his own self-interest by being committed to his craft.

Gilead creates similar constructs, but it releases women from the pressures of the other jobs they once held. Commander Putnam reminds Fred Waterford: "This is our fault. We gave them more than they could handle. They put so much focus on academic pursuits and professional ambition, we let them forget their real purpose. We won't let that happen again" ("A Woman's Place").

Women worked, so they didn't devote enough time to what they ought to do: keep a home and bear children. As the United States fell, so did the notion of a "working mother." In a "before" scene, we see June scolded by a nurse for not answering her phone when Hannah becomes sick at school. The passive aggressive conversation is an eerie sign of what is yet to come ("June").

Handmaids reproduce. Marthas cook and clean. This is how society ought to be organized. Along with Marthas (help) and Handmaids (surrogates), Gilead sorts women into categories of Econowives (working class women), Aunts (those who educate the handmaids) and Wives (the one percent) to ensure fulfillment of duty to God and His Will. To further demonstrate the separation, each class wears a certain color. The Marthas wear green, the Aunts wear brown, the Wives wear teal, the Econowives wear grey, and the Handmaids—to show off their fruitful wombs—wear red.

"Red's my color," June says when Serena completes an inspection of her dress.

"Well that's lucky," Serena smiles back.

On paper, Gilead has everything it needs. Food, water, shelter, and citizens performing roles they are biologically and morally suited for. So why is nobody happy?

How Does the Quiet Half of the Room Feel about Gilead?

Let's look back at *Republic*. According to Socrates, if everyone tends to their craft, they can provide basic necessities and other human goods not only for themselves, but also for each other. Essentially, the whole "perfect" city is eating, drinking, and having sex: it solves the basic human needs and creates a more efficient and expert production of goods. He says:

> They'll produce bread, wine, clothes, and shoes . . . they'll feast with their children, drink their wine, and, crowned with wreaths, hymn the gods. They'll enjoy sex with one another but bear no more children than their resources allow . . . they'll obviously need salt, olives, cheese, boiled roots, and vegetables of the sort they cook in the country. We will give them desserts, too, of course, consisting of figs, chickpeas and beans . . . they'll live in peace and good health, and when they will die at a ripe old age, they'll bequeath a similar life to their children. (372b–d)

Glaucon ridicules Socrates for conceiving of such a simplistic city. In fact, he calls it a "city of sows." And this language is important. Glaucon rejects this city not because it is a city of animals with basic needs (shelter, food, sex), but rather because Socrates includes singing, religious worship, technical crafts, and care for the family. Glaucon identifies a problem with this arrangement—because the people are satisfied, men won't achieve their full potential. The city lacks the masculinity of politics, war, and the honors that accompany war. Men need to feel special. Men need distinction.

The decision to use the word "sows" is noteworthy. "Sow," like "doe," "hen," "cow," and others, is a term that designates "female" and further highlights Glaucon's dislike for the feminine nature of the city. Plato, like his mentor Socrates, believes both women and men should participate equally in society. They believe in peaceful discourse rather than war and oppression.

Keep in mind that at the time, Ancient Greece reserved the political life for its male citizens, therefore Socrates's inclusion of women is subverting the culture in place. Glaucon feels that women belong exclusively in the private domain, much like Gilead proposes. Serena agrees with the separation as it supports traditional values. When asked by the Mexican ambassador if she's enjoying life in Gilead, she responds,

"I'm blessed to have a home and a husband to care for and follow."

The ambassador presses the issue further, "Back then, did you ever imagine a society like this?"

"A society that has reduced its carbon emissions by seventy-eight percent in three years?"

"A society in which women can no longer read your book . . . or anything else." Silence hangs in the room, and then Serena begins again.

"No, I didn't. God asks for sacrifices, Mrs. Castillo, that has always been His way, but He gives the righteous blessings in return and I think that it's safe to say that Gilead has been blessed in so many ways" ("A Woman's Place").

Serena is not speaking authentically here. First, we know Serena detests knitting, so she's clearly not entirely happy with her lot in Gilead ("Women's Work"). Second, though Gilead exists, allegedly, to create healthy babies at all costs, it can hardly be lost on anyone that they aren't good at producing and raising them. There isn't any evidence that Gilead is blessed in the way Serena claims. Serena once participated in society in the way Plato and Socrates advocated. She unwittingly played a pivotal role in ending that state of affairs once and for all.

Consider Gilead's success (or lack thereof) with babies in Season Two. When baby Charlotte (known as Angela in Gilead) becomes ill, the Gilead leadership faces a moral and ideological dilemma. Should they save baby Charlotte by getting her the care she needs from an acclaimed doctor, a *woman* forced to be a Martha, or should they let the child die to maintain their commitment to a regimented system of labor? ("Women's Work"). Janine's separation from Charlotte causes the baby to become very ill. It's only after they are reunited that the baby fully recovers.

In a different instance, June is stuck pumping milk in the Red Center while Serena Joy dotes on baby Holly (Nicole to Gilead) at home. And Serena is determined not to let June anywhere near her child, despite the fact that the baby needs breast milk. The general policies implemented by Gilead with respect to child rearing are certainly not policies that optimally promote the health and well being of the children involved.

Gilead claims it wants to create babies at all costs. It's clear, though, that's not really what it was designed to promote. Gilead was designed to keep men in power. The societal structure promotes men's interests—not anyone else's. Socrates is on the right track when it comes to equality for women. His ideas about division of labor might be less fruitful and, if Gilead teaches us anything, can actually be used in the service of injustice.

Waking Up

Serena eventually realizes her self-interests aren't in line with those in power. Early on, men don't allow her to speak at Gilead meetings, a decision she seemed content with at the time ("A Woman's Place"). After the bombing, she subverts laws in Season Two to push her agenda; however, Serena was still under the impression that her interests aligned with Gilead's. It wasn't until Eden's execution that she realized what the Gilead commanders truly want: to keep women submissive to men.

Eden seemed to be everything a young girl in Gilead should be. She was extremely pious—a true believer—and understood what God expected of her. Despite Nick's pleas to "claim she's pregnant," or to admit her sins, Eden remains true to her beliefs.

Did she disobey the rules? That depends on what values she's pursuing. Eden followed what she thought was God's law: to find true love and bring a child into a loving family. She didn't love Nick, so God wouldn't bless her with a child from him. For her to do what the men in power say that women in Gilead ought to do, she felt she needed to build a life with Isaac.

Eden's death absolutely wrecks Serena as she finally grasps what being a woman in her country means. Before that, losing some rights (working, speaking, writing another book) was a way to return to traditional values. She is comfortable inflicting pain on those beneath her station; we see her hit both June and Rita over the course of the show. The Aunts and Wives are perfectly willing to hurt the Handmaids. Women in Gilead will throw others under the bus—or up on the Wall—to save their own skin.

What baffles Serena more than anything else is the identity of the person responsible for bringing the punishments against Eden: Eden's own father turns her in for running away with Isaac. Her own father! As a new mother, Serena must ask herself if her—and her daughter's—interests align with Gilead's and, more importantly, with Fred's.

It appears that Serena has finally emerged from the cave. In Book VIII of *Republic*, Socrates introduces "The Allegory of the Cave." Essentially, a prisoner escapes from a cave where he has lived his whole life to find out that everything he thought he knew was both incomplete and somewhat misleading. Inside the cave, the guards show shadows of objects to the prisoners (the objects pass by a fire, which casts a shadow on the cave wall) and the prisoners believe those shadows are all there is to reality.

Serena is no longer convinced by the "shadows." She no longer believes that Gilead's policies, and even Gilead itself, are what the men marketed them to be—or even that they're good at all. She realizes in this moment that it's not just the Handmaids or the Marthas who face punishments. She understands Lily's fear when she spoke out at Janine's execution: If Gilead kills one of us, what will stop them from killing another? Eden was a true and faithful Wife. If she dies, what hope do Serena and the other women have?

Hoping to make things better for women (especially Nicole) in Gilead, she and the other Wives make a simple request. Like Socrates proposes in his city: give the children in Gilead the same education, regardless of gender. Young girls should be able to read the Bible, just like the boys. Serena even knowingly breaks the law and reads a passage from the Bible to illustrate her request in front of the all-male council. As we know, the Sons of Jacob reject this request and Serena loses half of her pinky for being so bold.

June is on the other end of the spectrum and knows her situation is horrific from the very first episode. Because she knows the truth, she is out of the cave far earlier than Serena and instead of making enemies and keeping other low-power individuals beneath her, she creates a community to give herself a better chance for survival. Along with strong friendships with Rita, Janine, and Emily, she repeatedly looks for opportunities to act in her own self-interests and not Gilead's. The audience cheers when they see June sneak around to sleep with Nick, because she enjoys it and because pregnancy keeps her safe. She repeatedly asks to see Hannah. She refuses to kill Janine. She reads a map to help her run away. She smuggles baby Nicole out.

Regardless of when the veil is lifted for them, both June and Serena can't unsee the reality of their situations once they understand their true position. The "good" and "just" society that Gilead proposes is only good for the white men in power.

In *Republic*, Socrates argues that justice is good for its own sake. This is where many of the characters in *The Handmaid's Tale,* at least the more powerful characters, go astray. They confuse justice with the pursuit of their own interests or the interests of the group to which they happen to belong. They forget, or maybe they never knew, that it is crucial to check your biases.

It Is in the Name of Duty

Generalizations tend to be made about whole classes of people in Gilead and beyond. Citizens of Gilead assume that women can only be wombs, cooks, or sexually frustrated wives. Many in our culture assume that people will be interested in certain things simply because of the arbitrary category to which they happen to belong. When we make those assumptions further, we stop doing what Socrates, Plato, and Aristotle thought was so valuable—we stop being curious.

For justice to exist in society, we need to know why we seek it. It's not to avoid consequences; we need to choose justice for its own sake and understand why justice for everyone is important. The two recognitions are crucially related to one another. If justice is good for its own sake for me, then it's good for its own sake for you.

Once we start to ask questions and try to understand one another, the reds, blues, greens and browns begin to fade away. We see the whole person, who they are and the challenges they face, not just what outfit they're wearing.

19
How Language Shapes Reality in Gilead

Enzo Guerra and Adam Barkman

Language—it's all around. Whether innate, simply learned, or a bit of each, it permeates the fabric of every human activity. Language is used to communicate ideas, give commands, and ask questions. It is universal, and yet, uniquely bound to different dialects and scripts around the world.

There are questions regarding how language shapes the perception of reality. As readers and viewers are surely aware, this feature of language is exploited to great effect in *The Handmaid's Tale*. Take the word "killing" for example. The word "killing," more often than not fosters a sense of grotesqueness, and maybe even a sense of moral wrongness. There seems to be a negative layer of interpretive judgment regarding the action of killing. It is simply the way one goes about understanding the word or phrase.

But is this layer of interpretive judgment justified? It may seem that this moral wrongness that is attributed to the word is fixed and unchangeable. But imagine soldiers in WWII "killing" the forces of the Nazi regime. This "killing" is in the name of protecting the human race from tyranny. "Killing" in this context seems justified, and perhaps even morally praiseworthy. In this context, it is at least defensible to say that the interpretive judgment that is often added to the word "killing," namely a moral wrongness, is completely reversed. It now fosters a sense of moral rightness. At the most basic level "killing" doesn't seem to have any inherent normative meaning. But words often get embedded with assumptions. This alteration can be a means to power.

The Republic of Gilead does an excellent job of altering words and phrases in such a way that contributes to its power. Ludwig Wittgenstein, one of the most prominent philosophers of the twentieth century, and perhaps *the* most prominent philosopher of language, gives quite an astounding and accurate insight into the nature of language. Let's hear what he has to say.

Philosophical Investigations

During his lifetime, Wittgenstein only published one book. But after his death, in 1951, many of his books were published posthumously. One of these is *Philosophical Investigations*, which gives two key insights helping to show how language can be used as a means to power.

The first key insight that Wittgenstein offers us is that words don't have a single fixed meaning or definition. As we saw with the word "killing," we often assume that words have fixed meanings. Wittgenstein claims that though words may have definitions, these definitions are subject to counterexamples. Let's say you want to define X. According to Wittgenstein, there will always be something that *is* X, but is excluded by the definition, or there will be something that *is not* X, but the definition may include it as such. Language is ultimately loose and malleable.

Wittgenstein uses the example of "a game." Though we can trace a thread of similarities between different conceptions of "games," the word has no single fixed meaning. *Merriam Webster* defines "game" as an "activity engaged in for diversion or amusement." But what if the activity is not done for diversion or amusement? Would it still be a game? Do you need to be consciously aware that something is a game before it actually is a game? What about common metaphors referring to life as a "game"?

It is a futile endeavor, according to Wittgenstein, to attempt to find precise boundaries of words and their definitions. There will always be a constant shifting of new ideas that can be put in or taken out to the definition of a game.

A common objection to this idea is the following: if there are no precise boundaries for words, then how can people even use words to communicate, which we obviously do? In response, Wittgenstein claims that words need not have precise boundaries in order for them to be useful. One person's conception of a chair may be different from another person's conception of a chair but if there is a thread of similarity between them (such as something you sit on), that is enough for communication to exist. New conceptions and ideas can be slipped in to refer also to something as a "chair" without communication ceasing to be viable. Words don't have fixed boundaries, and because this is so, they become easily malleable and can be moulded into referring to other things. There is a family resemblance between our various conceptions of "chairs."

The second key insight is tied to the first, and it is that the meaning of a word is determined by its use. This is to say that definitions are not prior to the words themselves. Instead, once a general understanding of a word is attained, in regards to its use, only then do definitions exist. Take for example the word "awful." Previously, this word was used to portray something that is full of awe. But as time went on, the usage of the word "awful" began to change. It began to be used as another adjective, something more negative. And this change resulted in a change of definition based on the usage of the word.

If one day everyone stopped using the word "hello" to mean a form of greeting, and starting using it as an insult, strange as it may be initially, the definition of the word would eventually change based on its usage. Or it could come to mean both a greeting and an insult. Words are malleable and can be changed, given enough time and consensus. They can go from meaning something positive to something negative and vice versa.

Even Offred gets a sense of this when she says,

> I sit in the chair and think about the word chair. It can also mean the leader of a meeting. It can also mean a mode of execution. It is the first syllable in charity. It is the French word for flesh. None of these facts has any connection with the others.

In other words, the word "chair" can only derive its meaning from its usage and context.

Assuming this understanding of language is reasonable, it's easy to see how words can alter reality and be used as a means to power. Given enough time and consensus, the use of a word can change its definition. This may cause individuals who may think words are fixed to believe that certain words mean whatever the party in power wants them mean. Or it can transform words with a positive connotation to words with a negative connotation. This is something The Republic of Gilead knows all too well.

Reality Warped in the Republic of Gilead

There are two main maneuvers Gilead uses to alter words, and their meanings, in order to acquire power. First, it introduces new words constructed out of previously existing words. Second, it creates new names for individuals and things that generate certain roles for those individuals or things to play in society.

The strategy of negation is a strategy of the first type. To read *The Handmaid's Tale* is to stumble upon unfamiliar and peculiar words like "unbaby" or "unwoman." Negation of this type is familiar to people who have read George Orwell's *Nineteen Eighty-Four*, in which the agents of Big Brother categorize certain citizens as "unpersons." This language is explicitly otherizing. In the context and usage of Gilead, an "unwoman" is the negating term for woman. It is a female who cannot integrate into the societal role that Gilead wants her to fill.

If a person is a feminist or lesbian in this republic, then that person is not even considered a woman at all. A woman,

according to Gilead, is a female who satisfies the socially constructed standards that the government has set in place.
Some of the standards include subordination to men and fulfilling their "biological destiny" to populate the Earth by
bearing children. Unwomen are also those who don't align
with the new culture's unique interpretation of the Bible. By
labeling a female an "unwoman," the Republic shames and
excludes her. You're in or you're out—there's no in-between.

Gendered language is motivational for many people. And
given enough time, the definition changes because of its
usage. So much so, indeed, that one day a person may accept
the new definition without questioning it. The standards for
what counts as a "woman" become whatever Gilead wants
them to be. And there are serious consequences—those who
are labeled "unwomen" are sent to the Colonies. This is a vir-
tual death sentence.

The same general analysis applies to the new term "unbaby." An "unbaby" is a newborn child that has some sort of
defect or unpleasant characteristic or set of characteristics.
In Gilead, having a child is a status symbol. The motivation
for having one does not appear to be to nourish and care for
another human being toward the goal of mutual flourishing. Instead, the motivation seems to be the mere possession of a scarce resource, like a big house or a flashy car. In
this dystopia, a child with defects won't fit the bill. The cultural motivation for having children in this society leads to
a fundamental change in what *even counts as a child*. A
child with defects does not meet the new standard for what
a baby *is*, and therefore gets referred to by a new, otherizing
name—"unbaby." "Unbabies" are, ultimately, disposable.
They are *things* rather than persons. In an alarming passage, an "unbaby" is referred to as a "shredder," hinting at
an even more disturbing picture of the fate of babies born
with defects.

By introducing the complement of a given word (the "non"
or "un"), a dichotomy—an opposition—is introduced. Gilead
manipulates its citizens through the use of word games. To
the members of this society, the consequence of challenging

the language of those in authority is typically not worth the shame and exile. Thus, language, in its most diabolical form, has the power to enslave.

Implicit Social Hierarchies

Another way Gilead goes about altering reality as a means to power is by using words to establish social hierarchies. Each member of society is given a certain title, such as "Commander" or "Handmaid." These titles dictate the roles that those individuals play in the culture. Some men, and only men, are given the title of "Commander." Such men have instant power. After all, a "commander" is one who has the power to command—to tell people what must be done. Citizens are already familiar with the way that word is used. If a person is given the title "commander," that person is in charge. In contrast, a "commander's wife" is not an authority figure like a commander, but is closely enough related to one that it is best to stay on guard around her. The Wife is the female who has the most legally respectable relationship to the Commander. Wives and husbands are engaged in a partnership.

That partnership may not be equal in Gilead, but it is a partnership nevertheless. A Wife is not to take charge as her husband does, but she does exercise some control over the other women in her household. Gilead uses the connotations of a previously existing word, "wife," to its advantage. Since the word has different connotations for different people (depending on what those people think the relationship between husband and wife should be), Gilead uses forced interpretations of scripture to reinforce exactly what its citizens should think of when they think of a "Wife" or a "Handmaid."

A "Handmaid" is one whose purpose is to serve. When Gilead sorts individuals into this group, they become the role the title describes. Of course, though the Handmaids are not inferior in any real way (in fact, they have a resource the society desperately wants, so one might even think of these people as advantaged!), the title implies a class struggle and automatically devalues them. There are no citizens, full stop.

There are only social roles. Individuals have no rights or responsibilities defined by anything other than the roles picked out by those words.

All of the other members of society have roles dictated to them by their names—Eyes, Marthas, Angels, and Aunts. Eyes watch over everyone to ensure that rules aren't being broken. Marthas, like the Martha in the Bible, brother of Lazarus, are in positions of manual servitude. Aunts help to guide their young charges to effectively fulfill the roles picked out by the names they are given. "Angels are, surprisingly, the soldiers. This is a particularly interesting strategy because the name paints Gilead's military interests with a veneer of moral righteousness. Gilead does a powerful thing by changing language—the rulers reinforce their authoritarian control.

Language plays a vital role in human affairs. There is often a misconception that the definitions of words are fixed. Wittgenstein pointed out that the meaning of a word can change with use. Because this is so, language has the potential to change people's perception of reality. As we've seen, this can have devastating consequences.

20
Under a Watchful Eye

CHAD TIMM

English playwright Edward Bulwer-Lytton once wrote in his play *Richelieu*, "The pen is mightier than the sword." But is it, really? I mean, under what circumstances would you want to stand toe to toe with a cattle-prod-wielding Aunt Lydia armed with only a ballpoint pen?

I've also been told that knowledge is power, but did the victims being smart or having knowledge ever stop the schoolyard bully from bullying? In the Republic of Gilead the bullies deprive others of their rights and persecute all those who stand in their way, often using violence to do it. Viewing the Republic of Gilead purely from the perspective of a brutal and oppressive dictatorship, however, doesn't explain why the Aunts, Marthas, or the Handmaids themselves co-operate and even support oppressive conditions.

Although some brutal acts of violence occur in Gilead, more subtle acts of power are played nearly every minute of every day, from the Ceremonies and Prayvaganzas to the Testifying and training to be a Handmaid. What's even more disturbing is that many of those who participate in these acts of violence, even against themselves, seem to agree with or believe in what they are doing! Maybe knowledge is power?

Power Is Knowing

To uncover the various ways power operates in the Republic of Gilead let's talk first about knowledge. Many philosophers throughout history have claimed that knowledge leads us to understandings of universal truths, whether about God in the heavens or the laws of nature governing the universe. French postmodern philosopher Michel Foucault (1926–1984), on the other hand, argues the relationship between knowledge and power is much more important and complex than you might think, and in fact knowledge *is* powerful and power *is* knowing.

Members of the Sons of Jacob, for example, claim that society should be led by men because God ordained it in the Bible. To these power-hungry masochists Gilead reflects progress towards realizing God's truth on Earth. Foucault would call BS on that claim. Instead of linking knowledge to any universal truth, Foucault researched under what conditions and in what circumstances someone could claim to know anything as the universal truth. In this way Foucault connects knowledge to power, instead of truth, because he argues that what is claimed as knowledge or truth of anything is directly linked to the power wielded by the person doing the claiming.

Let me break this down for you with an example. The leaders of Gilead grouped women based on their "ability" to procreate into categories like Wives, Handmaids, Aunts, Marthas, Econowives, and Unwomen while asserting that God had ordained it. Foucault tells us to look at the positions of power and influence held by those leaders which give them the authority to claim knowledge of God's truth in the first place. When the Sons of Jacob used their beliefs about the Bible to rally support for their cause and gain positions of power, they used that power to create these categories. Their followers, in turn, looked to them for leadership and guidance, further linking knowledge and power into a circular love fest that Foucault called a "regime of truth."

It's All in the Genes

Foucault built on a strategy developed by German philosopher Friedrich Nietzsche (1844–1900), called genealogy, where the philosopher critiques power relations in their historical context. For example, when studying concepts like madness, education, and sexuality, Foucault uncovered how experts had labeled people insane, sane, educated, homosexual or heterosexual throughout history.

Time and time again Foucault found that instead of a common definition or universal truth for insanity or sexuality, experts defined these concepts differently and their definitions varied widely across space and time. People in positions of power with respected credentials like degrees and licenses did the defining. This is especially true for government leaders and while analyzing the changing concept of government in eighteenth-century European societies, Foucault uncovered a shift in the way governments used power to control people.

Power that Disciplines

Up until the eighteenth century most European governments relied on what Foucault called sovereign power, or the outward and public acts of violence to maintain power and control, like the hangings for Gender Treachery in Gilead. Public torture and execution were common until eventually people had enough and started overthrowing governments.

In the French Revolution, for example, people oppressed by sovereign power responded in turn with their own violence and a bunch of heads rolled . . . literally. In the wake of these revolutions leaders looked for ways to not only control their people but to encourage their people to control themselves. Foucault called this new kind of power disciplinary power. While leaders used sovereign power to punish and frighten, disciplinary power worked by convincing people that doing what the leaders wanted was the right thing to do.

Examples of sovereign power are evident in Gilead, from the particicutions to the beating of Moira's hands and feet with the frayed end of steel cables. These examples, however, aren't enough to explain how the Sons of Jacob keep order and maintain control. We repeatedly encounter characters who govern or control themselves, who seemingly go against their own self-interest and instead play right into the hands of the government. Think of Aunt Lydia "teaching" the Handmaids about Unwomen in Gyn Ed, Handmaids like Janine who repent as sinners for being victims of sexual assault, or the Eyes who are everywhere and nowhere at the same time waiting to snitch on any transgressors.

These individuals act the way those in power want them to act without being physically forced to do so. This is the kind of power that interested Foucault, not the outward acts of forcible coercion. As Foucault says, "Power is anything that tends to render immobile and untouchable those things that are offered to us as real, as true, as good" (*Power, Moral Values, and the Intellectual*, p. 1), because this power encourages self-government and makes messed up and oppressive circumstances appear as natural.

May the Lord Open

Disciplinary power is imposed in Gilead through a systematic and carefully orchestrated process. Once in power, the Sons of Jacob define what beliefs and lifestyles are acceptable. Using a fundamentalist and manipulated interpretation of the Old Testament they deprive women of property and the right to work, they define heterosexuality as normative, and procreation is deemed the single most important role of society. Once these terms are defined, those in power use their leadership positions to identify and then sort people based on their criteria, like when Offred tells us "There are other women with baskets, some in red, some in the dull green of the Marthas, some in the striped dresses, red and blue and green and cheap and skimpy, that mark the women of the poorer men . . . Sometimes there is a woman all in black, a widow" (*The Handmaid's Tale*, p. 24). Once identified and sorted women are then confined to specific locations and "trained."

This is the exact process of enacting disciplinary power Foucault repeatedly uncovered in his analyses of the history of the mental institution, the prison, and the school. In *The History of Madness* Foucault describes the process by which the European field of psychiatry emerged in response to governmental attempts to silence political dissidents. Madness was defined by so-called experts, individuals who fit the description of insane were identified, sorted, and then confined to asylums. Foucault writes "In a single movement, the asylum . . . becomes an instrument of moral uniformity and social denunciation. The intention was to erect one form of morality as universal" (p. 495).

Instead of uncovering the "truth" of insanity, the definition of insanity depended on the context and the time, and those in power used their influence not only to silence their opponents but to shape the identities of those identified as mad. According to Foucault, "The body no longer has to be marked; it must be trained and re-trained" (*The Essential Foucault*, p. 45).

Foucault found examples of this training in the mental institution, prison, and even school. The "insane" and the "criminal" were taught to recognize and understand their so-called deviance, developing a new identity in the process. When Descartes famously claimed *Cogito ergo sum*, "I think, therefore I am," he asserted that we essentially have an identity and while we can question everything else about our existence, we know for certain we are thinking things in God's image. Foucault, on the other hand, would agree more with Offred when she writes "I tell, therefore you are" (p. 268). Instead of being born with a single identity that defines who we are, Foucault's analysis of disciplinary power shows us that our identities can be shaped by power relations. The reason the asylum, prison, and school are so effective in shaping identities is because they are perfect places to train minds and bodies.

The Red Center

Once Handmaids are identified, sorted, and confined they undergo "re-education" in order to fully embody the identity of the Handmaid. Aunts supervise the daily lessons in the Rachel and Leah Re-Education Center, otherwise known as the Red Center. It's funny that what happens at the Red Center is referred to as education. Actually it's not funny at all, but scary as Hell. One of the instructional strategies employed by the Aunts centered on using narrow selections from the Bible to teach the Handmaid's the importance of patriarchal procreation. "It's the usual story," Offred tells us, "God to Adam, God to Noah. Lie fruitful, and multiply, and replenish the earth" (p. 89). More than using the Bible narrowly, the Aunts make stuff up while teaching the Handmaids about their procreative duties. Since reading isn't allowed and the Bible is locked away, no one knows any better.

Another instructional strategy used by the Aunts involves showing old movies to teach the Handmaids about the horrors of the past and the dangers of a free and permissive society. These films typically highlight the dangers of allowing women to have freedoms in order to teach the Handmaids that giving up their freedom to read, to choose, or to move freely saves them from spiritual and even physical death. The Aunts' lectures inform the Handmaids that "Mind you, some of their ideas were sound enough . . . But they were Godless, and that can make all the difference" (p. 119). Although the training is oppressive and sometimes painful for the Handmaids, the Aunts teach them that they are a "transitional generation" and that they are making sacrifices so that those that come after them will have it easier, and will "accept their duties with willing hearts . . . because they won't want things they can't have" (p. 117). More than teaching them about an ideology or a vision for the future, the Aunts' instruction seeks to form new identities as Handmaids. The Aunts have so much power, according to Offred when describing Aunt Lydia, "We are hers to define" (p. 114).

Teachers from Hell

Aunts are powerful because they have credentials and have been given the authority to supervise the training by the leaders of Gilead. Their credentials and their position of authority allow them to decide what's taught, which in turn fills them with more power. Remember Foucault's point about power and knowledge? His research on the asylum and the prison demonstrate how the psychiatrist and the warden wielded similar power. Their power allowed them to control knowledge, which in turn gave them more power.

Let's pause for a second and address the elephant hiding in the corner of this page. If the Aunts in the Red Center are oppressive and wield disciplinary power as "teachers," then what about the thousands of teachers in public schools across the Republic of America? Foucault's point is not that all education is bad, or that all teachers or other "experts" are brainwashing Sons of Jacob. His point is that all power relations where there is a significant imbalance of power are dangerous and must be constantly evaluated.

In fact, for Foucault all human relationships involve power. Power is everywhere people are. Our marriages, our sibling rivalries, and our workplace banter all involve relations of power. Foucault tells us: "The problem with such practices where power—which is not in itself a bad thing—must inevitably come into play is knowing how to avoid the kind of domination effects where a kid is subjected to the arbitrary and unnecessary authority of a teacher" (*The Essential Foucault*, p. 40). The problem with the Aunts is that they use their position and power to repress and indoctrinate.

Do You Smell What the Aunts Are Cooking?

How do the Aunts know whether the Handmaids are picking up what they are putting down? Women and girls in the Red Center are learning when they demonstrate evidence of their new identities as Handmaids. They have learned when they "become" Handmaids both physically and psychologically.

Offred shows signs of her own learning when she tells us "Everything except the wings around my face is red: the color of blood, which defines us" (p. 8). and "The Republic of Gilead, said Aunt Lydia, knows no bounds. Gilead is within you" (p. 23). The Handmaids begin to see themselves through the lens of the Handmaid. The Handmaid internalizes what she's taught and it shapes how she sees herself and others. It defines her. Offred tells us "I avoid looking at my own body, not so much because it's shameful or immodest but because I don't want to see it. I don't want to look at something that determines me so completely" (p. 63). She continues, telling us "It has taken so little time to change our minds, about things like this." Whether she wants it to happen or not, and even though she struggles to remember the way things were, Offred is shaped by the disciplinary power of Gilead. She becomes a Handmaid.

Perhaps the most compelling example of disciplinary power among the Handmaids is that of Janine. When Janine shares her past life story of being gang raped and then getting an abortion Aunt Helena blames Janine and asks, "But whose fault was it?" The other Handmaids chant in unison "Her fault, her fault, her fault." Aunt Helena continues, "Who led them on? . . . [the Handmaids chant] She did. She did. She did" (p. 72). How can this be explained? How could these women, themselves confined to the Red Center, internalize their new identities so fully that they could blame a woman for being raped?

The New Normal

Becoming a Handmaid, actually internalizing the new identity of the Handmaid, is an example of how Foucault shows us that disciplinary power is normalizing. The defining, identifying, sorting, confining and then educating creates a new "normal." This new normal makes what was once strange, aberrant even, just the way things *are*, and it's in this way that disciplinary power is productive. Offred tells us, "Ordinary, said Aunt Lyida, is what you are used to. This may not seem ordinary to you now, but in time it will, it will become ordinary" (p. 33).

According to Foucault, "If I use my age, my social position, the knowledge I may have about this or that, to make you behave in some particular way—that is to say, I'm not forcing you at all and I'm leaving you completely free—that's when I begin to exercise power" (*Power*, p. 2). Offred embraces this power when she tells us "I resign my body, freely, to the uses of others. They can do what they like with me. I am abject. I feel, for the first time, their true power." This normalizing even further shapes the identities of those in power to the point they believe what they are doing is right!

There is one more element of disciplinary power that helps explain its effectiveness, and that element is continual observation and surveillance. Foucault points this out when he states "There is no need for arms, physical violence, material constraints. Just a gaze. An inspecting gaze, a gaze which each individual under its weight will end by interiorizing to the point that he is his own overseer, each individual thus exercising this surveillance over, and against, himself." Believing we are being watched at all times, but never knowing for sure, plays a vital role in the effectiveness of disciplinary power.

Under His Watchful Eye

Surveillance is one of the primary tools used by officials in Gilead to encourage the creation of compliant identities. We get the feeling that everyone is being watched, and that no one can truly be trusted. "We can feel their eyes on us as we walk in our red dresses two by two across to the side opposite them. We are being looked at, assessed, whispered about; we can feel it, like tiny ants running on our bare skins," Offred informs us (p. 214), and "Perhaps he was merely being friendly . . . Perhaps it was a test, to see what I would do. Perhaps he is an Eye." Because she never knows if she is actually being watched, or if the people looking at her are Eyes for the government, she behaves as expected. Not only does she behave, but as we've seen earlier, at times she actually *believes* in what she's doing.

In his book *Discipline and Punish* Foucault used genealogy to analyze the birth of the modern prison system and how it worked hand in hand with government leaders to exert disciplinary power. Foucault describes how British utilitarian philosopher Jeremy Bentham (1748–1832) devised architectural plans for a special kind of prison, called the Panopticon. The Panopticon would be a circular shaped prison with each floor comprised of cells facing a common central guard tower. The prisoner could only see out the cell door and all they see is the bright light shining from the guard tower in the center of the prison. The prisoners are told they are being watched at all times but never know if they actually are because the guard tower has windows of opaque glass. The prisoners can see shapes and shadows behind the glass, but never know for sure if the guard is actually there.

This is eerily similar to the black vans in the *The Handmaid's Tale*, with the white eye painted on the side because, "the windows of the vans are dark-tinted, and the men in the front seats wear dark glasses: a double obscurity." Just as the prisoner in the Panopticon never knows if they are being watched, but must assume they are at all times, Offred also never knows who is a friend or foe and who is watching.

The uncertainty of this surveillance makes the disciplinary power of observation, of the gaze, even more profound. Foucault tells us that "Bentham laid down the principle that power should be visible and unverifiable." Visible in the sense that the inmate will always have the image of the tall central guard tower in their mind, assuming they are spied on at all times. Unverifiable because they can't know for sure, but they must assume they are.

Do you think Bentham designed the Panopticon this way just to save money so they could do without a ton of guards? Nope. Observation is the final piece to the disciplinary power puzzle. Offred, Ofglen, Janine, Moira, the Aunts, Marthas and everyone else in Gilead cannot escape the gaze of the eyes. Initially the gaze tells you that if you misbehave, if you deviate from the rules, you will be caught and punished. In time the gaze becomes more than something outside of you, instead penetrating you deeply and becoming a part of your new identity. The fear of being seen and punished is no longer conscious and "behaving" and following the "rules" just becomes the way things are supposed to be. It becomes normal.

Biopower

Unfortunately it is frighteningly easy to find elements of Gilead's reactionary vision emerging in the Republic of America today. Growing religious fundamentalism, nationalistic rhetoric, and the criticism or outright repression of civil liberties like freedom of speech and expression by our elected officials is commonplace. The loud and hateful rhetoric spewed by some of our leaders, however, doesn't frighten me as much as the silent support for those views granted by millions of Americans.

One of the more subtle ways disciplinary power operates in the United States today, as it does in Gilead, is in the way every aspect of a woman's life is placed under regulatory control. Foucault called this use of disciplinary power "Biopower." Sexual intercourse, birth control, pregnancy, childbirth, and eventually the end of life become objects of study, they are medicalized, credentialed experts use their positions of power to declare what is the medical truth, lawmakers use their positions of power to legislate those truths, and in turn more power is given to the experts and lawmakers. Sure, medical experts and lawmakers are concerned about the health and well-being of mothers, but the medicalization of women's health can also lead to the intensification of social control over women's bodies.

Under His Watchful Iowa

In Gilead women's bodies are medicalized and regulated to the point that their reproductive potential completely defines them, both legally and psychologically. Offred tells us "I'm taken to the doctor once a month, for tests: urine, hormones, cancer smear, blood test . . . now it's obligatory" (p. 59).

On May 4th 2018 the governor of Iowa signed a fetal heartbeat bill into law representing the most restrictive antiabortion law in the United States. According to the law it is illegal for a physician to perform an abortion if a fetal heartbeat is detected, which is generally about six weeks into a pregnancy. Ignoring the fact that it contradicts *Roe v. Wade* and supporting the bill she signed the governor of Iowa stated, "This is bigger than just a law. This is about life. And I'm not going to back down from who I am or what I believe in" (*Des Moines Register*, May 4th 2018). This bill raises many important questions, but the question most relevant to Foucault might be: How does this bill reflect an imbalance of power relations with the potential to be oppressive? In what ways are Iowans repressing women's rights?

Speaking of disciplinary power, Foucault noted "Relations of power are not in themselves forms of oppression. But what happens is that . . . organizations are created to freeze the relations of power, hold those relations in a state of asymmetry, so that a certain number of persons get an advantage." How does Iowa's fetal heartbeat bill tip the scales of power and further demonize and oppress women? And, for Offred's sake, how can a woman sign a bill that restricts the rights and freedoms of women?

The era of fake news, fake facts, and twitter tirades is upon us. If the election of 2016 wasn't enough to shake the foundations of postmodern philosophy for me, then engaging in a recent straight-faced discussion about why the Earth is actually round with a group of my students who swear it is flat shook me to the core. I mean, after reading this chapter you might even be questioning the truth of everything. But don't miss Foucault's point. Never accepting anything as definitive doesn't mean that nothing is true. Questioning everything we accept as truth makes us hyper-aware of the ways in which power operates to create and control us.

Foucault once said "I believe that one of the tasks, one of the meanings of human existence—the source of human freedom—is never to accept anything as definitive . . . no aspect of reality should be allowed to become a definitive and inhuman law for us" (*Power, Moral Values, and the Intellectual*, p. 1). It's easier to imagine all the power in the hands of a certain few, like major arteries we could cut to kill the beast. Foucault's philosophy, on the other hand, demonstrates how disciplinary power operates more like small capillaries running throughout all of our bodies, and it's impossible to ever completely stop the flow.

Yet She Resists

I find hope in *The Handmaid's Tale* because despite the horrific and oppressive situation in Gilead, Offred never fully submits to disciplinary power: she resists. She resists when she says "My name isn't Offred, I have another name . . . I keep the knowledge of this name like something hidden, some treasure I'll come back to dig up." She resists when she says "The night is mine, my own time, to do with as I will" (p. 37), and she resists when she gets the urge to steal something, anything, because "It would make me feel that I have power" (p. 81). Actually writing *The Handmaid's Tale* is the ultimate act of resistance. Despite the imminent threat of punishment or death, and despite the fact her identity is no longer completely her own, she still resists.

Throughout Foucault's many analyses of disciplinary power he consistently uncovers examples of resistance, because disciplinary power doesn't rest on universal truths. Instead of blaming Foucault and postmodernism for the era of Trump, we would do well to heed his call to refuse to accept the way things are as the truth and to "Rise up against all forms of power— but not just power in the narrow sense of the word, referring to the power of a government or one social group over another" (*Power, Moral Values, and the Intellectual*, p. 1).

Resisting disciplinary power doesn't require marches or demonstrations, although those are always welcome. Resisting requires small acts of refusal and the curiosity to create new relations. Offred's refusal helped bring down Gilead. Just think what your refusal could do?

Part VI

Gilead in the Rearview Mirror

21
A Response to Professor Pieixoto

Darci Doll

In 2195 the keynote speaker, Professor James Darcy Pieixoto, at the Twelfth Symposium on Gileadean Studies discussed the authenticity and historical context of the manuscript commonly known as The Handmaid's Tale. *Professor Pieixoto argued that, assuming the authenticity of the document, "Our job is not to censure but to understand," a comment that received ample applause (*The Handmaid's Tale, *p. 383).*

Professor Pieixoto was adamant that the real emphasis ought to be on establishing authenticity and ascertaining the identities of the mentioned individuals. The latter is identified as being a means to achieve the former in addition to having historical value. For Professor Pieixoto, the intellectual curiosities only involve the factual components of the document and the Gileadean Age; he notes that, at least in part, this is essential because we only see minor glimpses of history and those glimpses are through our anachronistic lenses.

Thus, it is deemed more important to focus on the objective facts and not subjective interpretations. We are not able to judge the goodness (or absence thereof) of the Gileadean Age because we are lacking the perspective and experiences that would enable us to do so thoroughly and accurately.

While Professor Pieixoto makes some good points and has a sizeable following of fans and comrades sharing his ideology, others argue that his position is morally problematic and considerably dangerous. What follows is an example of this dissenting view presented by Professor Anadicrad as the keynote address from the Thirteenth Symposium on Gilead-ean Studies.

Welcome and thank you for your attendance. I want to thank the Gileadean Research Association for allowing me to present this year's keynote address. I welcome the opportunity to, in a word, respond to and challenge last year's keynote address, "Problems of Authentication in Reference to *The Handmaid's Tale*," presented by Professor Pieixoto. By now, it's safe to assume that you are all intimately familiar with this piece; it has gained ample fame (and in some circles infamy) over the last year. Professor Pieixoto is correct that we can only view historical events through an anachronistic lens, that we cannot truly understand these events in the same way as those who lived them. He is wrong, and dangerously so, in the assertion that this requires a purely descriptive analysis, that we should only identify and focus on the objective factual elements of the Gileadean Age and should not attempt what's known as a prescriptive analysis. A prescriptive, or normative, analysis provides a value judgment about something, to give a rationale as to why something is deemed good or bad. Or, to paraphrase Pieixoto, to praise or censure as we deem appropriate.

Pieixoto stated, "As all historians know, the past is a great darkness, and filled with echoes. Voices may reach us from it, but what they say to us is imbued with the obscurity of the matrix out of which they come; and, try as we may, we cannot always decipher them precisely in the clearer light of our own day" (p. 394).

I concur that we can only decipher historical times through our current lens. Not being present in a time period means that we are tasked with translating the past into an anachronistic lens. What we can glean from historical accounts will always be incomplete and subject to misunderstanding. However, it does not follow that we ought not to condemn or praise societies for their past actions. We can, for example, acknowledge the reasons people had for their choices whilst also acknowledging that those reasons may not have been ideal. To take a strictly descriptive approach to history is to undermine the value of the lessons that history can impart to us. Historians, and I would argue philosophers, have the obligation not only to relay the information, but to provide us with a normative explanation of these events if for no other reason than to help us avoid repeating mistakes.

The Goddess of History has also provided us with materials from philosophers, many of whom who died years (if not millennia) before the rise of Gilead. One such philosopher, Aristotle, argued that people need to use practical wisdom to understand the world around them and to identify the difference between virtuous and vicious (or morally good or bad). We then need to create a system (which includes education, societal structures, and virtuous relationships) that allows people to cultivate the virtuous behaviors into habitual traits and to avoid the cultivation of vices. This is the route to flourishing (*eudaimonia*) on the individual and, arguably, also on the social level; this is the ideal towards which we strive and which we should seek to attain.

If the citizens of a society fail to do this, the society may end up developing in a way that is morally bad and harms its citizens. Gilead is a prime example of this: the architects designed the society in a way that capitalized on a lack of information, an acceptance of problematic views, and a guise of social benefit. Specifically, they reinforced the idea that women are valuable in respect to reproductive activities as well as heteronormative patriarchal norms to create the caste system that we saw in the Gileadean age.

These norms were reinforced by keeping people ignorant, forbidding autonomy, and imposing an extreme penal system. Gilead required heteronormativity, forced procreation, and forbade any relationships outside of utility. These tools protect the totalitarian regime, condition citizens to be compliant, and eliminate or minimize subversive tendencies. As Piexioto noted, one of the architects had allegedly said, "Our big mistake was teaching them to read. We won't do that again." Thus, Gilead was constructed intentionally to avoid the cultivation of virtues that would contribute to human and social flourishing; instead, it was a totalitarian regime that was particularly horrifying to women and LGBTQ individuals.

Thus, it is not sufficient to merely *describe* Gilead and establish the authenticity of our records. We must also *evaluate* Gilead and the contributing factors that allowed it to rise to power. Texts such as Aristotle can help us understand the framework of an ideal society and the moral criticism of Gilead. Combined with philosophers such as Simone de Beauvoir, we can demonstrate the moral (and descriptive) insufficiency of equating women as a second sex whose value comes from procreative abilities. The Goddess of History requires that we learn from these mistakes, we need to call out and address the evil of the society, use our resources to cultivate virtues and eradicate vices. This society will promote individual flourishing as well as a society that sees the error of a heteronormative, patriarchal society; by doing this, we will flourish and (may) attain moral virtue Under Her Eye.

To illustrate this, I will utilize the works of an Ancient Greek Philosopher, Aristotle, who lived and died in the fourth century B.C.E. Aristotle lived in Greece, was a student of Plato, a teacher (amongst his students was Alexander the Great), founded a school, and wrote on a variety of philosophical topics including metaphysics and logic. He may be best known for his theories on ethics.

If we were to adhere to Pieixoto's standard, we might not have much more to say about Aristotle; the description would be sufficient. However, several thousand years later, we can still benefit from the wisdom of this philosopher. Despite the historical gaps, his writing still has the power to shape the values of individuals and a society. This, at least in part, is why Aristotle (and reading in general) was banned in Gilead. Those in power knew that reading could shape ideas beyond a descriptive measure. They forbad reading to ensure that they had control over the thoughts and values of Gileadean citizens.

Someone like Aristotle would have been deemed especially dangerous as he argued we have an obligation to cultivate practical wisdom to identify the habits that contribute to the attainment of *eudaimonia,* or flourishing. Such an emphasis on education and *eudaimonia* would have been disastrous for Gilead; Aristotle encourages independent thought and analysis of values in a way that is in direct opposition to the narrative established in Gilead. Despite Pieixoto's claim, acknowledging the normative aspect of Aristotle is important for at least two reasons: first, it provides us with a standard by which we can evaluate historical events; second, this standard can help us shape and mold our own society in a way that is morally justifiable.

First, we can use Aristotle to provide an ethical analysis of the Gileadean age in a manner that can account for its contemporary state and will be efficient, even through an anachronistic lens. Aristotle's view of ethics relied on what is often translated as practical wisdom. This wisdom is cultivated through a rigorous examination of what we perceive to be true versus what is actually true. So in our case, history affords us with the opportunity to see whether people's assumptions of truth aligned with what is actually true.

In this case, the gods of history have gifted us the benefits of hindsight. This practical wisdom can be used to ascertain whether the society cultivates habits that allow individuals to habituate character traits that are consistent with virtuous behavior. For Aristotle, this means the ability to determine or identify the golden mean in a situation; that is, whether an action is between excess and lack of a certain character trait. As an example, this means that when we're trying to find the golden mean regarding honesty it requires that we identify the proper amount of honesty; too much honesty is a vice as is too little honesty.

The virtuous trait of honesty, then, is knowing when to be honest, to what degree and in what manner. It's using your practical wisdom to reason through a situation to identify what will most likely align with virtue. If done often enough, this will become a matter of habit and the reasoning will become second nature; intentional reasoning will only be needed for new or especially difficult dilemmas. The virtue of honesty, then, isn't necessarily being brutally honest one hundred percent of the time; it's having the wisdom to know that honesty is generally the right policy, but the degree of truthfulness will vary depending on the circumstance.

So the real question is whether Gilead was encouraging its citizens to cultivate practical reasoning and the ability to habituate the habits they deemed virtuous after this consideration. One of the questions that follows is whether the categorization of women and men based on their reproductive abilities is appropriate.

Gilead defines women by their biological sex and affords men the consideration of being defined (at least in some circumstances) by their rational abilities. Because of this delineation, the roles of women within society are reduced to their abilities to reproduce. Women who are fertile are (at least in theory) revered and, unless they are a wife, are granted the position of Handmaids. Other women are assigned tasks based on other abilities, such as cooking, providing assistance to a household.

Some may be granted the "freedom" of being an econowife, while others are penalized and sent to the colonies to do hard labor until they die. It should be noted that Aristotle, too, defined roles of women by their biological function. However, since his time, there have been competing views challenging this and arguing that women and men ought not be reduced to their biological function and that women are not de facto inferior to men based on their reproductive abilities. One such person is the twentieth-century philosopher, Simone de Beauvoir. De Beauvoir argued that reducing people to their biological sex will undermine the value of the individuals and fail to give a fair, clear recognition to the inherent values within people. It also fails to account for the fact that biological sex and reproductive abilities are not reliable markers for a person's abilities.

I propose that we uphold the Aristotelian standard of using our rational capacities to choose traits that contribute to the habituation of the virtues and the attainment of *eudaimonia*. However, we should make sure that we are extending this to all individuals independent of their reproductive abilities or biological expressions. Aristotle argued that we have the obligation to allow for this; therefore, an ideal society would be one that helps cultivate *eudaimonia* for all of its citizens.

As Gilead requires a heteronormative standard (that is, a society that focuses on heterosexuality and relationships determined by the ability to procreate) and emphasizes the problematic emphasis on fertility and utility, they are interfering with individual's ability to establish relationships that contribute to *eudaimonia*. If we were to follow Pieixoto's guidance, we would not be able to take this approach; we'd be merely forced to describe what had happened.

The final problem with merely describing the Gileadean age is that it would prevent us from criticizing the fact that Gilead kills and disposes of unwomen, people who are unuseful, gender traitors, people who exercise autonomy, who believe in the "wrong" religion, who *read*. This is wrong because it denies the damage committed by Gilead and the harm to the people within the walls of Gilead. Moreover, it means that we may not take the time and effort to prevent this from happening again. If we don't look at the wrongdoings of the past, we will repeat these atrocious acts (or worse ones). The descriptive account will be useful, but we cannot sacrifice the moral obligation to provide a prescriptive analysis under Her Eye.

References

Adorno, Theodor W. 2013. *Aesthetic Theory*. Bloomsbury.

Arendt, Hannah. 1964. *Eichmann in Jerusalem. A Report on the Banality of Evil*. Viking.

———. 1976 [1951]. The *Origins of Totalitarianism*. Harcourt Brace.

———. 1998 [1958]. *The Human Condition*. University of Chicago Press.

Aristotle. 1936. On Colours. In Aristotle, *Minor Works*. Harvard University Press.

———. 1999. *Nicomachean Ethics*. Hackett.

———. 2018. *Rhetoric*. Hackett.

Atwood, Margaret. 2003. Orwell and Me. *The Guardian* (June 16th).

———. 2013. My Hero: George Orwell. *The Guardian* (January 18th) <www.theguardian.com/books/2013/jan/18/my-hero-george-orwell-atwood>.

———. 2017. On What "The Handmaid's Tale" Means in the Age of Trump. *New York Times* (March 10th).

Aurelius, Marcus. 1983. *The Meditations*. Hackett.

Baudrillard, Jean. 1994 [1981]. *Simulacra and Simulation*. University of Michigan Press.

———. 2016 [1976]. *Symbolic Exchange and Death*. Sage.

———. 2017 [1970]. *The Consumer Society: Myths and Structure*. Sage.

Beauvoir, Simone de. 2011 [1949]. *The Second Sex*. Vintage.

———. 2015 [1948]. *The Ethics of Ambiguity*. Kensington.

Benhabib, Seyla. 1993. Feminist Theory and Hannah Arendt's Concept of Public Space. *History of the Human Sciences* 6:2.

References

Benjamin, Walter. 2004. A Child's View of Color. In *Walter Benjamin: Selected Writings, Volume 1, 1913-1926*. Harvard University Press.

Boethius. 2001. *Consolation of Philosophy*. Hackett.

Bourdieu, Pierre. 2010. *Sociology Is a Martial Art: Political Writings by Pierre Bourdieu*. New Press.

Braun, Thom. 2007. *The Philosophy of Branding: Great Philosophers Think Brands*. Kogan Page.

Build Series. 2017. Ann Dowd on "The Handmaid's Tale" and "The Leftovers." Youtube (22nd June) <www.youtube.com/watch?v=DyDWFcJBwZE>.

CBC Radio. 2017. How Margaret Atwood's Puritan Ancestors Inspired *The Handmaid's Tale* <www.cbc.ca/radio/tapestry/religion-utopia-or-dystopia-1.4143654/how-margaret-atwoods-puritan-ancestors-inspired-the-handmaid-s-tale-1.4143718>.

Curtis, Kimberley F. 1995. Hannah Arendt, Feminist Theorizing, and the Debate Over New Reproductive Technologies. *Polity* 28:2 (Winter).

Derrida, Jacques. 2016 [1967]. *Of Grammatology*. Johns Hopkins University Press.

Du Bois, W.E.B. 2002. *The Souls of Black Folk*. Penguin.

Epictetus. 1983. *The Handbook (The Encheiridion)*. Hackett.

Field, Shivaune. 2018. Author Margaret Atwood On Why "The Handmaid's Tale" Resonates in 2018. *Forbes* (July).

Foucault, Michel. 1980. *Power/Knowledge: Selected Interviews and Other Writings, 1972–1977*. Vintage.

———. 1988. Power, Moral Values, and the Intellectual. *History of the Present* 4 (July).

———. 1990. *The History of Sexuality, Volume 1: An Introduction*. Vintage.

———. 1995. *Discipline and Punish: The Birth of the Prison*. Vintage.

———. 2006. *History of Madness*. Routledge.

Freud, Sigmund. 1958. Thoughts on War and Death. In Benjamin Nelson, ed., *Creativity and the Unconscious*.Harper.

———. 2016 [1929]. *Civilization and Its Discontents*. Martino.

Goethe, Johann Wolfgang. 1970. *Theory of Colors*. MIT Press.

Hardin, C L 1988, *Color for Philosophers. Unweaving the Rainbow*, Indianapolis: Hackett, 122.

Hemingway, Ernest. 1995 [1952]. *The Old Man and the Sea*. Scribner.

References

Itten, Johannes. 1970. *The Elements of Color: A Treatise on the Color System of Johannes Itten Based on His Book The Art of Color*. Van Nostrand Reinhold.

Kant, Immanuel. 2012 [1785]. *Groundwork of the Metaphysics of Morals*. Cambridge University Press.

Klawiter, Maren. 1990. Using Arendt and Heidegger to Consider Feminist Thinking on Women and Reproductive/Infertility Technologies. *Hypatia* 5:3 (Fall).

Levinas, Emmanuel. 1988. Useless Suffering. In R. Bernasconi and David Wood, eds., *The Provocation of Levinas: Rethinking the Other*. Routledge.

———. 1998 [1974]. *Otherwise than Being or Beyond Essence*. Duquesne University Press.

Marx, Karl. 1974 [1867]. *Capital: A Critical Analysis of Capitalist Production*. Volume 1. Lawrence and Wishart.

McCoy, Marina. 2015. The City of Sows and Sexual Differentiation in the *Republic*. In Jeremy Bell and Michael Naas, eds., *Plato's Animals: Gadflies, Horses, Swans, and Other Philosophical Beasts*. Indiana University Press.

Mill, John Stuart. 2002 [1861]. *Utilitarianism*. Hackett.

Mitchell, Stephen. 1987. *The Book of Job*. North Point Press.

Morrison, Patt. 2017. Margaret Atwood on Why *The Handmaid's Tale* Is More Relevant Now than Ever. *Los Angeles Times* (April 19th) <www.latimes.com/opinion/op-ed/la-ol-patt-morrison-margaret-atwood-hulu-handmaiden-20170419-htmlstory.html>.

Neiman, Susan. 2001. What Is the Problem of Evil? In Maria Pia Lara, ed., *Rethinking Evil: Contemporary Perspectives*. University of California Press.

———. 2015 [2002]. *Evil in Modern Thought: An Alternative History of Philosophy*. Princeton University Press.

Orwell, George. 1961 [1949]. *Nineteen Eighty-Four*. Signet.

Plato. 1992. *Republic*. Hackett.

Renteln, Alison Dundes. 1988. Relativism and the Search for Human Rights. *American Anthropologist* 90:1 (March).

———. 2004. *The Cultural Defense*. Oxford University Press.

Reuters. 2017. Margaret Atwood: The Handmaid's Tale Sales Boosted by Fear of Trump. *The Guardian* <www.theguardian.com/books/2017/feb/11/margaret-atwood-handmaids-tale-sales-trump>.

Rocheleau, Matt. 2017. Chart: The Percentage of Women and Men in Each Profession. *Boston Globe* (March 7th).

Rorty, Richard. 1995. Ironists and Metaphysicians. In Walter Truett Anderson,ed., *The Truth about the Truth*. Putnam.

Ryan, Maureen. 2018. Ann Dowd on "The Handmaid's Tale," Aunt Lydia, and the Miracle of Forgiveness. *New York Times* (August 20th).

Sartre, Jean-Paul. 1992 [1943]. *Being and Nothingness: A Phenomenological Essay on Ontology*. Simon and Schuster.

Seneca.1969. *Letters from a Stoic*. Penguin

Timm, Chad. 2017. Only Deadpool Is Sane. In Nicolas Michaud and Jacob Thomas May, eds., *Deadpool and Philosophy: My Common Sense Is Tingling*. Open Court.

Tronto, Joan C. 1994. *Moral Boundaries: A Political Argument for an Ethic of Care*.

———. 2013. *Caring Democracy: Markets, Equality, and Justice*. NYU Press.

Wittgenstein, Ludwig. 1977. *Remarks on Colour*. Blackwell.

———. 2009 [1953]. *Philosophical Investigations*. Blackwell.

Mayday Members

EMILIANO AGUILAR teaches philosophy at the Universidad de Buenos Aires (UBA)—Facultad de Filosofía y Letras (Argentina). He has published philosophical pieces about science-fiction in journals such as *Lindes* and *Letraceluloide* and chapters in *Orphan Black and Philosophy*, *The Man in the High Castle and Philosophy*, *Giant Creatures in our World: Essays on Kaiju and American Popular Culture*, *Twin Peaks and Philosophy*, and *American Horror Story and Philosophy*.

ADAM BARKMAN got his PhD at the Free University of Amsterdam and is Professor of Philosophy at Redeemer University College. He is the author or editor of a dozen books, most recently *Making Sense of Islamic Art and Architecture* (2015) and *A Critical Companion to James Cameron* (2018). He has also written over eighty articles or book chapters, many having to do with philosophy and film.

FERNANDO GABRIEL PAGNONI BERNS teaches at the Universidad de Buenos Aires (UBA). He conducts seminars on international horror movies and has published chapters in the books *Divine Horror*, edited by Cynthia Miller, *To See the Saw Movies: Essays on Torture Porn and Post 9/11 Horror*, edited by John Wallis, *Critical Insights: Alfred Hitchcock*, edited by Douglas Cunningham, *Time-Travel Television*, edited by Sherry Ginn, and *The Man in the High Castle and Philosophy*, edited by Bruce Krajewski and Joshua Heter. He is at work on a book about the Spanish horror TV series *Historias para no Dormir*.

CARI CALLIS lives and works in Chicago. She's grateful for its diverse culture and neighborhoods, and fortunate to work with brilliant women filmmakers, writers, actors, producers, painters, poets and educators from all across this city of "big shoulders," this city of big demonstrations led by women who are never silent. She's an associate professor in Cinema and Television Arts at Columbia College Chicago and working on a novel about Marie Leveaux, the Voodoo queen of New Orleans. The award-winning short film *Towing* that she wrote has screened in film fests around the world and was recently sold for international distribution.

ANNA DE VAUL is a poet and a professor of creative writing and literature. One of her favorite pastimes is geeking out over a good dystopia or apocalypse, as long as it's fictional.

DARCI DOLL is a Philosophy Professor at Delta College. Her works have appeared in many volumes, including *Orphan Black and Philosophy*, *The Princess Bride and Philosophy*, and *Mr. Robot and Philosophy*.

CHARLENE ELSBY is the Philosophy Program Director and Assistant Professor of Philosophy in the Department of English and Linguistics at Purdue University Fort Wayne. Formerly IPFW, the institution closed its Women's Studies and Philosophy Departments effective January 1st 2017. The administration characterized the closures as in-line with national trends.

MIHAELA FRUNZ is Associate Professor at the Department of Philosophy, Babes-Bolyai University of Cluj-Napoca, Romania. She teaches courses on ethics and philosophy of communication. She has written several books and articles on these topics and she is editor of the *Journal for the Study of Religions and Ideologies*.

IULIA GRAD is lecturer at the Department of Communication, Public Relations, and Advertising at Babes Bolyai University of Cluj-Napoca, Romania. She obtained her PhD in philosophy in 2012, with a thesis on Martin Buber. Her main research interests are philosophy of communication, communication ethics, and symbolic structures in media communication, with a particular focus on advertising. She has published two books and numerous scholarly articles in national and international journals.

RICHARD GREENE is Professor of Philosophy at Weber State University. He also serves as Executive Director of the Intercollegiate Ethics Bowl, and as the Director of the Richard Richards Institute for Ethics. He is the author of the forthcoming book *Spoiler Alert! It's a Book About the Philosophy of Spoilers*. He has co-edited sixteen books on pop culture and philosophy, including *The Princess Bride and Philosophy, Twin Peaks and Philosophy*, and *American Horror Story and Philosophy*. He is the co-host of the philosophy and pop culture podcast *I Think, Therefore I Fan*.

ENZO GUERRA is an independent scholar interested in ethics and the philosophy of religion. His recent publications include a chapter on Aristotelian conceptions of forgiveness in *The Philosophy of Forgiveness* (2018) and an article on the philosophy of humor in *Scott Adams and Philosophy: A Hole in the Fabric of Reality* (2018).

RON HIRSCHBEIN's interdisciplinary Ph.D. from Syracuse reflects his varied interests in social philosophy, cultural studies, and war and peace issues. He's published five books and numerous articles in these areas. He is researching the advent of nihilism in popular culture and working on a volume with an Arab colleague tentatively entitled: "Two Semites Confront Anti-Semitism." In addition to teaching philosophy and war and peace studies at California State University, Chico, he's served as a visiting professor at University of California campuses in San Diego and Berkeley, and at the UN University in Austria.

ERICA A. HOLBERG is Assistant Professor of Philosophy at Utah State University. Her research explores the question of how communities contribute to the transmission and internalization of values and pleasures and so whether it is possible to have good pleasures in a bad society.

TIM JONES teaches a range of Humanities subjects to Foundation and BA level at the University of East Anglia in Norwich.

The first draft of his bio filled half of this entire book, but then he re-read his chapter and decided it'd be inappropriate.

CHRISTOPHER KETCHAM (www.chrisketcham.com) earned his doctorate at the University of Texas at Austin. He teaches business and ethics at the University of Houston Downtown. Besides extensive work in popular culture and philosophy, his other interests include the ethics of Emmanuel Levinas and Gabriel Marcel, and East-West comparative philosophy. As Atwood has done in *The Handmaid's Tale*, it's important to look at the palimpsests we uncover in our own lives and relationships to others. What has been crossed out or written over in the document or our own lives may be as or more important than what has been written anew.

LEIGH KELLMANN KOLB is an assistant professor of English and journalism at East Central College in Missouri. She's contributed to *Sons of Anarchy and Philosophy*, *Philosophy and Breaking Bad*, *Twin Peaks and Philosophy*, and *Amy Schumer and Philosophy*. She's also written for *Vulture* and *Bitch Magazine* and serves as a screener and juror for multiple Missouri film festivals.

GUILLAUME LEQUIEN teaches philosophy and cinema studies at Paris Science Lettres University in Paris, France. He's mostly interested in philosophy of cinema and pop culture. He spends most of his time trying to find new ways of teaching, reading science fiction books and watching both old movies or new TV series alike. Promoting animal rights and reading Margaret Atwood made him wish only women were in charge for a change.

TRIP MCCROSSIN teaches in the Philosophy Department at Rutgers University, where he works on the nature, history, and legacy of the Enlightenment. Looking at first for an occasion, any occasion to channel Offred's "Seriously! What the actual fuck!!," occasions have turned out to be so many, arising so often, that now he can't seem to *stop* saying it.

EDWARDO PÉREZ is an Associate Professor of English at Tarrant County College in Hurst, Texas. He has contributed essays to *1984 and Philosophy*, *Doctor Strange and Philosophy*, *SNL and*

Philosophy, *Disney and Philosophy*, and *Black Mirror and Philosophy*, writes philosophical blogs on andphilosophy.com, and manages the website lightsabertoss.com.

RACHEL ROBISON-GREENE earned her PhD in philosophy at the University of Massachusetts, Amherst in 2017. She is a regular columnist for the ethics periodical *The Prindle Post*. She has edited or co-edited twelve books in pop culture and philosophy, including *Twin Peaks and Philosophy*, *The Princess Bride and Philosophy*, and *Peanuts and Philosophy*. She teaches philosophy at Utah State University. She is co-host of the philosophy and pop culture podcast *I Think, Therefore I Fan*.

STEPHANIE ST. MARTIN received her BA in Communications and Perspectives (Philosophy Honors Sequence) from Boston College. Upon graduation, she received the Bernard Lonergan, SJ scholarship for excellence in philosophy and went on to earn an MA in Philosophy from Boston College in 2010. As well as being a modern philosopher, Stephanie is an inbound marketer, SEO, and social media expert. She currently serves as Marketing Manager for Archetype (a Boston consulting firm) and serves on University of South Florida MUMA College of Business Advisory Board. She has contributed to works popularizing philosophy, including *The Red Sox and Philosophy*, *The Rolling Stones and Philosophy*, and *What Philosophy Can Tell You About Your Lover*.

CHAD WILLIAM TIMM is an Associate Professor of Education at Simpson College in Indianola, (Under His Watchful Eye) Owa. Chad used to teach *The Handmaid's Tale* and *Nineteen Eighty-Four* in a first year seminar on dystopias, but given the recent political climate he teaches them in a seminar on current political issues. He looks forward to the day when he can again say *The Handmaid's Tale* represents dystopian thinking rather than the current political reality.

SETH M. WALKER is a doctoral student at the University of Denver, studying religion, new media, and popular culture. He has contributed chapters to *Jurassic Park and Philosophy*, *Orange Is the New Black and Philosophy*, *The Walking Dead and Philosophy*, *The Americans and Philosophy*, and *American Horror*

Story and Philosophy—and edits *Nomos Journal,* an online magazine on the intersection between religion and popular culture.

SAMANTHA WESCH is a Canadian graduate student from Edmonton, Alberta. She holds an MA in Philosophy from the University of Toronto and a BA (Hons) in Philosophy from the University of Alberta.

MARIANA ZÁRATE teaches philosophy at the Universidad de Buenos Aires (UBA)—Facultad de Filosofía y Letras (Argentina). She integrates the research group on horror cinema "Grite" and has published in *Racism and Gothic: Critical Essays, Bullying in Popular Culture: Essays on Film, Television, and Novels,* edited by Abigail Scheg, and *Projecting the World: Classical Hollywood, the "Foreign," and Transnational Representations,* edited by Russell Meeuf.

Index

1984

AND PHILOSOPHY
IS RESISTANCE FUTILE?

EDITED BY EZIO DI NUCCI AND STEFAN STORRIE

ALSO FROM OPEN COURT

1984 and Philosophy

Is Resistance Futile?

Volume 116 in the Open Court series,
POPULAR CULTURE AND PHILOSOPHY

EDITED BY EZIO DI NUCCI AND STEFAN STORRIE

"*Beware! If Ignorance is Strength, this book will turn you into a ninety-eight-pound weakling.*"

　　—ERIC J. SILVERMAN, author of *The Prudence of Love* (2010)

"*Why does* Nineteen Eighty-Four *resonate today as much as it did in 1984 or 1949? Because the topics discussed are deeply philosophical—and scary as sh@t.*"

　　—ROBERT ARP, author of *1001 Ideas that Changed the Way We Think* (2013)

"*Have you ever wondered how those online retailers knew about your favorite kind of double-stuffed Oreo? Were you surprised when they recommended the perfect gift for your niece's First Communion? Big Brother might still be watching but so are his younger siblings Google, Facebook, and Amazon. This enlightening volume is a must-read for those of us wondering what it means to watch and be watched in today's frightening digital age.*"

　　—ROBERTO SIRVENT, author of *Embracing Vulnerability* (2014)

EZIO DI NUCCI is Associate Professor of Medical Ethics at the University of Copenhagen. He is the author of *Ethics without Intention* (2014) and *Mindlessness* (2013).

STEFAN STORRIE has written the *Routledge Guidebook to Berkeley's Three Dialogues* (2018) and is the editor of *Berkeley's Three Dialogues: New Essays* (2018).

ISBN 978-0-8126-9979-1

**AVAILABLE FROM BOOKSTORES AND
ONLINE BOOKSELLERS**

For more information on Open Court books, go to
www.opencourtbooks.com.